PROBLEMS OF DISADVANTAGED AND DEPRIVED YOUTH

Publication Number 954

AMERICAN LECTURE SERIES®

A Publication in

The BANNERSTONE DIVISION *of*
AMERICAN LECTURES IN SOCIAL AND
REHABILITATION PSYCHOLOGY

Editors of the Series

JOHN G. CULL, Ph.D.

Director, Regional Counselor Training Program
Department of Rehabilitation Counseling
Virginia Commonwealth University
Fishersville, Virginia

and

RICHARD E. HARDY, Ed.D.

Diplomate in Counseling Psychology (ABPP)
Chairman, Department of Rehabilitation Counseling
Virginia Commonwealth University
Richmond, Virginia

The American Lecture Series in Social and Rehabilitation Psychology offers books which are concerned with man's role in his milieu. Emphasis is placed on how this role can be made more effective in a time of social conflict and a deteriorating physical environment. The books are oriented toward descriptions of what future roles should be and are not concerned exclusively with the delineation and definition of contemporary behavior. Contributors are concerned to a considerable extent with prediction through the use of a functional view of man as opposed to a descriptive, anatomical point of view.

Books in this series are written mainly for the professional practitioner; however, academicians will find them of considerable value in both undergraduate and graduate courses in the helping services.

PROBLEMS OF

DISADVANTAGED AND

DEPRIVED YOUTH

JOHN G. CULL

RICHARD E. HARDY

CHARLES C THOMAS • PUBLISHER
Springfield • Illinois • U.S.A.

Published and Distributed Throughout the World by

CHARLES C THOMAS • PUBLISHER

BANNERSTONE HOUSE

301-327 East Lawrence Avenue, Springfield, Illinois, U.S.A.

© 1975, by CHARLES C THOMAS • PUBLISHER

ISBN 0-398-03171-1

Library of Congress Catalog Card Number: 74-5155

Library of Congress Cataloging in Publication Data

Cull, John G.
    Problems of disadvantaged and deprived youth.

    (American lectures series, publication in the Bannerstone Division of American lectures in social and rehabilitation psychology).

    1. Socially handicapped children—Addresses, essays, lectures. 2. Socially handicapped—Rehabilitation—Addresses, essays, lectures. 3. Social work with youth—Addresses, essays, lectures. I. Hardy, Richard E., joint author. II. Title [DNLM: 1. Cultural deprivation. 2. Education, Special—U. S. 3. Poverty—U. S. LC4091 P962 1974]

HV1421.C84   362.7'04'2   74-5155

ISBN 0-398-03171-1

Printed in the United States of America

X-2

To an educator *par excellence*

MAURINE BULLOCK BOWERS

for her concern

The following are some of the books which have appeared in the Social and Rehabilitation Psychology series:

PROBLEMS OF ADOLESCENTS: SOCIAL AND
PSYCHOLOGICAL APPROACHES
Richard E. Hardy and John G. Cull

JUVENILE CRIMINAL BEHAVIOR AND DRUG ABUSE
Richard E. Hardy and John G. Cull

BEHAVIOR MODIFICATION IN REHABILITATION
SETTINGS: APPLIED PRINCIPLES
John G. Cull and Richard E. Hardy

GROUP COUNSELING AND THERAPY TECHNIQUES
IN SPECIAL SETTINGS
Richard E. Hardy and John G. Cull

REHABILITATION OF THE URBAN DISADVANTAGED
John G. Cull and Richard E. Hardy

CLIMBING GHETTO WALLS: DISADVANTAGEMENT,
DELINQUENCY AND REHABILITATION
Richard E. Hardy and John G. Cull

SPECIAL PROBLEMS IN REHABILITATION
A. Beatrix Cobb

MEDICAL AND PSYCHOLOGICAL ASPECTS OF DISABILITY
A. Beatrix Cobb

AVOCATIONAL ACTIVITIES FOR THE HANDICAPPED:
A HANDBOOK FOR AVOCATIONAL COUNSELING
Robert P. Overs, Elizabeth O'Connor and Barbara Demarco

CONTRIBUTORS

PATRICIA G. ADKINS, Ph.D.: Director, Early Learning Center, El Paso, Texas; Division Director, Region XIX Education Center; Director of EPDA Institute in English for Speakers of Other Languages. Formerly, Associate Professor of Speech Pathology and Linguistics, University of Texas at El Paso; Past-President, Organization of Mexican-American Teachers of English. Advisor, El Paso Public Schools Special Education Advisory Council; Advisor, Texas Regional Council of Governments. Dr. Adkins has contributed more than twenty publications to the professional literature in education. Dr. Adkins is author of *Speech for the Bilingual Spanish-Speaking Student* and *Structured Experiences for Developmental Learning*.

HARVEY R. AUSTRIN, Ph.D.: Professor of Psychology, St. Louis University, St. Louis, Missouri; Consultant in Psychology, Veterans Administration, Head Start, and Jefferson County (Missouri) Health Department. Formerly, Director of Clinical Training, St. Louis University; Associate Professor of Psychology, Temple University; Assistant Professor of Psychology, The Ohio State University; Chief Clinical Psychologist, Chief of Clinical Psychology Training Unit, Veterans Administration Regional Office, Indianapolis; Clinical Psychologist, Columbus (Ohio) State School; and Clinical Psychologist, Bureau of Juvenile Research, Columbus, Ohio. A Diplomate in Clinical Psychology, ABPP and a Fellow of the American Psychological Association, Dr. Austrin has contributed extensively to the professional literature in clinical and school psychology, and mental health.

ROBERT H. BRUININKS, Ph.D.: Associate Professor of Education, University of Minnesota. Formerly Research Associate, Research and Development Center in Education of the Handicapped; Research Associate, Institute on Mental Retardation and Intellectual Development; Teacher, Peabody College summer demonstration project. Dr. Bruininks has been a consultant in special education to the Ramey Air Force Base, Puerto Rico; research consultant to the Metropolitan School System of Nashville, Tennessee; the Higginsville State School in Missouri; the South Dakota State Department of Education; the Division of Special Programs for the Los Angeles Public Schools; Special Education Section of the Minnesota State Department of Education; the Minnesota State Department of Public Welfare. His research interests are in mental retardation, special learning disabilities, and program and curriculum evaluation. He has contributed extensively to the professional literature in special education.

MILDRED R. BUCK, Ph.D.: Clinical Psychologist, Psychological and Psychiatric Dept., Pupil Personnel Services, St. Louis Public School System; Professor, University of Missouri, Professorial Lecturer, St. Louis University; Director, St. Louis Association of Black Psychologists' Mental Health Center; Vice President, Mental Health Association of St. Louis; Board of Directors, Missouri State Association for Mental Health; Board of Directors, Health and Welfare Council of Metropolitan St. Louis; Education Comm., Urban League of St. Louis; Consultant, St. Louis City Jail and Juvenile Detention Division; and various organizations and agencies in St. Louis Metropolitan area; expertise in sensitivity training, group process, psychotherapy, and education. Dr. Buck has contributed to the professional literature in these areas.

HARRIET C. BURGER, R.N.: Nurse-teacher in charge of childcare program with the Board of Cooperative Educational Services, Port Chester, New York. Mrs. Burger received her R.N. degree in 1961 from the Bellevue School of Nursing a B.S. in Nursing from New York University in 1956 and her M.A. in Special Education from New York University in 1970. She has held various positions in the field of nursing.

LAMORE JOSEPH CARTER, Ph.D.: Associate Dean of the College and Professor of Psychology and Education, Grambling (State) College, Grambling, Louisiana; Adjunct Professor of Psychology and Education, Kansas State University, Manhattan, Kansas; Institutional Self-Study Consultant, Commission on Colleges, Southern Association of Colleges and Schools, Atlanta, Georgia; Vocational Consultant, Bureau of Hearings and Appeals, Social Security Administration; Member, Board of Directors, Black Educators' Council for Human Services (BECHS); Diplomate, American Board of Professional Psychology; Fellow, American Association on Mental Deficiency (FAAMD); Formerly Dean of Faculties, Texas Southern University, Houston, Texas; Post-Doctoral Research Fellow, Commission on Colleges, Southern Association of Colleges and Schools; Distinguished Visiting Professor of Psychology, Morehouse College, Atlanta, Georgia; Visiting Lecturer, Northeast Louisiana University, Monroe, Louisiana. The following are some of the books Dr. Carter has coauthored: *Mentally Retarded Children: Their Characteristics, Needs and Education; Toward the Professional Preparation of Elementary School Teachers; Teaching and Learning in the Model Classroom.* Dr. Carter has contributed more than 25 publications to professional literature in psychology and education.

JOHN G. CULL, Ph.D.: Professor and Director, Regional Counselor Training Program, Department of Rehabilitation Counseling, Virginia Commonwealth University, Fishersville, Virginia; Adjunct Professor of Psychology and Education, School of General Studies, University of Virginia, Charlottesville, Virginia; Technical Consultant, Rehabilitation Services Administration, United States Department of Health, Education and Welfare, Washington, D.C.; Editor, American Lecture Series in Social and Rehabilitation Psychology, Charles C Thomas, Publisher; Lecturer Medical Department, Woodrow Wilson Rehabilitation Center; Formerly, Rehabilitation Counselor, Texas State Commission for the Blind; Rehabilitation

Counselor, Texas Rehabilitation Commission; Director, Division of Research and Program Development, Virginia State Department of Vocational Rehabilitation. The following are some of the books which Dr. Cull has coauthored and co-edited: *Drug Dependence and Rehabilitation Approaches, Fundamentals of Criminal Behavior and Correctional Systems, Rehabilitation of the Drug Abuser with Delinquent Behavior,* and *Therapeutic Needs of the Family.* Dr. Cull has contributed more than sixty publications to the professional literature in psychology and rehabilitation.

EDMUND T. DIMOCK, M.S.W.: Program Supervisor, Youth Crisis Services, Children's Home Society of California, Chico, California; and Lecturer, Social Welfare and Corrections Department, California State University, Chico. Formerly, Child Welfare Supervisor, Protective Services, Shasta County Welfare Department, Redding, California; Instructor, Shasta College, Redding; Consultant, Mercy Hospital, Redding, and Casework Supervisor, San Diego County Department of Public Welfare, San Diego, California.

RUSSELL A. DUSEWICZ: Director, Pennsylvania Research in Infant Development and Education Project; Senior Research Associate, Pennsylvania State Department of Education. The following are some of the books Dr. Dusewicz has authored or coauthored: *Student Attitude Factors Affecting Achievement in the Urban School; The KDK-Oseretsky Tests of Motor Development: A Group Testing Technique; Drive Theory and the Nature of Reinforcement.* Dr. Dusewicz has also contributed more than 25 publications to the professional literature.

EDGAR G. EPPS, Ph.D.: Marshall Field IV Professor of Urban Education, The University of Chicago: Member, Assembly of Behavioral and Social Sciences, National Research Council; Technical Consultant, National Institute of Education, U. S. Department of Health, Education, and Welfare; Associate Editor, *American Sociological Review*. Formerly Director of Behavioral Science Research, Tuskegee Institute; Research Associate, Institute for Social Research, The University of Michigan; Professor of Sociology, Florida A. and M. University. Dr. Epps has edited the following books: *Black Students in White Schools* and *Race Relations: Current Perspectives*. Dr. Epps has also edited special issues of the *Journal of Social Issues* and the *School Review*.

ROBERT M. HANSON, Ed.D.: Director of Special Education, Second Supervisory District of Westchester County, New York. Dr. Hanson received his M.Ed. from the University of Nevada and his Ed.D. from Syracuse University. He is a member of the American Association of School Administrators, Council for Exceptional Children and past president of the New York State Association of Special Education Administrators.

RICHARD E. HARDY, Ed.D.: Diplomate in Counseling Psychology (ABPP), Professor and Chairman, Department of Rehabilitation Counseling, Virginia Commonwealth University, Richmond, Virginia; Technical Consultant, United States Department of Health, Education, and Welfare, Rehabilitation Services Administration, Washington, D. C.; Editor, American Lecture Series in Social and Rehabilitation Psychology, Charles C Thomas, Publisher; and Associate Editor, *Journal of Voluntary Action Research*. Formerly Rehabilitation Counselor in Virginia, Rehabilitation Advisor, Rehabilitation Services Administration, United States Department of Health, Education, and Welfare, Washington, D. C.; former Chief Psychologist and Supervisor of Professional Training, South Carolina Department of Rehabilitation and member of the South Carolina State Board of Examiners in Psychology. The following are some of the books which Dr. Hardy has coauthored and coedited: *Drug Dependence and Rehabilitation Approaches, Fundamentals of Criminal Behavior and Correctional Systems, Rehabilitation of the Drug*

Abuser with Delinquent Behavior, and *Therapeutic Needs of the Family.* Dr. Hardy has contributed more than sixty publications to the professional literature in psychology and rehabilitation.

OLIVER D. HENSLEY, Ph.D.: Professor and Director, Research and Projects, Northeast Louisiana University, Monroe, Louisiana; Chairman, Research Committee, Society of Research Administrators; Editor, *Society of Research Administrator's Notebook;* Technical Consultant to public schools throughout the United States, to various government agencies, and to universities. Dr. Hensley has directed numerous programs concerned with improving public schools in newly integrated communities. He has been an administrator and teacher in public schools and in institutions of higher education. Dr. Hensley is the author of several articles on bussing as a factor promoting racial integration and is also the author of articles on the acceptance and adoption of educational innovations.

CYNTHIA A. KALLAN: Mrs. Kallan is a learning disabilities specialist. She is presently employed by the New York City Board of Education, Office of Special Education, as a psycho-educational evaluator of children with learning disabilities. Prior to her employment with the NYC Board of Education, she acted as consultant to the Learning Rehabilitation Services, Maimonides Hospital Mental Health Center in Brooklyn, New York. Here she developed a pilot program in perceptual-motor therapy, and learning rehabilitation and participated in their diagnostic screening and studies of learning disabled children. She has contributed another article "Rhythm and Sequencing in an Inter-sensory Approach to Learning Disabilities," which appeared in the February 1972 issue of the *Journal of Learning Disabilities.* She has lectured on the subject at various colleges in the New York City area, and has been a panel discussant at the ACLD Conference in February 1970.

SAUL S. LESHNER, Ph.D.: Professor of Management, Temple University; Regional Counseling Consultant, Manpower Administration, U. S. Department of Labor. Member of the Board of Trustees, Eagleville Hospital and Rehabilitation Center. Formerly, Executive Director, Jewish Employment and Vocational Service of Philadelphia. Fellow in the American Psychological Association and Pennsylvania Psychological Association, and member of the National Rehabilitation Association, American Personnel and Guidance Association, Philadelphia Society of Clinical Psychologists. Dr. Leshner has contributed forty professional publications in vocational rehabilitation, manpower development, counseling, mental retardation, aging, disadvantaged youth, work evaluation and vocational education.

ALLAN C. ORNSTEIN: Associate professor of education at Loyola University of Chicago. Author of ten books including: *Race and Politics in School/Community Relations* (Goodyear, 1974), *Metropolitan Schools: Administrative Decentralization vs Community Control* (Scarcrow Press, 1974), and *Reforming Metropolitan Schools* (Goodyear, 1974) with Daniel U. Levine and Dorey A. Wilkerson.

ROBERT B. PHILLIPS, M.Ed.: Special teacher for children with learning disabilities with the Board of Cooperative Educational Services, Port Chester, New York. Received his B.A. in 1955 from Lincoln University and his M.Ed. in 1962 from the University of Pittsburgh. He has taught children with various disabilities, including brain-injured and mentally retarded. Member of the New York State Teachers Association, National Education Association, American Association of Mental Deficiency and New York Association for Brain Injured Children.

BARBARA RIEGEL, M.S.W.: Assistant Chief, Social Services, North San Diego County District Office, Department of Public Welfare. Formerly Child Welfare Supervisor, Foster

Home Licensing Supervisor in San Diego County; Social Worker in private practice, Family Service Association, and San Diego County Department of Public Welfare. Ms. Riegel has also written "Group Meetings with Adolescents in Child Welfare," *Child Welfare,* July 1968.

MARTIN A. SILVERMAN, M.D.: Senior Psychiatrist, The Child Development Center of the Jewish Board of Guardians, New York, New York; Clinical Instructor in Psychoanalysis, Division of Psychoanalytic Education, Department of Psychiatry, State University of New York, College of Medicine, Downstate Medical Center, Brooklyn, New York. Formerly Instructor in Psychiatry, Department of Psychiatry, University of Rochester School of Medicine and Dentistry, Rochester, New York. Dr. Silverman has contributed a number of publications to the professional literature in psychiatry and psychoanalysis.

MARJORIE KAWIN TOOMIM, Ph.D.: Received her doctorate from the University of Southern California. She has held several positions of responsibility in the Los Angeles area. Currently Dr. Toomim is in private practice. Her areas of interests are community, psychology, child development, humanistic psychology and separation counseling.

ALEXANDER J. TYMCHUK, Ph.D.: Assistant Professor of Psychology and Psychiatry, and Psychology Coordinator, University Affiliated Facility, Center for the Health Sciences, University of California, Los Angeles, California. Consultant, Los Angeles County Experimental Education for Autistic Children Project. He has written *The Mental Retardation Dictionary,* edited a book of readings on the psychology of the exceptional child and has contributed thirty articles to the professional literature in psychology and special education.

EVA WOLFSON, B.A.: Educational Consultant, Division of Day Care, Department of Health of the City of New York. Formerly Educational Director, Goddard-Riverside Head Start, New York, New York; Educational Consultant, Preschool Liaison Project, The Child Development Center of the Jewish Board of Guardians, New York, New York.

PREFACE

ONE OF THE MOST significant problems facing our society, and specifically professional practitioners in diverse medical and social disciplines, is concern for youth who have been physically, psychologically and socially marred due to deprivation and disadvantagement. Deprivation and disadvantagement have been with us always—they are a most persistent problem. However, only when the factors of affluence and technology have become so advanced do we recognize, by a stark contrast, the real impact of these factors on our culture. By recognizing the problem and by mobilizing our efforts to obviate the lasting effects of deprivation and disadvantagement not only can we add quality to many lives but to the total society since there will be more citizens capable of contributing to the welfare of the society.

The purpose of this text is to take a small, tentative step toward the erosion of these problems. We hope to communicate the parameters of the problems of disadvantagement and dependency. We are identifying many areas in which these conditions have impact. From this identification we feel the magnitude of the problem will be evident and perhaps some readers will be motivated to take the next step which is outlining the approaches in the mobilization effort to overcome the effects of these conditions of disadvantagement and deprivation.

We are very grateful to the contributors for their efforts in revising their materials when we felt it was necessary to do so. We appreciate the help from Joanie Tiller and Libby Wingfield for their untiring clerical help and from Margie Alexy for her help in all the library research which was required in the development of this text. Lastly, we are most appreciative of the support and encouragement we received from our wives.

John G. Cull

Richard E. Hardy

Stuarts Draft, Va.

xvii

CONTENTS

Part Two

IMPLICATIONS OF DISADVANTAGEMENT
AND DEPRIVATION

PROBLEMS OF DISADVANTAGED AND DEPRIVED YOUTH

CHAPTER 1

WHO ARE THE DISADVANTAGED?

Allan C. Ornstein

EDUCATORS WHO SPEAK OF or write about the disadvantaged tend to categorize them somewhat arbitrarily into one or more of the following areas of deprivation: economic, racial, geographical, social, cultural, cognitive, and/or emotional. The explanation of each category, including the descriptions and characteristics, focuses on their weaknesses and cumulative deficits. This is the traditional and most prominent school of thought. It is based on the writings of the 1940's and 1950's, which described the plight of lower-class youth as well as of racial minorities and emerged as "common wisdom" in the 1960's—when the two groups, that is lower-class and racial minority youth, began to appear interchangeably under the label "disadvantaged."

Although the author tends to agree that lower-class youth and racial minority youth are disadvantaged in our schools and society, and will return to this theme below, there is a danger of oversimplifying this relationship, of dichotomizing students solely into lower and middle class and categorizing all minorities into lower class and all whites into middle class. Similarly, it invites stereotyping; reinforces a segregated rather than an integrated view of society; and reflects, in part, a cultural bias. The author will attempt to go beyond this one-sided, often simplified approach of describing the disadvantaged in terms of a racial, ethnic, or socioeconomic group.

In describing the disadvantaged, Robert J. Havighurst (Havighurst, 1964) tend to follow the traditional approach. He refers to their family, personal, and social group handicaps, and tends to sort them into observable groups mainly at the bottom of the

American society in terms of income, as well as in racial and ethnic groups, hence, trapping the uncritical reader, and educator, too, into describing the disadvantaged solely in terms of low income and race.

What may be considered as a reaction to the "negative" literature on the disadvantaged is the attempt to list and define the "positive" characteristics or strengths of the disadvantaged. This treatment tends to romanticize the poor and implies that their teachers have no real respect for, or understanding of, them. Comparing both schools of thought, the literature that portrays the disadvantaged negatively implies that the student, or his family and environment, is mainly to blame for his school failure; the literature that presents a "positive" view of the disadvantaged blames the teachers and schools.

Frank Riessman's (Riessman, 1964) writings are indicative of the new and growing trend to describe the disadvantaged as having many positive characteristics—a physical orientation, hidden verbal ability, creative potential, group cohesiveness, informality, sense of humor, etc. By using the word "disadvantaged" in the title of the paper, which describes these "positive" characteristics, as well as "deprived" in his noted book, *The Cuturally Deprived Child*, Riessman unwittingly endorses the standards of the school of thought and of middle-class school and society which he criticizes. In this connection, Riessman currently uses the term "poor" youth, with the mistaken conviction that this is a more positive term, in referring to the disadvantaged or deprived.

An extension of the philosophy of the positive portrayal of the disadvantaged is the contention that these children and youth are not culturally deprived, that they have a culture of their own, and that most of us fail to recognize this because of our middle-class standards in measuring and judging them. Those who argue this viewpoint refer to the "culture of poverty." In doing so there is a propensity to glorify the poor, which seems almost ludicrous, for slums are ugly and slum life is painful. Also, there is a tendency to claim that the poor do not want to become like the middle class, which seems equally ludicrous, for the poor, even those who are trapped in the culture of poverty, wish to break their chains of penury, which connotes a striving toward a middle-class income level and a simultaneous change in values and life style.

Although Oscar Lewis (Lewis, 1966) was not writing directly to an educational audience or about the disadvantaged, his concept of the culture of poverty, which reflects his deep respect and concern for the poor, is the basis of the writings in which the term "culturally deprived" is rejected and poverty is ennobled. For Lewis, the culture of poverty is a way of life shared by poor people, transcending rural-urban, regional, and national differences. Poverty across the globe is more than just a story of deprivation, disorganization, and dispiritedness. It has a structure, organization, and rationale—a sense of community and group values. Although the poor are marginal and helpless now, Lewis warns they have a deep resentment toward the establishment, toward the "haves," and that they represent a potentially powerful and world-wide political force. Lewis claimed that about ten million Americans live in the culture of poverty. Although blacks are not the only people who constitute this bottom group, their liberation movement—from chattel to black power—represents both ends of the continuum of the culture of poverty, the emerging first of the "third world."

Many educators now contend that middle-class, suburban youth can no longer be taken for granted either; these youth, for the greater part, feel aimless, useless, cynical, and alienated— deeply worried about their future—or they even question if there will be one. Similarly, many are in revolt against their parents and against the technological aspects of society: bigness, bureaucratization, impersonality, careerism, etc.

His slum counterpart may live in a fatherless home, but the suburban adolescent may be seriously lacking in parental attention; often both parents work in the day and attend social activities in the evening. While the poor slum youngster may swipe hubcaps, push heroin, or give birth to an illegitimate child, the affluent suburban adolescent may steal automobiles, trip on LSD, or visit grandmother.

The suburban child, according to the recent literature, lives in a saran-wrapped, protective, and limited environment, engulfed by growing provincialism and prejudicial attitudes toward other social groups. Alice Miel's (Miel, 1967) findings denote this alarming situation: The average suburban elementary pupil is bigoted and hypocritical about other racial, religious, ethnic, and socioeconomic groups. Materalism, selfishness, conspicuous consumption, cheap abundance, and an uneasy conformity pervade.

There is a tiny band of ultraprogressive critics of teachers and schools, whose "wisdom" seems couched in the rhetoric of angry exaggeration, who tend to gush over and review each other's books: Coles, Friendenberg, Hentoff, Holt, Kohl, Kozol, and Schragg, to name a few. For them, the schools are factories of failure, classrooms are cages, and teachers are unproductive frauds. These critics broaden the concept of the disadvantaged to include almost all students, regardless of their color, income, geographical location, etc. Their teachers and schools short change them; therefore, they are unable to fulfill their learning potential. Thus, students do not fail schools; teachers and schools fail them.

John Holt (Holt, 1964) as indicated above, espouses this type of philosophy. He observes the way students manipulate their teachers and adopt strategies of fear and failure. The longer the student goes to school, the more bored, answer-centered, and stifled he becomes. Even worse, according to Holt, most teachers are unaware of their students' strategies and the way they think or feel.

Finally, the term *disadvantaged* is nebulous and relative; educators need to agree upon and define this term, rather than vault off in several directions. For the author's purpose, and he makes no liberal or fashionable pretense about it, any student who falls below the school standard is disadvantaged. In this connection, the research shows there is a substantially high positive correlation between (1) low school achievement and low-income youth and (2) low school achievement and racial minority youth. Similarly, there is a high positive correlation between low income and racial minority groups.

To the author's knowledge, there is no school yet in which low-income youth or minority youth are not overtly or covertly discriminated against—where they have an equal educational opportunity, regardless of the amount of compensatory educational input or quota of school interracial mixing.

The school by its very nature and function is a white-oriented, middle-class institution, and one of its main functions is to perpetuate the white, middle-class society, despite our lip service that the schools should shape society. Teachers, by the level of their education and income, tend to adopt and mirror middle-class values, despite the few radicals who would have us believe the opposite, who are usually squashed by the system or elevated by it into another position. Achievement tests, school texts, and curriculum objectives still reflect a middle-class fair-skinned bias —despite our notions about (presently nonexistent) culture-free tests and token integrated primers and courses in black history. All our rhetoric about reorganizing the school system and redistributing power, under the philosophy of integration, decentralization, and/or local control, will not change the system; the carbon copy, xeroxing process will continue: bright students will be siphoned off from stupid students; the former will continue to be awarded gold stars while the latter receives demerits.

For purposes of school achievement, it does little good for the student to possess other skills, abilities, positive strengths, or a different culture, unless the school system changes. Granted, the white, middle-class student may reject school and society; nevertheless, when all the other variables are held constant (although some may be vague or unidentifiable), he has a "more equal chance" than the minority, and/or lower-class student for obtaining the proper credentials—a college degree—and becoming a part of the very power structure he may condemn. He may decide to accept or reject the myth of the dominant culture, but at least he has his choice.

Thus, our concern should be realistically directed toward those youth who seem destined to drop out of school or to graduate as functional illiterates, i.e. the American poor and minority youth who are more prone to becoming educationally disadvantaged.

REFERENCES

Havighurst, R. J.: Who are the socially disadvantaged? *J Negro Educ,* 33:210-217, 1964.

Holt, J.: *How Children Fail.* New York, Pitman, 1964.

Lewis, O.: *La Vida.* New York, Random, 1966.

Miel, A.: *The Shortchanged Children of Suburbia.* New York, Human Relations Press, 1967.

Riessman, F.: The overlooked positives of disadvantaged groups. *J Negro Educ,* 33:225-231, 1964.

Riessman, F.: *The Culturally Deprived Child.* New York, Har-Row, 1962.

CHAPTER 2

PRIVATION OR DEPRIVATION: A DISCUSSION ON THE "CULTURALLY DEPRIVED" CHILD

CYNTHIA A. KALLAN

CULTURALLY DEPRIVED children are not deprived of stimulation. Rather they are deprived of distinctive stimulation. Sensory stimulation, sheer amounts of light or sound, for instance, is not to be equated with symbolic or intellectual stimulation. Actually, to be deprived of something, an individual must first have experienced the stimuli, then suffer its loss. In the case of the culturally deprived, I would venture to say, the suffering is from privation rather than deprivation.

Who is the disadvantaged child? We used to call him "the slum child," "the poor white," "the migrant." He may be white or Negro, he may be a mixture of many ethnic cultures. His place in our society is delineated by his socioeconomic environment. If poverty is considered, he has been classed as "disadvantaged." Poverty is defined as characterizing a family with an annual income of less than $3,000 per year.

Riessman describes the culturally deprived child as follows: a) He is physical and visual, rather than aural; b) he is content-centered, rather than form-centered; c) he is externally oriented, rather than introspective; d) he is centered on a problem, rather than on an abstraction; e) he is inductive, rather than deductive; f) he is spatial, rather than temporal.

One out of every three children in our school system is classed as culturally deprived, disadvantaged, or as a retarded reader. A retarded reader is generally regarded as one who is reading a year or more below grade placement. The culturally deprived

11

child is not culturally deprived. Rather, he has been reared in a culture and society that is different from his middle-class counterpart. He has a life style of his own. He is nonverbally oriented and motoric. He lives to survive for today and is quick to take advantage of an opportunity that will afford him pleasure. He is creative, in that he can figure out a way to "circumvent the law when the law is irrelevant to his life," or to play basketball without the trappings of a gymnasium. He orients spatially, through the physical world, but often does not tune in on temporal orientations, the abstract world.

The child of poverty, of whom we are speaking, suffers from a distinct kind of stimuli privation. He lacks differentiation of visual stimuli in his world. His figure-ground perceptions are inadequate; eye-hand controlled movements are noticeably inadequate. He keeps himself occupied, and out of trouble by watching TV or listening to a blasting radio. He does not learn to relate to his environment through touching and manipulating his surroundings. Language, *per se,* is clouded through limited verbal communications with others. Sound is everywhere but auditory discrimination is inadequate. He has no play room, no picture books, few people who would talk to him, no one to read to him, no blocks or games that would normally stimulate his middle-class counterpart. How can he prepare himself for school? He does not recognize forms, shapes, sizes, contours, textures, etc. He is not deprived; in his case, again, this is a privation of selected stimuli.

Like any young child, he thrives on a just but firm atmosphere. He is very literal and responds to a structured, functional set of guidelines. It is quite clear that the present educational system has not been able to reach these children, for it is structured to approach the middle-class child, with middle-class teachers who come from middle-class teacher education programs. Society has not provided educational leadership training necessary for new supplementary technologies to filter through to the teacher training programs.

A major problem is that the education system tends to ignore some well-established knowledge about human development that could be applied for the benefit of these children. Cognitive psychologists of today have taken the work of Piaget a step further than originally outlined. Piaget painstakingly observed and recorded children's cognitive development in much the same manner as Gesell set norms for the average child's development and growth. Erickson and Freud have outlined for us the stages of psychosocial and psychosexual progression of personality development. The works of these men have given us standards to be used as guideposts in understanding the physical, cognitive and social growth of the child.

Most feel that an individual's achievement in life depends very largely on what he has been helped to learn before the age of four. The passage of time and "waiting until he matures" may cause irreparable damage. Studies of the disadvantaged child, the child with a developmental lag in his perceptual-motor functioning, and the child whose personality development has been fixated in a stage of his maturation processes, have shown that active intervention through learning therapy and psychotherapy have been successfully utilized to rehabilitate such a youngster. Time, used inappropriately in rehabilitating and intellectually stimulating the children of the slums, increases the cumulative deficit ratio.

Until about eighteen months of age, the children of poverty and middle-class families perform along parallel lines. In some respects, such as motor performance, the poorer class infants seem slightly ahead. At about eighteen months, when babies begin to talk, they move from the physical to the cultural environment. It is here that the curves of development take widely divergent forms. Middle-class toddlers begin by investigating their world of toys, speech and games under the guidance of interested adults. But the children of poverty in their crowded, disorganized, noisy homes, learn that the best way to stay out of trouble is to keep quiet. By kindergarten age the I.Q. scores of these children of poverty run five to fifteen points below their middle-class peers.

Piaget tells us that language becomes internalized as an instrument of thought. A child uses language even when he does not speak. Piaget calls it inner speech; speech for oneself, as opposed to speech for others. Preschoolers speak out loud, an intermediate stage during which their voiced egocentric speech fulfills the functions of inner speech.

A child who learns a restricted linguistic code from his lower working class parents also learns that nothing really important is ever transmitted by language. In his family, the strongest messages take nonverbal forms; gestures, inclinations, actions, spankings—where are the family lectures on values, attitudes, motivations, ethics and morals to which the middle-class child is exposed? A mother's teaching style is a better predictor of a child's school achievement than is his I.Q. Since the child's central task is to deal with the environment and learn to focus on ideas, deprivation seems to be a deprivation of meaning in early cognitive relationships between mother and child.

Head Start does not appear to have produced any lasting change in children's understanding of their language skills or in their ability to learn. By the age of five or six, slum children trail so far behind their middle-class counterparts, that from an educational point of view, they are already remedial cases. Improving their behavior is not enough; socialization is not enough. Enrichment such as field trips or clay modeling is not enough. In eight weeks, can a child from the slums catch up to his more fortunate classmates? What he needs is intensive, systematic training to bring him closer to the verbal and abstract level required for success in school.

Carl Bereiter and Sigfried Engelman, working in the slums of Urbana, Illinois, devised a system of conceptual awakening in the disadvantaged child of preschool age. Some call it the pressure cooker approach. This is a misnomer, for with an understanding of how the slum child approaches life, it is the logical way to stimulate him: noise, participation and an urgency about learning. Language, loud and intense, is an instrument of learning and thinking. This was rescue operation. However, it was successful and can be justifiably applied to the middle-class preschool program, albeit, without the reinforcement of the physical noisy atmosphere. One can stimulate conceptualization in the preschooler!

Deutsch emphasizes the urgency of early childhood education, for intervention later may be wasteful. The essential element is simply that for the child who is inadequately equipped to handle what school has to offer, it is up to the system to develop compensatory strategies through a program of stimulation appropriate to his capabilities. Deutsch strongly recommends a flexible, ungraded grouping of children in the elementary school that will permit individuals to complete, for example, a given three-year block of work in four years or perhaps in two years. This will reduce discouragement on the part of the slower children and make it possible for the more able to accelerate and/or enrich their learning.

If we were to match the needed skills with the developmental stages of a child's growth as Hunt suggests, the child should be enrolled in a formalized school situation beginning at age four. He would then find himself in a systematically enriched environment encompassing his pre-operational and pre-conceptual stages. De Hirsch proposes an interim class for the children with a developmental lag in their perceptual skills. Deutsch would like to carry this concept further with ungraded classes up to and including the second grade. Riessman, too, recommends that there be a transition period in the school where the deprived child is awakened, through his visual and kinesthetic senses. He will then be able to progress to the conceptual level where verbalization can occur without immediate sensory cues.

Volume upon volume has been written, each proferring similar recommendations. Question: What concrete steps has the System taken to heed the advice, suggestions and recommendations offered by men of knowledge and experience?

REFERENCES

Bereiter, C., Engelmann, S.: *Teaching Disadvantaged Children in Pre-School.* Prentice-Hall, Englewood Cliffs, N. J., 1966.
de Hirsch, K. et al.: *Predicting Reading Failure.* New York, Har-Row, 1966.
Deutsch, M. et al.: *The Disadvantaged Child.* New York, Basic, 1967.
Hunt, J. McV.: *Intelligence and Experience.* Roland Press, New York, 1961.
Piaget, J.: *The Language and Thought of the Child.* Cabain, Marjorie (Trans.) New York, Meridian Books, 1967.
Pines, M.: *Revolution in Learning.* New York, Har-Row, 1967.
Riessman, F.: *The Culturally Deprived Child.* New York, Har-Row. 1962.

CHAPTER 3

PERSONALITY AND THE ECONOMICALLY DISADVANTAGED CHILD*

Alexander J. Tymchuk

T HE MEMBERS OF THE President's Panel on Mental Retardation (1962) concluded that the greatest number of persons classified as mentally retarded are mildly retarded with no demonstrable organic basis for their retardation. Further, these members reported that the majority of those labelled mildly retarded come from impoverished families with considerable overlap between mild mental retardation and impoverishment.

Inherent in the definition of mental retardation is the intellectual or cognitive deficit on which the definition is made. Remediation programs, therefore, have stressed cognitive factors in an attempt to overcome the debilitating effects of poverty upon the intellectual development of these children. This emphasis upon cognitive factors alone has caused an even greater neglect than there has been in the past of noncognitive factors that have been shown to influence how the child from an impoverished background will approach a new learning situation and will assimilate the new information presented in that situation. These nonintellective or personality factors are important and should be taken into consideration before any cognitive training can effectively take place. These factors may also play a key role in the initial assessment of the level of intelligence of these children.

*The writing of this paper was supported in part by Maternal and Child Health Grant Number 927, Interdisciplinary Training in Mental Retardation.

16

This article presents some of the evidence to show that an emphasis must also be placed upon personality factors as well as upon cognitive factors in intervention programs with mildly retarded children from impoverished backgrounds. A hypothetical view of how personality becomes an integral part of intellectual functioning in these children will also be presented.

Hunt's View of the Development of Intrinsic Motivation

Despite a paucity of theoretrical statements on the personality of the disadvantaged child, Hunt (1969, 1972) has provided an initial conceptualization of that personality. Hunt (1963) originally postulated that man was motivated in part at least to learn new material because of the motivation inherent or instrinsic in the processing of that new information. Hunt explained this intrinsic motivation as being in opposition to extrinsic motivation or motivation for external reasons (e.g., money). As part of his conceptualization of the development of intrinsic motivation, Hunt adapted the test-operate-test-exit or TOTE unit of Miller, Galanter and Pribram (1960). In the TOTE unit the individual perceives a stimulus, compares it with his past experience and performs a behavior based upon his past learning. If the stimulus is too incongruous with his past experience, the person's behavior may be to withdraw; if the stimulus is too familiar, the response may be boredom. Somewhere in between is an optimum of incongruity.

Hunt believes that the poverty situation is not conducive to the development of intrinsic motivation and hence the retardation that some of these children show is due not to an inherent incapacity to learn, but to inefficient means of processing new information related specifically to their personality structures.

In Hunt's conceptualization there are three stages in the development of intrinsic motivation in which the need for an optimum of incongruity or the problem of the match plays an integral part.

In Hunt's schema, stage one in the development of intrinsic motivation is the orienting response which appears in all infants. The child orients towards stimuli and variations in those stimuli.

When there is no variation as in orphanages (Dennis, 1960), children soon stop orienting because of the lack of change in stimulation. Stage two involves the child in actively attempting to move towards, to grab or to suck the stimulus and to begin recognition of objects, places or events. The baby is beginning to be able to explore and to predict his environment. He is learning in the absence of extrinsic reinforcers. In stage three the child's repeated encounters with objects, events and places have become too familiar and now he has a memory or the basis with which to compare new information. He becomes interested in *novelty*. This interest in novelty usually occurs by the end of the first year (Piaget, 1936). Now, the child, if he has been encouraged in the past, will seek new experiences. If these new experiences are too incongruous with his past experience, he will withdraw (e.g., fear of unfamiliar faces), but there must be some incongruity or novelty involved so that he will strive for it. Rats will even endure electric shock to get from their familiar nests to an unfamiliar cage where novel objects were available to manipulate (Nessin, 1930, referred to in Hunt, 1963). On the other hand, lack of stimulation, as in the case of college students in an unstimulating environment, causes extreme boredom and agitation (Bexton, Herson and Scott, 1954). Festinger (1957) has found that people withdraw from information that is too incongruous with their own.

The child's interest in novelty now motivates him to explore new objects where he has to move to get to them and he begins imitating adult language sounds. The development of language provides him with another means of finding new information. With the development of language, the child learns that objects have names (labelling) and begins classifying them in finer classes. This is the development of abstract language. The parent must now provide for encounters with experiences that have the proper degree of incongruity. If the parent does not provide him with these new and various encounters, the infant may begin performing self-stimulating behaviors or begin to lag developmentally. This developmental lag is precisely what occurs in the impoverished environment; the lag is not only in cognition, but also in personality and motivation.

Hunt's conceptualization of the development of intrinsic motivation has important implications for the study of the mildly retarded from impoverished environments because it provides a model that might help us understand how personality variables might affect intellectual development.

Early Experience of the Mildly Retarded Child From An Impoverished Background

In Hunt's first stage the infant orients itself to variations in stimulation. In the typical home in a poverty environment there are many children, a great deal of noise and little variation in light (Deutsch, 1965). There is little or no variation in the type of stimulation; the child has little chance to respond to changes in stimulation so that stage one may be delayed. Although some may consider that early developmental landmarks would not be affected by a stable environment, evidence has shown that the appearance of fisted swiping and grasping, both part of the development of eye-hand coordination, can be hastened through varying stimulation (White and Held, 1966). Greenberg, Uzgiris and Hunt (1968) found that whereas infants with mobiles over their cribs showed the eye-blink response at age seven weeks, in those without mobiles, it appeared at age ten weeks.

The importance of these data lies in the fact that these early developmental behaviors form the basis of later behaviors and any delay is magnified by a cumulative effect. Further evidence comes from a study in which groups of infants at seven, eleven, fifteen, eighteen and twenty-two months of age from middle- and lower-class families were studied for the attainment of the notion of permanence, for the development of schemas, foresightful behavior, imitation and verbal facility. The middle-class infants did better on all variables. In addition, overstimulation in the home was correlated with a poorer performance; that is, an infant reared in a crowded home where the television was always on, was less advanced than one who was raised in a moderately and directly stimulating environment (Wachs, Uzgiris and Hunt, 1967). Schoggen and Schoggen (1971) have reported the same type of home conditions with the poor; in professional homes, interaction between infants and parents is directed and purposeful.

Pavenstedt (1965) and Malone (1966) have identified family disorganization as another factor in the early experience of these children that appears to be critical in the child's development. The stable families lived in clean, but unstimulating homes; the mother was authoritarian, but the children were not neglected. In the unstable family the children were neglected, radios blared, no one responded to infant demands. No child owned anything exclusively, none approached the adults for comfort, nor did they expect requests to be filled. They did not follow directions.

Hertzig, Birch, Thomas and Mendez (1968) in studying middle- and lower-class Puerto Rican mothers found that whereas the former appeared to be concerned about when their children could assume responsibility and encouraged task-mastery, the latter discouraged such attempts by their children and did little talking with them. In testing, the lower class children made fewer responses and did more poorly than their middle-class peers.

In Hunt's stages two and three, in the poor environment there would be little opportunity for the child to seek and explore, to have his environment respond to him and to find novelty. Exploratory behavior and questions are squelched by punishment and are not encouraged in the poverty situation (Gray and Klaus, 1965).

Children from impoverished environments then have few opportunities to learn, typically encounter fewer objects than middle-class children and live in an environment continuously and unvaryingly low in stimulation. These children have little opportunity to interact verbally with adequate language models; their questions go unanswered or are squelched; they are seldom asked to describe events; their ingenuity is seldom rewarded; and they have little opportunity to learn to take the initiative, to give up present satisfactions for larger ones later or to take pride in problem-solving achievement (Hunt, 1972).

By the time the economically disadvantaged child who comes from such an environment reaches school age, he is ill-prepared to participate in a classroom where self-control, attention, task-mastery, achievement, motivation, and adequate language are required. In terms of Hunt's model the incongruity may be too much and he may withdraw. The effects of his environment may be so debilitating that he may never catch up to his middle-class peers. Through school, this child will withdraw from too difficult problems showing fear of failure and performing some tasks only if the reward is enough, but seldom for the satisfaction that task-mastery brings.

There is evidence that the personality of mildly retarded children from impoverished backgrounds develops in this fashion. This personality is independent of any cognitive ability but yet has a great effect upon how that cognitive ability is displayed. For this reason, it is vitally important that attention be paid to change this personality structure to one that helps performance in our current middle-class society. At the end of this chapter, we will discuss some ways in which this can be done.

Evidence for Personality Structure Peculiar to the Mildly Retarded

There is evidence available that the present conceptualization of the development of a personality structure peculiar to the mildly retarded may be valid.

Manifest Anxiety and Achievement

One would expect to find higher anxiety scores in these children particularly when placed in an unfamiliar testing or school situation because these are too incongruous to their experience. Several studies have shown that mildly retarded children have significantly higher manifest anxiety scores than do their middle-class peers (Cochran and Cleland, 1963; Feldhusen and Klausmeier, 1962). In addition, Haywood and Dobbs (1964) have reported that their lower-class group scored significantly higher than did their middle-class group on both a manifest anxiety and a tension avoiding scale and on an extrinsic motivation scale. Several other studies have found that high test anxiety scores and poor test performance are related for mildly retarded subjects (Reger, 1964; Silverstein, 1966).

Self-Concept, Curiosity, and Fear of Failure

Self-concept appears also to be related to level of manifest anxiety. Katz (1970) for example, found that among Negro boys from a high poverty area, low achievement, anxiety and self-devaluation were significantly interrelated as well as being related to the boys' perceptions of low parental acceptance and high parental punitiveness. Other studies have shown high positive correlations between manifest anxiety scores and teachers' ratings of maladjustment, between self and desired self, and with the tendency to nominate oneself or to be nominated by one's peers for negative roles in a sociometric situation (Cowen, Zax, Klein, Izzo and Trost, 1965).

Evidence has also been reported that children from impoverished backgrounds show a lower need for achievement compared to their middle-class peers (Rosen, 1956; Merbaum, 1962) and are generally socially immature with a higher chance of dropping out of school and for acting out delinquent behavior (Eisenthal and Sherman, 1969).

There is some evidence that mildly retarded children are less curious than their middle-class peers and data have been reported showing that this curiosity is directly related to the mother's curiosity (Saxe and Stollak, 1971) and to the mother's support (Minuchin, 1971). Highly curious lower-class children tend to have a better self-concept than their less curious peers (Minuchin, 1971).

Part of this lack of curiosity or novelty-seeking may be due to the original lack of support in the home environment, but later in school situations, to a fear of failure. Malone (1960) stated that the person who has low self-esteem is strongly motivated to avoid failure and will set goals so low that he need not strive to prove himself. This failure avoidance has serious implications in the education of the mentally retarded where an attempt is made to motivate the person to try new tasks, to guess and to use new language. Research has shown that following experimental failure on a task, retarded children will even blame themselves for the failure when in reality they had nothing to do with that failure (MacMillan, 1969; MacMillan and Keogh,

1971). After an experimental failure experience, the performance of mildly retarded children has regressed; that is, they make more errors and perform more slowly. And after experimental failure, when given a choice of doing a task previously completed or similar to an earlier one, or attempting a new task, mildly retarded children will invariably select the former, shying away from the threat of potential failure in a novel situation (Weblink and Stedman, 1966). Middle-class children will select new tasks after failure and will improve in performance (Gardner, 1966).

Motivation-Orientation

A number of researchers have identified that retarded children will work for an opportunity to interact socially with the experimenter (e.g. Zigler and Williams, 1963). Zigler, Butterfield and Capobianco (1970) in a ten-year follow-up study of institutionalized retarded children from backgrounds of varying degrees of deprivation, found that the motivation for social reinforcement in those who came from the more deprived environment decreased most and concluded that institutionalization was more socially depriving for those children from less deprived backgrounds than for those from more deprived backgrounds.

Other researchers have found that mildly retarded children are less likely to be intrinsically motivated and are usually extrinsically motivated. Those who are intrinsically motivated will work more efficiently for the opportunity to do another task (Haywood and Weaver, 1967) and are more likely to be overachievers (Haywood, 1968a). Children who are extrinsically motivated are interested in safety, comfort and monetary reward; will avoid situations inducing tension (Haywood and Dobbs, 1964); perform significantly worse on a visual size discrimination task than those who are intrinsically motivated (Haywood and Wachs, 1966); will work more efficiently for money and are more likely to be underachievers.

More research is needed to determine if the mildly retarded child from an impoverished background is in fact extrinsically motivated and if this personality trait is related to his past experiences of failure, to a poor self-concept, to low achievement motivation and to heightened anxiety in formal testing and academic settings. In addition it must be determined how these traits affect learning and whether or not they can be prevented or changed.

How Personality May Affect Cognition

Correlations between intelligence test performance and scholastic achievement are between .50 and .70 thereby accounting for only 25 to 50 per cent of the variance associated with predicting achievement from I.Q. (Haywood, 1968b; Zigler and Butterfield, 1968). Stanford, Dember and Stanford (1963) have reported that manifest anxiety scores and I.Q. predicted reading performance by third grade children equally well, but that accuracy of prediction increased when the two predictors were combined. In addition, scores on Haywood's (1968b) motivator hygiene test can account for up to 30 per cent of the variance associated with the prediction of scholastic achievement among educable mentally retarded children, 10 per cent for intellectually average children and 0 per cent for intellectually superior children. Finally, Dave (1963) and Wolf (1964) have reported that a scale of home environment conditions correlate .69 with I.Q. and .80 with academic achievement.

These data, although correlational, indicate that noncognitive or personality factors can affect cognitive performance. Other evidence suggests that changing these noncognitive factors may in fact improve cognitive performance. Zigler and Butterfield (1968) have found that testing Head Start nursery school children before and after familiarization to the testing situation, significantly increases their I.Q.s compared to a group that was tested without familiarization. These gains are the same as those found in a contrast group that participated in a compensatory program.

These results were replicated by Zigler, Abelson and Seitz (1973) and by Kinnie and Sternlof (1971). These results suggest that economically disadvantaged children do perform more poorly on standardized tests and in schools because of a heightened anxiety as a result of their unfamiliarity with such situations, but that an adaptation experience allays this anxiety. It would be of interest to have an independent measure of anxiety (e.g. galvanic skin response) before and after such familiarization to determine if this is in fact what is occurring.

Portuges and Feshbach (1972) reported a study in which children from economically disadvantaged backgrounds imitated teachers' behaviors significantly less than did their middle-class peers. This finding is only suggestive but may indicate some inhibition on the part of the economically disadvantaged child to perform in a school setting.

Conclusion

The mildly retarded child, coming as he most often does from an economically disadvantaged environment, is ill-prepared to perform adequately in a standardized testing or academic situation. Early deprivation and inadequate training practices appear to have inculcated a personality structure that early in life may be characterized by apathy and unresponsiveness and later by a fear of failure, high test anxiety, a low need for achievement, a lack of interest or satisfaction in task-mastery, and a poor self-concept. Hunt's model of the development of intrinsic motivation serves as a useful conceptualization of how the economically disadvantaged child's interaction with his environment appears to shape his personality structures.

There are data to suggest that the environment can be manipulated so as to enhance rather than hinder adequate intellectual functioning. Familiarization to the testing situation is one such manipulation and there are others. Early intervention, either through a preventive parenthood concept where people before they become parents are trained how to foster both the cognitive and the personality growth of their child, or later through child care centers should be of the first priority. There is a great deal of evidence that parental support and reinforcement (Bee, Van Egeren, Streissguth, Nyman and Leckie, 1969), maternal warmth (Radin, 1971) and curiosity (Minuchin, 1971; Saxe and Stollak, 1971), prior exposure to strange stimuli (Endsley, 1967), and parental verbal intervention (Jones, 1972) will affect how a child from an impoverished background will achieve on standardized tests and in an academic setting. These parental behaviors are noncognitively related and yet affect how these children perform on cognitive tasks.

Providing self-selection of difficulty in school relates to Hunt's view of incongruity. If a child approaches a problem that is too difficult, he will withdraw; however, if he can select his own level of incongruity, he will succeed and be rewarded by that success thus providing for the basis of intrinsic motivation. The teacher must inculcate, through the use of social and other types of reinforcement, satisfaction in achievement.

These children should be encouraged to take the initiative, to explore, to be curious, to try new solutions. They should be encouraged to delay gratification for some later larger goal and be encouraged for persistence and effort in the attainment of that goal. Whether or not such efforts would have long-term effects must be empirically determined; however, the evidence indicates that they would.

REFERENCES

Bee, H., Van Egeren, L., Streissguth, A., Nyman, B. and Leckie, M.: Social class differences in maternal teaching strategies and speech patterns. *Dev Psychol, 1*:726-734, 1969.

Bexton, W., Heron, W. and Scott, T.: Effects of decreased variation in the sensory environment. *Can J Psychol, 8*:70-76, 1954.

Cochran, I. and Cleland, C.: Manifest anxiety of retardates and normal matched as to academic achievement. *Am J Ment Defic, 67*:539-542, 1963.

Cowen, E., Zax, M., Klein, R., Izzo, L. and Trost, M.: The relation of anxiety in school children to school record, achievement, and behavioral measures. *Child Dev, 36*:685, 1965.

Dave, R.: The identification and measurement of educational process variables that are related to educational achievement. Unpublished doctoral dissertation. Chicago, University of Chicago, 1963.

Dennis, W.: Causes of retardation among institutional children: Iran. *J Genet Psychol, 96*:47-59, 1960.

Deutsch, M.: The role of social class in language development and cognition. *Am J Orthopsychiatry, 35*:78-88, 1965.

Eisenthal, S. and Sherman, L.: Psychological characteristics of neighborhood youth corps enrollees. *J Consult Clin Psychol, 33*:420-425, 1969.

Endsley, R.: Effects of differential prior exposure on preschool children's subsequent choice of novel stimuli. *Psychonomic Science,* 7:411-412, 1967.

Feldhusen, J. and Klausmeier, H.: Anxiety, intelligence, and achievement in children of low, average, and high intelligence. *Child Dev.* 33:403-409, 1962.

Festinger, L.: *A Theory of Cognitive Dissonance.* Evanton, Row, Peterson, 1957.

Gardner, W.: Effects of failure on intellectually retarded and normal boys. *Am J Ment Defic,* 70:899-902, 1966.

Gray, S. and Klaus, R.: An experimental preschool program for culturally deprived children. *Child Dev,* 36:887-898, 1965.

Greenberg, D., Uzgiris, I. and Hunt, J.: Hastening the development of the blink response with looking. *J Genet Psychol,* 112:167-176, 1968.

Haywood, C.: Psychometric motivation and the efficiency of learning and performance in the mentally retarded. In Richards, B. (Ed.): *Proceedings of the First Congress of the International Association for the Scientific Study of Mental Deficiency.* Reigate, England, Michael Jackson Publishing Co., Ltd., 1968a.

Haywood, H.: Motivational orientation of overachieving and underachieving elementary school children. *Am J Ment Defic,* 72:662-667, 1968b.

Haywood, H. and Dobbs, V.: Motivation and anxiety in high school boys. *J Personality,* 32:371-379, 1964.

Haywood, H. and Wachs, T.: Size-discrimination learning as a function of motivation-hygiene orientation in adolescents. *J Educ Psychol,* 57:279-286, 1966.

Haywood, H. and Weaver, S.: Differential effects of motivational orientations and incentive conditions on motor performance in institutionalized retardates. *Am J Ment Defic,* 72:459-467, 1967.

Hertzig, M., Birch, H., Thomas, A. and Mendez, O.: Class and ethnic differences in the responsiveness of preschool children to cognitive demands. *Monogr Soc Res Child Dev,* vol. 33, 1, Whole No. 117, 1968.

Hunt, J.: Motivation inherent in information processing and action. In Harvey, O. (Ed.): *Motivation and Social Interaction.* New York, Ronald, 1963.

Hunt, J.: *The Challenge of Incompetence and Poverty.* Urbana, U of Ill Pr, 1969.

Hunt, J.: The role of experience in the development of competence. In Hunt, J. (Ed.): *Human Intelligence.* New Brunswick, N. J., Dutton, 1972.

Jones, P.: Home environment and the development of verbal ability. *Child Dev,* 43:1081-1086, 1972.

Katz, I.: A new approach to the study of school motivation in minority group children. In Allen, V. (Ed.): *Psychological Factors in Poverty.* Chicago, Markham, 1970.

Kinnie, E. and Sternlof, R.: The influence of noncognitive factors on the

IQ scores of middle- and lower-class children. *Child Dev, 42*:1989-1995, 1971.

MacMillan, D.: Motivational differences: Cultural-familial retardates vs. normal subjects on expectancy for failure. *Am J Ment Defic, 74*:254-258, 1969.

MacMillan, D. and Keogh, B.: Normal and retarded children's expectancy for failure. *Dev Psychol, 37*:579-586, 1971.

Malone, C.: Fear of failure and unrealistic vocational aspirations. *J Abnorm Soc Psychol, 60*:253-261, 1960.

Malone, C.: Safety first: Comments on the influence of external danger in the lives of children of disorganized families. *Am J Orthopsychiatry, 36*:3-12, 1966.

Merbaum, A.: Need for achievement in Negro and white children. *Dissertation Abstracts, 23*:693-694, 1962.

Miller, G., Galanter, E. and Pribram, K.: *Plans and the Structure of Behavior.* New York, HR&W, 1960.

Minuchin, P.: Correlates of curiosity and exploratory behavior in preschool disadvantaged children. *Child Dev, 42*:939-950, 1971.

Pavenstedt, E.: A comparison of child rearing environment of upper-lower- and very low lower-class families. *Am J Orthopsychiatry, 35*:89-98, 1965.

Piaget, J.: *The Origins of Intelligence in Children.* Cook, Margaret (Trans.): New York, Intl Univs Pr, 1952.

Portuges, S. and Feshbach, S.: The influence of sex and socioethnic factors upon imitation of teachers by elementary school children. *Child Dev, 43*:981-989, 1972.

President's Panel on Mental Retardation. Washington, D. C., U. S. Government Printing Office, 1962.

Radin, N.: Maternal warmth, achievement motivation, and cognitive functioning in lower-class preschool children. *Child Dev, 42*:1560-1565, 1971.

Reger, R.: Reading ability and CMAS scores in educable mentally retarded boys. *Am J Ment Defic, 68*:652-655, 1964.

Rosen, B.: The achievement syndrome. *Am Sociol Rev, 24*:47-60, 1959.

Saxe, R. and Stollak, G.: Curiosity and the parent-child relationship. *Child Dev, 42*:373-384, 1971.

Schoggen, M. and Schoggen, P.: Environmental forces in the home lives of three-year-old children in three population subgroups. *DARCEE Papers and Reports,* vol. 5, no. 2, 1971.

Silverstein, A.: Anxiety and the quality of human-figure drawings. *Am J Ment Defic, 70*:607-608, 1966.

Stanford, D., Dember, W. and Stanford, B.: A children's form of the Alpert-Haber Achievement Anxiety Scale. *Child Dev, 34*:1027-1032, 1963.

Wachs, T., Uzgiris, I. and Hunt, J.: Cognitive Development in Infants of Different Age Levels and From Different Environmental Backgrounds.

Paper presented at the meetings of the Society for Research in Child Development, New York, March, 1967.

Weblink, G. and Stedman, D.: Unpublished manuscripts, George Peabody College, 1966.

White, B. and Held, R.: Plasticity of sensory motor development. In Rosenblith, J. and Allensmith, W. (Eds.): *Readings in Child Development,* 2nd ed., and *Educational Psychology.* Boston, Allyn, 1966.

Wolf, R.: The identification and measurement of environmental process variables related to intelligence. Unpublished doctoral dissertation. Chicago, University of Chicago, 1964.

Zigler, E. and Williams, J.: Institutionalization and the effectiveness of social reinforcement: A three-year follow-up study. *J Abnorm Soc Psychol, 66*:197-205, 1963.

Zigler, E. and Butterfield, E.: Motivational aspects of changes in IQ test performance of culturally deprived nursery school children. *Child Dev, 39*:1-14, 1968.

Zigler, E., Butterfield, E. and Capobianco, F.: Institutionalization and the effectiveness of social reinforcement: A five- and eight-year follow-up study. *Dev Psychol, 3*:255-263, 1970.

Zigler, E., Abelson, W. and Seitz, V.: Motivational factors in the performance of economically disadvantaged children on the Peabody Picture Vocabulary Test. *Child Dev 44*:294-303, 1973.

CHAPTER 4

RUNAWAY YOUTH: CAUSES FOR RUNAWAY BEHAVIOR

Richard E. Hardy and John G. Cull

Background
Additional Reasons for Negative Attitudes on the Part of Society in General
Importance of Peer Groups and Role Models
References

THE RECENT discovery of the sadistic slayings and secret graves of twenty-seven boys in Houston, Texas has helped in focusing much needed attention of parents, professional helping persons including policemen and others on problems of the teenager who leaves home as what has been called a runaway. The number of young runaways has been estimated to total anywhere from six hundred thousand to one million a year (Parade, 1973).

BACKGROUND

Anthropologists tell us that the most persistent institution in the history of mankind has been the family unit which has been traced as a phenomenon back to the dawn of man. The family has seemed to be impervious to external pressures which impinge upon this unit or external pressures which impinge upon the individuals within it; however, we are now seeing increased evidence within our culture that the family is no longer immune to pressure and change as it once was. In fact we are now seeing many types of pressures which are weakening solidarity. Family disharmony seems on the increase as divorce rates soar, not only in our country and culture, but across the world. Perhaps the most persistent attacks on the family unit have centered around questions relating to the effectiveness and purpose of the family. The family now serves a weakened roll in inculcating the social and moral values of our society. Other institutions have assumed responsibility for this role and an increased emphasis in molding the opinions and attitudes of young persons has been taken on by their peers. The attacks on the viability and practicality of family units commenced with lower-class families; however, the questions of the efficacy of a family unit have spread to the middle and upper classes so that now it is a generalized concern among sociologists, anthropolgists, psychologists and marital counselors.

More and more social scientists are becoming confronted with clients whose basic problem is that of a deteriorating family unit. The spectacle of the deteriorating family is depressing. Figures now show that approximately 50 per cent of delinquents come from broken homes. The fact that families are increasingly being broken by desertion and divorce is of immediate concern and even among those family units which remain intact, there are exhibited many problems of a social and emotional nature; alcoholism, other drug addiction, crime and suicide are now rampant.

The family has been frequently cited as the villain of many social evils but with regard to delinquency and runaway behavior there has been a substantial agreement that the family is to blame.

The difficult and puzzling stage of adolescence brings about many profound problems. As Mead has aptly stated, "Parents have been rearing unknown children for an unknown world since about 1946" (Mead, 1972).

The rejection of either or both parents by the child is certainly an important factor in demonstrated, aggressive behavior on the child's part. Many children feel rejected and react with overt aggression toward parents and the family units. Rejected children generally show a marked tendency toward an increased resistance and quarreling in relationship with adults. They also show considerable sibling rivalry.

Many family members who are confronted with a child's hostile-progressive or delinquent behavior react very negatively. In addition to the problems of financial or social misfortunes, the family as a unit is generally ill-prepared to deal with these situations. Often there are real communication problems because there are definite differences in values, especially between the outside peer culture and the individual's family.

There are some early signs which can indicate possibilities for runaway behavior. Some of these include resentment of authority figures in the home and school, resentment of over-protection, open conflicts, resentment of discipline, loss of interest in school subjects, impulsivity associated with permissiveness, heavy influence of juvenile peer group, antisocial attitudes, general frustration and need for compensatory behavior and involvement with drugs.

It is important for parents and others to understand the self-concept. Often persons who are prone toward runaway behavior show inadequate self-confidence and see themselves in negative ways. An individual who maintains a negative self-concept often continues to behave in accordance with his concept by way of expressing hostility. Counseling sessions with a social worker, rehabilitation counselor, psychologist or other helping professional person can be beneficial if this individual is keenly tuned in to the subculture of youth and current mores and patterns of behavior. Professional service workers and parents must be willing to look into the conditions that produce attitudes toward runaway behavior. These include the environment of the home and the interrelationships between the individual runaway and his parents and peer associates. Every effort should be made to get children inclined toward becoming involved in meaningful activities, if not possible within their home, at least within their community areas. Projects in which students can find meaning through helping others are often of substantial value in modifying negative self-concepts and poor attitudes toward the community, home and society in general. If at all possible, families should attempt to have joint projects of mutual interest. These can help in maintaining and improving relationships among family members. Projects should be selected by the family team and not forced upon younger family members by parents or older relatives or siblings.

Another helpful resource is that of grandparents or other relatives who are at least one generation removed from the youth; in that they are more removed there is less ego involvement. Children can often go to such persons and find considerable positive regard and acceptance. In some cases, grandparents may be very helpful in that they constantly reinforce positive self-appreciation in the young person.

The parent may also wish to consider allowing the young person to get a job in order to become more self-sufficient. This can improve concept of self and cut down on the amount of time which is used negatively. It should be remembered that most young people get quite bored with themselves, their friends and their family units. This is partially due to the large amount of unproductive time which many of them while away.

ADDITIONAL REASONS FOR NEGATIVE ATTITUDES ON THE PART OF SOCIETY IN GENERAL

Rapid Social Change

Institutions such as the church, the family, governmental structures of service, the university, and other educational systems are changing so rapidly that many persons are losing their anchor points for emotional stability. People look around them and find little or no certainty in their jobs, in their family life, or in traditional and religious beliefs formerly held sacrosanct. All of us are deeply influenced by the effects of the mass media such as television. These media depict to us what the outside world seems to have. The outside world seems to have so much more than so many think they have.

Diminishing Value of Work

In the early days of the development of this country, the Protestant Ethic played a most important part in bringing about advancements in agriculture, technology, and the social services.

The amount of hard work which an individual did was a direct indication in many cases of his status in the community. Work for work's sake was highly respected. The Protestant Ethic is now much less an influencing factor on attitudes of persons toward work than it once was. In fact, by the year 2000 it may well be that family attitudes in teaching children such characteristics as dependability and diligence related to work may be drastically modified. Society is moving toward a much greater leisure time involvement. At the present time the effects of this accelerating movement away from the Protestant Ethic are being felt. This means that convincing persons that the way to success is through hard work of an honest nature is becoming even more difficult. Even vocational specialists such as vocational rehabilitation counselors in state and federal agencies are now talking about deemphasizing the vocational aspect of rehabilitation services, which in itself indicates some drastic changes in the philosophy of many persons in the social service area on vocations and work.

With an increased amount of leisure time and a deemphasis on full work days or full work weeks, there is more time for all types of activities, including unlawful activities. There seems to be a definite emphasis toward getting what we want the easy way. This emphasis is perpetuated and reinforced by many white collar workers who are able to get around the law by various methods. An example is the landlord who puts enough pressure on tenants to receive monthly payments for rent but does not maintain his buildings according to city ordinances. Persons often see different applications of the law applied according to socioeconomic status of the individual accused. Sentences can vary enormously depending on whether an individual brings an attorney with him to court, whether the offense is a traffic violation or a more serious one.

IMPORTANCE OF PEER GROUPS AND ROLE MODELS

Pressures for conformity come from all sides. Persons in the ghetto feel pressure to conform to the customary behavior of persons in the ghetto. These behavioral pressures are particularly strong among the adolescent groups and especially influential among adolescent boys. The emphasis seems to be on beating the system somehow, and this attitude should not be considered an unhealthy emphasis. It represents the wish of most Americans—to somehow get established and find happiness within a social system which is now in constant turmoil and within a society which is in many ways unhealthy.

In order for the person from the ghetto to beat the system, he must either "fake out" some bureaucratic program such as the Department of Public Welfare and get on the public dole, or behave as two different persons. He must demonstrate one type of behavior which will secure his position within his own peer group and demonstrate another type of behavior which will allow him to secure employment in the outside world. His only other alternative is to leave his peer group and those things which he has felt important in order to enter another man's world. It is much easier for all of us to remain in a world which we have known and adjusted to than to modify behavior in order to become members of a different society. Think how difficult it would be for most of us to move into a culture different and distinct from our own. The same types of problems, equal in complexity, exist for persons who are from impoverished areas, either rural or urban, when they face finding employment and security in the world of work.

Another problem which often leads to crime and runaway behavior is the lack of sufficient role models for individuals to follow. One of the earliest influences on all persons is that of the parents and much of the child's early play involvement is concerned with the work behavior of adults. When adults within the family are not able to work, children simulate the behavior which they exhibit and this behavior is often characterized by frustration and idleness.

REFERENCES

Mead, Margaret: A conversation with Margaret Mead: On the anthropological age. In *Readings in Psychology Today*. Del Mar, CRM Bks, 1972.
Parade Magazine, October 7, 1973.

CHAPTER 5

THE CHILD OF DIVORCE

MARJORIE KAWIN TOOMIM*

What Is Lost?
The Mourning Process
References

THE CHILD OF DIVORCING parents must cope with a multitude of losses. While on the surface it appears that he has lost only the easy availability of a parent, in fact he has lost much more. He has lost a basic psychosocial support system. His own dynamic structure has been molded by this system; the fibers of his being have been interwoven with those of his family members in a way which, if not altogether positive for growth, were at least familiar and in some way balanced. With the dissolution of the structure, the child must now find new support systems.

The process of coping with loss is the same, whether the loss is of a person, a relationship, or a possession; whether the cause of loss is death, divorce, or a marked widening of psychosocial distance (Bowlby, 1961). Losses must be mourned in order to satisfactorily end a relationship and to allow new persons and relationships to fulfill one's needs.

How the child copes with the loss and the mourning process is crucial to his future development. A certain level of ego-strength, psychic energy, and external support is necessary to carry the mourning process through to completion. Few children

---

*The author wishes to thank Lillian Freeman and Pamela Kawin for their assistance in the preparation of this paper.

have the capacity for healthy mourning before the age of three and a half years (Siggins, 1961). Few children of divorcing parents have the requisite external support at any age.

In divorce, the problem of accepting loss and properly mourning is complicated by the difficulty of discriminating the exact nature of the various losses. Even when the father deserts, his loss is not clear and the child may feel justified in hoping for his return, though, in fact, there is no hope.

Divorce losses are difficult to discriminate. Parents compound the problem by ignoring or denying that such losses exist. Some parents are too absorbed in their own pain to help the child appropriately; some do not recognize the various losses, naively believing that only the person of the father is gone. Parents may even state that the child has not lost his father at all—or claim they will now have a better relationship because they will see more of each other. Where such denial of the reality of loss occurs, the parent and the child cannot share mutual thoughts and feelings, or explore alternative ways of meeting needs together. The gap grows wider and losses mount. Parental failure to help in this trying time also alienates the child from himself. The child cannot cope with the overwhelming nature of his feelings. He defends against them. He denies, represses, withdraws, regresses, projects, detaches. He retains in fantasy what is not there in reality and he does not adequately deal with the loss.

Incomplete mourning leaves a reservoir of painful memories and feelings experienced as an undercurrent of depression. A rigid defense system guards against the awareness of ambivalence and pain and is a distorting screen through which subsequent realities are passed, misperceived, and misconstrued. The pain of the loss remains buried, occasionally surfacing when defenses are lowered or reminders of the loss transcend the defense barrier. Energy must constantly be expended to hide the pain. Distortion of reality creates difficulties in living; avoidance of stimuli which might bring the pain to the surface leads to a narrowing of life-space. Loss follows loss as the individual finds himself only partially alive, unable to partake of whole areas of existence. Energies bound in denying and avoiding the reality of loss and its associated pain are not available for use in positive growth and development.

Loss hurts; it leaves scars; it diverts one's life-course. Acceptance of loss provides freedom to explore other alternatives in life and to have other experiences. Denial of loss leaves a gaping hole that may only be covered over. There is constant fear of falling into the darkness below. Denial of loss leaves a vacuum in which no substitute relationship can flourish. Needs are left unsatisfied. The feeling of loss pervades one's life. Acceptance of loss and healthy, complete mourning provide a stable base for future growth.

Some of the trauma of divorce can be prevented by advance planning. Divorcing parents prepare themselves by a long period of questioning, expressing feelings, protesting and despairing, exploring alternatives in fantasy or in fact. Much of their mourning process is experienced in the context of the marriage. The child, on the other hand, is not prepared for this major change in his life. Furthermore, he must adjust to sudden loss in a chaotic family setting.

Parents need to respect the ways in which the child copes with divorce. His stress is great, his capacities limited. He does what he can to protect himself from what might be overwhelming stress. The parent may guide his adjustment patterns with tenderness and love, not with criticism and anger. The divorce adjustment takes years, during which time the dynamics need to be worked through repeatedly as the child's emotional strength and conceptual abilities mature. Young children almost universally deny some aspects of their situation. The aware parent can help the child integrate the realities the child brings to awareness as his strength grows. Insistence that the child see the whole reality at once will only bring resistance and move him further into denial and fantasy.

The following sections—"What Is Lost," "The Mourning Process," and "How the Child Defends Against Loss"—describe in detail the complexities of divorce from the child's point of view. They are written to alert parents and counselors to interactions which often occur for children of divorce. With this knowledge and parental self-awareness, the strain of divorce can be minimized. A good divorced family structure may even allow for growth not possible to attain in the failing marriage. They are not intended to deter parents from divorcing—only to help them enter into this new family relationship intelligently and with care. Divorce may be the most important event in your child's life.

WHAT IS LOST?

Loss of Faith and Trust

A tacit contract is entered into by parents upon the birth of a child. The parents, in effect, promise to establish a firm psychosocial base from which the child can grow. In return, he is expected to remain with the parents, to develop and mature. The child in a two-parent family generally expects that the parental unit will continue to be available to him until he no longer needs it. Most parents encourage this belief by assuring the child of their love, concern, and intention to maintain the family structure. Most parents, experiencing a strain in their relationship, are especially vocal in such reassurance hoping to allay his fears and make him feel secure. They do not want him to be unnecessarily upset, just in case they are able to remain together.

For the child, it does not matter how unhappy the parents are together or how reasonable and right that they separate. He only sees that they have been unable to solve their problems in such a way as to maintain *his* security. Even where a parent is cruel or the strain in the relationship is so great that divorce would ultimately benefit him the child has no assurance that his lot will improve. He feels betrayed. He may feel so hurt that he never trusts again. The younger the child, the less he can understand, the more his need for both parents, and the more his need for a stable family unit, the more divorce will leave him feeling betrayed, angry, hurt and untrusting.

The hurt, untrusting child is in the uncomfortable position of needing help from parents who have just betrayed his trust.

The likelihood of finding someone outside of the family to help him through this difficult time varies with the age of the child and his level of socialization. Very few children under six years of age have this ability. Beyond six, the willingness to ask for and receive help, the willingness of the parents to allow him to form a closer relationship with another adult or good friend, and the availability of a suitable, supportive individual are crucial factors.

Many children at this point deny their dependency needs and withdraw rather than trust either a parent or a parent-substitute. Or they may remain aware of unfulfilled dependency needs and feel helplessly angry. The child who remains aware of dependency needs and refuses to trust, places himself in the precarious interpersonal situation of feeling unsatisfied and of being unsatisfiable. He has laid the grounds within himself of a double-binding situation that may persist into adulthood where he simultaneously demands and rejects love. As a result, his needs remain unmet and he remains frustrated.

Parents are generally advised (Despert, 1962) not to distress their child unnecessarily by telling him of their difficulties before they separate just in case things can be patched up. My experience with family crisis is that the child is aware of conflict but does not understand it. Mistrust grows in such an interpersonal setting. Parental honesty builds trust. Parents can be open about the seriousness of their difficulty without burdening the child with unnecessary details, fighting in his presence, or using him in their struggle. Rather, they can *talk about* the fact that they have problems and how they are trying to solve them. The child usually can understand the parents' situation if it is discussed in terms of the child's own difficulties with playmates. Care *must* be taken to understand the extent of his ability to deal with the details of the conflict.

The separation counseling model provides an optimum situation in which the child can be prepared for divorce. Such an approach not only builds trust, but also provides the child with an effective model for conflict resolution. Even the concept that separation may be a constructive step in problem-solving may help the child. Knowing when to end a relationsunp — sign of strength and success, not of failure.

Maintaining open communication between parent and child helps to build his trust and provides a strong support for him. Only thus can the parents help the child cope with the many changes with which he will be faced as he grows in a divorced family. It is important that parents understand the child's experience of divorce, the logical and moral systems under which he operates at various developmental stages and the ways in which this particular child copes with stress. Without this understanding the parent runs a high risk of being misunderstood and rejected.

Respect for the child's attempts to cope with his difficulties will also increase parental availability and support. The child who feels accepted will be more likely to keep the parent informed of how he perceives the changes in his life, and will ask for continued clarification of his thoughts and feelings. As the child develops, he is increasingly capable of conceptualizing and integrating the whole reality of divorce.

Loss of the Child-Mother-Father Relationship

In an intact family, the child has a child-mother relationship, a child-father relationship, and a child-parents relationship. Each parent gives him something; each provides a measure of support, control, nurturance, etc. Together they complement and supplement each other. Even parents in conflict represent a unit. In fact, they represent a very strong unit if, for example, the child has learned to use one as a rescuer when he displeases the other, or if he has learned to gratify his needs by using their divergence to manipulate.

Unless he has assumed a large portion of child-care functions, the father of the infant from zero to eighteen months is more important for his role than for his person. The infant is primarily involved at the interpersonal level with his mother, especially in executing the difficult task of breaking his symbiotic bond with her and establishing his individuality (Mahler, 1971; McDevitt and Settlage, 1971). The father now represents a vital source of support for the mother, permitting her to give the child consistent care so that he may gradually learn to cope with separation according to his daily needs and capacity to tolerate stress. The father also represents a safe person the child can go to as he explores away from his mother. Relating to both father and mother gives him social skills necessary for complex interpersonal relationships. After the eighteenth month he is still able to hold symbolic representations of objects in his mind. Between the eighteenth and thirty-sixth month, he is still involved in the critical separation-individuation processes. Now father loss is important, for he is vulnerable to people coming and going, to marked variations in patterns of living, and to the absence of the father as an individual, not just to his role. The Oedipal experience of the three- to five-year-old are difficult to work through in a disrupted family. The time of the disruption in terms of the child's place in and resolution of Oedipal conflicts is vital. Parental relationships with other potential rivals intensifies the Oedipal crisis.

The child whose parents stay together during the vital period in which basic identification patterns are established will gain ego-strength. Even though parents differ markedly, the child is better able to take from each in an integrated way when they are together. It is also easier to talk about these differences with parents while they are together. Divorced parents seldom are able to talk about each other with good feeling, particularly when value and life-style differences are involved. As parents separate, differences tend to become accentuated and criticized. What the child perceives of his parents is then filtered through this screen of negativity. A parent may be so anxious to pass his value systems on to a child and mitigate the values of the other parent that he pushes too hard. Such an approach leaves the child confused and likely to reject the values of *both* parents.

The older the child, the less difference between parental value systems and the greater their ability to treat each other with respect after divorce, then the less serious will be the loss of the parental unit for the child. Maintenance of open communication between the parents minimizes the loss of the parent-unit for the child. As step-parents are added to the child's extended family, such open communication greatly aids his ability to integrate a new relationship with its attendant value system and changes in control and dependency patterns.

Loss of the Pre-divorce Mother

It is generally the custom for children of divorce to remain in their mother's custody. Therefore, I am going to conceptualize the child's changing relationship with his mother in these terms.

The divorcing mother is in the process of changing her life. She must cope with her own feelings of loss and anxiety. She must find alternative ways of satisfying the needs formerly met by her marriage. She may have to find or change work. She may begin to look for other interpersonal relationships. She probably needs to lower her socioeconomic level, which means she may become less giving of things that cost money while, simultaneously, she is giving less of her time and attention. The child then feels rejected. Conversely, a divorcing mother may change her relationship with her child by turning to him for need-gratification. She may begin to spend too much time with him, to use him for her emotional support. This child feels smothered.

Many mothers at this time become quite inconsistent. Some quickly try to be both mother and father, precipitously changing nurturance and control patterns rather than waiting for a new interpersonal balance to evolve. The mother, concerned with her own adjustment, is less available and less sensitive to the child, leaving him with more cause and opportunity to break rules. At the same time that she provides this latitude, the mother may be more punitive or harsh when she does realize that her limits have been violated. Or she may be more harsh because she must deal with control issues when she is overburdened by her own problems. She may then react to her own punitiveness by guilt and overconcern. She may become overpermissive and allow too much freedom because she feels guilty about the divorce or feels this kind of giving will make up for the child's loss. She may be just too overwhelmed by her own adjustment problems to expend her energies in child-control.

That is something she can "always do later." Perhaps the school or a "Big Brother," or the "father-when-he-comes-over" will do it for her. She may use her energy to get a new husband-father who will assume the child-control function for her. Sulla Wolff (1969), discussing children of deceased fathers, notes that adjustment was better when their homes were kept intact by mothers who were independent, hard-working, and energetic and who took on the working role with little conflict. Qualities of warmth and affection deemed of primary value for the married mother are less important for the separated mother. Mothers who clung to their children for support, especially their sons, impeded their maturation. Sons of such mothers tended to be tied to the mother and had difficulty establishing a good sexual adjustment.

Personal qualities of mothers seldom change a great deal as a result of divorce. Some mothers feel relieved at the resolution of their marital conflicts and thus are more relaxed with their children. However, if they become heavily involved in dating during this euphoric period their children feel deprived and rejected. Mothers who feel depressed and overburdened by the stress of divorce, though they stay home, are experienced as rejecting by their children. However, the mother responds to divorce, the ways in which the child has learned to cope with her are no longer altogether satisfactory. Some change must be effected in order to function well with her again. In addition, the post-divorce child has different needs and so requires new maternal qualities and behaviors. Thus, pre-divorce reciprocal-role relationships are lost, and post-divorce relationships must be established.

Children tend to idealize the pre-divorce mother and may try to cling to the fantasy that somehow they can get her to change back to her old self. Feelings of guilt, inadequacy, frustration, and anger arise when they cannot. At times, they believe that the return of the pre-divorce mother will bring the father back. These manipulations of the post-divorce child serve only to create greater stress for the post-divorce mother. She thus becomes even more "different" than she was. The clinging child is further alienated.

A mother who is fairly stable emotionally, has a firm sense of values, and has established pre-divorce support-systems for herself in addition to those provided by her husband and the marriage relationship, is less likely to change much within herself after divorce. She will, as a result, be more accessible to adapt to her child's changing needs.

If the father cannot provide for the family's support, the mother should establish a work pattern and child-care facilities before separation. Thus, her stress is reduced at the time of divorce and the child is given an opportunity to cope with this change within the frame of an intact family. The mother who is unable to cope with the changes in her life comfortably should seek counseling. She thus minimizes the loss of the pre-divorce child-mother relationship.

Loss of the Pre-divorce Father

In a divorce in which the father leaves the home, the father-child relationship changes drastically and precipitously. In the ordinary family, the father works regularly, and thus is available to the child in a more limited and structured way than is the mother. After divorce, the structure becomes more rigid and highly limited in time and space. Thoughts and feelings the child may wish to communicate to the father or the sharing of activities must wait until the appointed time. And at that time, both the psychological and the physical space in which father and child meet are often not conducive to the delayed communication or activity. Maintaining a flowing, comfortable, in-depth relationship is ordinarily difficult for many fathers and their children; it is almost impossible under divorce conditions. Time with father is often time to be close "whether you feel like it or not." The closeness, if achieved, must be broken off at the appointed time or "Mommy will be mad" or "because Daddy has other plans for the evening." Many children will not open themselves to closeness under these conditions. Many will not tolerate the pain of repeated separation and loss. It is like reliving the divorce with each contact. Many children are fussy and angry with their mothers after a happy day with father.

On-going reciprocal role-relationships between father and

child are disrupted in the event of divorce where father leaves the home. The only roles that are traditionally given to the absent father are those of financial supporter, giver of fun-times and extra goodies, and person who leads the child to much of the outside world through trips, talk of work or business, etc. If the father has held the traditional role of disciplinarian, he cannot do this well at the end of the week or over the phone. Also, he may be reluctant to discipline the child on his visiting day for fear of leaving the child with a bad feeling about him.

In the pre-divorce family with an active father, his authoritarian role contributes enormously to the ethical-moral value structure of the home. If the father has held the role of rescuer in mother-child struggles, his help will now be rejected by the mother as interference and side-taking unless she actually solicits it. The child may have difficulty accepting the father's help because of mixed feelings and divided loyalties. He may even use such help against the mother or of trying to take him from the mother.

The father's role as provider of the "masculine principle" in the child's life is difficult to maintain on a limited contact. Visiting the child or going out to have fun cannot replace the feeling that exists when a father actively lives in the home. This feeling is one of almost magical strength and protection against evil or powerful forces. It often transfers from the man to the child, even though by adult standards he might be considered weak and ineffectual. The concept of father as strong protector is further threatened by maternal criticism of the father. Also, the fact that the father does not return or is prevented by the mother from returning home and thus putting the child's world "right" again may be evidence to the child that he does not have the power to help at this important juncture in his life.

Biller's (1971) review of research studies of sons with absent fathers indicates that the loss of the father as a role model has more effect on boys before the age of six than after. Boys with absent fathers tend to be less aggressive and less interested in sex-role stereotyped activities than are boys whose father remained in the home. However, the effects of father-absence on sex-role stereotyping may be mitigated by the mother's positive attitude toward the absent father and other males, and by her generally encouraging her boy's masculine behavior. Father-absence does not significantly affect the sex-role stereotyping of girls.

The continued availability of the post-divorce father in part determines how much is lost. However, the child's fantasy relationship with the father may be more significant than his actual presence. For example, an adolescent girl of sixteen had maintained constant contact with her father through wish-fulfilling day-dreams and fantasies since his desertion in her third year. The fantasies were reinforced by his monthly support check, one letter and one gift a year, and her mother's constant complaints about him. On the other hand, a twelve-year-old girl whose parents divorced when she was four and a half often refused to respond to her father's daily telephone calls and went with him Sundays only reluctantly at the mother's urging.

Father-absence in divorce is ambiguous. Unless he has deserted totally, he is clearly available to the child at some times. Children believe their fathers could make contact by phone or could come "if they really wanted to" or if they loved the child enough, etc. The post-divorce father is there-but-not-there. Such a frustrating situation predisposes the child to respond with father-idealization and clinging or with resentful rejection.

Any action that minimizes the ambiguity of the post-divorce father's place in the child's life minimizes his loss. His new role must be clearly defined. Time commitments must be honored. Even if the father sees the child irregularly, he will maintain the child's trust if he is clear about his availability. It is always better if the child and father work out their relationship together without maternal guidance. The mother's role is to accept and support whatever solution they reach.

Many children idealize their divorced father as a way of denying their loss. (See below.) Such idealization, though often hard for the mother to accept, needs to be respected. Both parents can assist the child in expressing and accepting ambivalent feelings. Tolerance for ambivalence is essential to perceiving the father as a whole person with both positive and negative qualities.

Loss of Environmental Supports

Many divorcing families move from one home to another. Such a move means the child will lose his familiar surroundings. Most children lose a special room in which was found safety, security, and refuge. Older, more socialized children lose friends, school, neighboring adults, perhaps youth organizations and leaders. Environmental supports become more meaningful as familiar parental supports disintegrate. Creating new supports at a time of stress, weakened ability to trust, and negative feelings about oneself are difficult problems. The effect of losses can be disabling and should not be underestimated. Divorcing families should not move unless it is essential. If it is essential, staying in the same neighborhood reduces the loss.

The Loss of the Pre-divorce Child

The child, after family dissolution, is not the same as he was before. So pervasive are the changes in his intimate relationships and environmental supports that his feelings and perceptions of himself and others are profoundly affected.

Children are less secure after divorce. They question, with justification, parental ability to maintain a stable environment. They trust less. Dependency and control relationships become difficult.

One of the major disruptions the child of divorce experiences is a discontinuity in identification. Before the divorce, he had been able to assimilate and integrate qualities from both parents with a reasonable degree of freedom. After divorce, the parents are realistically changed. In addition, the child perceives them differently. Generally one is idealized and the other depreciated. Furthermore, if parents criticize each other the child may be afraid to identify with qualities formerly deemed acceptable. With these changes in identification models, the child may now reject formerly acceptable parts of himself which are like a parent he now rejects. He may also experience conflicting feelings about qualities that are now unacceptable to one or the other parent because they are reminders of the divorced partner. Conversely, a child may purposely emulate the qualities of one parent to anger the other, or he may seek to become like the absent parent in order to keep the feeling of closeness. Such major identification shifts cause a changed, usually lowered, self-image.

Most children experience an unrealistic sense of guilt and responsibility about the divorce. This contributes to feelings of failure, inadequacy and lowered self-esteem. Before the age of seven, the child's view of justice is one of retribution. He believes anything bad that happens must be punishment for his wrongdoing. Parental quarrels must be about him; the divorce must be his fault. In addition, the child believes that if his parents loved him, they would reunite; therefore they do not love him. "Perhaps," he thinks, "I am unlovable. What did I do wrong?" The young child's omnipotent fantasies create a fear of his own power as well as an awareness of helplessness. This issue of power becomes central for the child whose parents divorce during his second through fourth year. At this age, a thought is equivalent to action. To be angry with a parent, to wish him gone, and then to find him in fact gone is translated by the child into, "He left because I got angry." The situation is further complicated for the two- to four-year-old in that he often entertains destructive fantasies when frustrated. His inability to conceptualize future time and permanence leaves him the freedom to say "I'm going to chop you up" with little fear (Stone and Church, 1968). However, when loss really occurs, he grows fearful of his anger and magic power. On the other hand, he finds himself powerless to right "his" wrong or to reunite his parents. For example, a thirteen-year-old girl whose parents divorced when she was four announced to her mother one day, "I guess I won't try to get you and Dad together again." This child had devoted nine years of her life to the accomplishment of an impossible task. She saw herself inadequate and a failure. Indeed, so much of her energy was directed to this hopeless project that she had not developed ego-skills necessary for effective functioning in the real world.

In addition to manipulating to reunite his parents, the child may play one against the other or express anger when in fact he feels intolerable fear and sadness; as a result he ends up rejecting parents who care for and love him. He may regress to lower levels of functioning to increase his security. He may feel guilt if his manipulations *are* successful. These manipulations often bring both parental criticism and self-criticism. Thus a negative self-concept is reinforced by those on whom he depends, by those with whom he identifies, and by himself. The child who feels himself "bad" then clings to parents seeking reassurance that he is loved and wanted. Such reassurance from parents who are so deeply involved in the child's conflicting feelings and manipulations is seldom meaningful. They often serve only to reinforce his negative self-image.

The stability of the parent-child relationship is threatened by divorce. Before the age of seven, a child thinks in terms of authoritarian morality (Flavell, 1963; Wolff, 1969). Rules are sacrosanct and cannot be changed. What is right for one person must be right for all. Thus, it is not difficult to conceive that if it is right to divorce a parent, why is it not right to divorce a child? If one parent can reject the other for "breaking a rule" or being difficult to live with, why could not the child be rejected for exceeding some limit? He also stays out late, gets angry, likes someone besides mommy or daddy, etc. To tell the child he is not divorceable is difficult, for he is effectively been divorced by the parent who has left him. What assurance does he have that his remaining parent will not also leave? In socioeconomic settings where foster-home or boarding school placement is common, such fears may be quite realistic.

A very complex group of feelings are associated with separation from a person on whom one has come to depend. A child must learn to cope with these feelings as he separates from the symbiotic mother-child relationship, from parents and friends as they come and go or from toys as they are lost. In an optimal growth situation short-term separations and minor losses are experienced in such ways that the child learns to deal with the attendant anxiety. Gradually, he learns to depend on his own resources for self-support. He learns to trust that those on whom he depends will be available when needed, even though they are not available all the time. The child from birth through the third year is constantly struggling with the task of separating. Even after this he remains vulnerable to devastation from major losses until he has developed sufficient ego-strength, self-confidence, interpersonal skills and support systems outside of the family to feel that he can survive if the parent is not physically available to help him cope with problems. This level of development seldom occurs before the sixth or seventh year. It may never develop for the child who comes from a strife-ridden home or who has been unable to adjust after overwhelming separations resulting from, for example, major illness, hospitalization or prolonged parental absence. Also, it may never develop if the child perceived the birth of a sibling in terms of parental loss. Separation anxiety assails this weakened child at any age when traumatized by the flood of losses which accompany divorce.

Any separation produces simultaneously a complex set of emotions. These include love, anger, fear, sadness, helplessness, hopelessness and—especially for children—guilt.

Love includes feelings of dependency, attachment and need. Without these feeling no loss would be experienced. Perceived abandonment, hurt, frustration of needs and wants satisfied by the lost person or relationship breed *anger*. *Fear* is experienced in terms of being alone; of further abandonment; of one's own vulnerability; of the possibility that one's own destructive powers may have been responsible for the loss. *Sadness*, the hallmark of loss, is the feeling when something of value has gone and can never be again, the sorrow from impoverishment of the self, the finality of an ending. *Helplessness* is the knowledge that one is not omnipotent; one did not have the power to prevent the loss. Life will continue without the lost person or relationship. *Hopelessness* is the acceptance of the reality and finality of the loss. Even if the lost person returns, it is never the same. The memory and experience of loss alters the relationship. The greatest problem for the post-divorce child is accepting the hopelessness of reinstating the family. *Guilt* usually accompanies loss, especially for the child who still believes he is all powerful. Guilt is proportional to the perception of his responsibility for the loss, and for his wish that the loss would occur.

How the child copes with this complex set of emotions has a major effect on his subsequent development. The overwhelming force and confusion of these feelings is often too great and he turns them off. He detaches emotionally. Sometimes one of these emotions is more acceptable than the others and this one dominates when any of the others are felt. Thus, his first response to any emotional stimulus becomes anger or tears or fear or sometimes even love. A child can seldom deal with this complex of intense feelings alone. He needs parental support to allow their full expression as well as to gain tolerance for ambivalent feelings.

Parents can provide this support by discussing with the child their feelings related to the separation. This does not mean the parent should overwhelm the child with emotion. Rather, the parent can let the child know he also feels sad, sometimes scared, and sometimes glad about the divorce; angry and at the same time loving and needing; helpless and struggling; hopeless about the past and hopeful about a realistic future; guilty and simultaneously justified in separating; aware of everyone's pain.

The loss of inner security and sense of self-worth through divorce is the greatest loss of all. It is also the loss which can most easily be prevented, given parental awareness and skill in helping the child through this critical experience.

Divorcing parents should be particularly careful of the child two to seven years of age. He is most in need of complete parenting and the least able to understand the complexities of divorce. The child from seven on is thus in a better position to adjust. The adolescent has the complex emotional interactions that are inherent to divorce. Also, the adolescent is in the process of separating from his parents. He is the least affected by divorce.

Divorcing parents will best be able to help the child maintain a positive self-image if they accept the special ways he perceives and conceptualizes events in the outside world, his emotional capacities, and his defense patterns. Such accepting parents will be less reactive to divorce-related manipulations, emotional outbursts, and defense maneuvers. The accepting parent can control himself and the child better, help him understand, accept himself, and guide him in ways which will build his self-image.

THE MOURNING PROCESS*

The fact that a child's parents divorce is much less important for his future development than how he reacts to the experience. Does he perceive the divorce as a punishment? Does he find the experience overwhelming? Does he compliantly appear accepting while secretly he is angry and too afraid to express anger? Does he rebel openly? Does he manipulate to get his family back together? Does he also expect to be rejected? Does he recognize his losses and mourn them, or does he cover over the pain and leave an empty space inside?

The healthy mourning process involves a) accepting the reality of the loss; b) experiencing fully and accepting the complex of feelings which are always associated with loss (love, anger, fear, sadness, helplessness, hopelessness and sometimes guilt); c) finishing "unfinished business" associated with the loss: resolving ambivalent feelings, expectations, disappointments, things left unsaid or undone, etc. (Tobin, 1971); d) gradually releasing the lost person or relationship. This may be accomplished in active involvement with the separating person if open contact can be maintained. Where loss is sudden and contact is lost, introjecting the lost one or maintaining a fantasy relationship with him gives the mourner time to master the experience. Ties are then gradually cut while strength develops and alternative ways to gratify needs are explored; e) establishing new ways to gratify needs.

---

*For full discussion of the healthy mourning process see Bowlby, 1961; Fenichel, 1945; Jacobsen, 1971; Volkan and Showalter, 1968.

How Can the Child Be Helped to Complete the Mourning Process?

Acceptance is the essence of healthy mourning. Parents can help the child by accepting their own loss and their own loss-associated feelings. The separation process is essentially the same for all members of the family, even though the specific losses differ. The more deeply the parents explore and understand themselves, the better they will understand and support their child. When both parents address their attention to this process, they form a parent-unit for the child. Such a unit mitigates the loss of the child-mother-father unit of the married family.

The parent will help most by focusing on the reality of the child's feelings about his many losses; these are the most immediate in the awareness of everyone concerned. Feelings may be indirectly expressed, but a parent who is in touch with his own emotional experience will be likely to attend to the underlying real feeling. Thus, for example, a child who is fussy after a good day with his father is probably sad and defends against this feeling with anger. It does little good to *ask* a young child what he feels, for he has limited ability to put his deep feelings into words. The empathic parent can look at the child's body, his behavior, and his external situation and make some guess about the child's feelings. In the above example a mother might say:

Mother: You looked sad as you came in—before you got angry with me. Did something special happen that made you feel bad?

Child: Oh . . . No . . . We went to the zoo and had chocolate ice cream.

Mother: It must be hard for you to have fun with Dad and then have to leave him. I sometimes feel sad after we have a nice phone conversation. I wish then we could have stayed together. Then I get angry because we couldn't. I almost wish sometimes we didn't have the good times, because I feel lonelier when they are over.

Child: Why can't Daddy come in the house with me when he brings me home?

Mother: Oh, I didn't realize that was important to you.

Child: Well, I asked him to tuck me in bed like he used to, and he said he couldn't come in the house with me.

Mother: I will talk to him about that tomorrow and see what we can do.

> I can understand that you would like him to tuck you in. It really feels good to have a Daddy do that, doesn't it? If you will accept a substitute, I would like to tuck you in tonight while you tell me about the zoo.

By this focusing on underlying feelings, the child brought to the foreground one of the losses which was important for him, the tuck-in ritual with daddy. He was able to express his anger about the loss of this child-father interaction. He acted out his ambivalence. It was accepted and a resolution offered. We may assume he felt a sense of rational control over his life and accepted a substitute need—satisfied for the evening. He may also have trusted his parents would work together to give him at least a symbol of something important to him. A fight was avoided and support was given at a crucial time. The child accepted his own needs and feelings as well as effective mothering. Had the mother reacted with anger to his anger, he would have felt less trusting of her sensitivity and caring for him. He would have felt guilty, angry, and afraid at a time when he was especially needy and sad. He probably would have gone to bed pouting, brought his mother back to him with numerous demands (water, blankets, another story, etc.). Perhaps he would have had a nightmare and come to her to relieve his fear.

This issue could have been handled by his father directly. As it was, his mother had to accept the responsibility for dealing with the problem. The father had reinforced his own idealized image as all-giving but failed to deal with the whole child. The following type of father-child interaction would have been appropriate:

Child: Will you come in and tuck me in tonight? You haven't done that for such a long time.

Father: I'd really like that but I don't feel comfortable in the house any more.

Child: But it is still your house. Besides, you told me you were just divorcing mother, that you were not divorcing me. I want you to come in and tuck me in tonight.

Father: Wait a minute. There are about three things going on here. Let's get them straight. First of all, I heard you say you wanted me to have some time or do something that would feel close for both of us. You thought about my tucking you in as a way of doing that. Second, you brought up the whole issue of the divorce and my place in the house and the family now. Third, you became demanding and angry, and I started to get mad about being forced to do something for you.

Child: OK. Forget it.

Father: No, I don't want to forget it. Let's try to work it out. I miss the things we used to do together that just came easily when I was living in the house, like putting you to bed or reading with you or watching TV. I enjoy our Sundays and the zoo was fun, but we don't have much opportunity to just be quiet together. And you and Mommy and I are never together as a family.

Child: The house isn't much fun without you. Mommy is always tired and busy now. And she has that other guy here all the time. If she marries him, you can't ever come back?

Father: Oh, did your wanting me to come in the house have something to do with wanting me to come back to live there?

Child: Well, will you?

Father: No, I won't come back. Mommy and I have found that we are much better off living apart. I know it hurts you and that both Mommy and I lose a lot in our relationship with you. But I also remember how much we used to fight and how afraid you were that we might hurt each other. We weren't very good for you that way, either.

Child: I don't remember the fights very much any more, just the good times. Mommy talks about the fights, but I don't like to listen to her when she does that. She tries to take me away from you. She doesn't want me to like you.

Father: I can't say what Mommy wants or is trying to do. I think Mommy and I had better get together and work out more of our differences. It sounds as though you are being put in the middle between us, and I don't like to see that. I will call Mommy in the morning.

Child: OK. But what about tonight?

Father: Well, I will go to the door and see if Mommy would object to my putting you to bed tonight. But, I don't think that will solve the whole problem. Next week let's go to my apartment and have a regular "Sunday at home" instead of doing something special.

Child: Could I invite a friend to come along?

Father: Sure. Now I'll go and talk to Mom.

In this interaction, the father was able to set limits on the child. He shared his feelings of loss; he took responsibility for the divorce with his wife, and relieved the child of the pressure of trying to reunite the family. He took an active role in the family interaction and understood the child's need for closeness with him in a less formal arrangement. The request that a friend join them for the "day at home" is indicative of conflicting feelings about such imtimacy. It appears that his son holds un-repressed resentment toward him. He would do well to arrange to wrestle with this child during his day at home, or find some other activity that will allow for expression of ambivalent feelings.

By interactions such as the one noted above, communication paths are maintained, trust is built, losses for the child are clarified and defined. The defined loss can be accepted, and substitute gratifications can be found. Hundreds, perhaps thousands of such interactions are required to accomplish the task of complete divorce mourning. It must be done over and over again.

It is important to recognize that divorce losses change as the child develops. For example, parents who remain so estranged that the father is not allowed in the house will create discomfort for the child at all special events throughout his life where families come together (birthdays, graduations, weddings, etc.). He loses his fantasy of family unity at each of these events.

It is to be hoped that effective parent-child interactions will teach the child to cope with each loss successfully as it comes to awareness. In time he will need parental support only when he is so confused that he cannot sort out the issues himself.

All of us defend against loss because it is overwhelming. Parents must respect the child's perception of his own strength and only help him confront reality when he shows readiness to accept help, much as sexual information is gradually given. He will turn away or misperceive what is said to him if he feels he cannot absorb the reality.

The child needs to finish "unfinished business" with his parents and confront his feelings about them in the present (Perls, 1969; Tobin, 1971). It must be remembered that there are actually great changes in the parents as well as the child as a result of the divorce. Children need to work through their "unfinished business" with the pre-divorce parents in the context of how he was then as well as how he is now. The following example illustrates this point:

Child: Mom—why don't you ever cook any more?

Mother: I do cook—I make dinner and breakfast and fix your school lunches.

Child: But I remember you used to be cooking everyday when I got home from school. You made cookies and cakes and things.

Mother: Oh, that was before the divorce. Now I am at work when you come home from school.

Child: That is how I always think of you in the kitchen when I came home from school. I liked the good smells and helping you.

Mother: Sounds like you really miss that part of me.

Child: Yes. Like you aren't my mother now, 'cause my mother was always in the kitchen when I got home from school.

Mother: You sound sad—like you really lost me.

Child: I am sad. (Child hits the sink.)

Mother: Are you angry, too?

Child: Well—it's not your fault and you had to work.

Mother: No, it's not my fault, but you can still be angry that I don't have time to bake now and that you feel like you lost your mother.

Child: I don't feel right getting mad at you. You do so much now. I mean, you work so hard.

Mother: Are you feeling that I work so hard that you don't get enough mothering now? Like you are deserted now?

Child: Well, it would be nice if we could have more fun. You are always so tired, now.

Mother: I miss the good times we had, too. I remember now that we used to talk a lot when you came home from school. You told me about what you did and I liked baking with you. I have lost touch with that part of you. When I cook dinner now, you are watching TV and I am so rushed to put dinner on the table I don't cook the same things. I remember now that you would chop things for me and stir things that took time. Now I use a lot of frozen food. Asking you to set the table is a lot different from asking you to cook with me. No wonder you resent setting the table now and you didn't before.

Child: I didn't realize the difference either. And I can't talk to you about my stuff anymore. At dinner now you always answer the phone because it might be a date calling. (Child looks away and starts to move away.)

Mother: (Moving toward the child) I feel sad, too. I don't want to lose you in all the changes that have happened since the divorce.

> Let's sit down now and see how we can get back some of the
> good things we have had together. Would you sit on my lap
> for a while?
Child: (Nods ascent and starts to cry.)

Too much was brought forth in this interaction to be dealt
with at the moment. Sadness, anger, and love were the dominant
emotions. The anger was directed both at the mother and at her
dates.

In a therapeutic setting, the child ideally would have hit some
mother-symbol (pillow, chair) while the mother held the child
so that the complex of feelings, love, anger, hopelessness, etc.,
could have emerged together. After the feelings had been expressed, the two could more easily find the closeness they once
had. Some mothers would be able to cope with such an interaction outside of a therapeutic setting. Mother and child together would mourn the irretrievable loss of the mother-in-the-
kitchen-when-I-come-home-from-school ritual, and find another
mutually satisfying activity that would allow two-way open
communication. The child would also, at some time, deal with
feelings of resentment toward the mother's suitors, her tiredness
and general unavailability. The child's present needs would be
assessed. There may be something particularly difficult to discuss at this time which would have been easier to bring up in
the earlier "kitchen" setting. Or, if the time between the remembered interaction and the present is very long, perhaps the
child needs some way to regress as a defense against a present
stress. The conflict between anger engendered by frustrated
needs for mothering, and guilt or overconcern about the mother's
additional burdens could be explored. No feelings are expressed
in the above interaction about either the divorce or the father.
Interventions that might have been appropriate include: "If
Dad were here, then things would be the same as they were."
"Sometimes I wish we had never divorced. Things would be
easier then." "Even if Dad were still here, I had planned to go
to work at this time." Also, no mention was made of possible
changes in the child's situation. For example: "Then we were
so far from people, you had no one to play with. Now we live

in a neighborhood with lots of children and you play after school." "You seemed frightened then, and hung on to me a lot. Now you seem to be having more fun with friends. Is that right?"

How Does the Child Defend Against Loss?

Dominant in the constellation of defenses of the child who cannot mourn his losses is either premature detachment or internalization of the lost one or some combination of these.

Premature detachment (Bowlby, 1961; Deutsch, 1937; Heinicke, 1965) is evidenced by passive withdrawal, active rejection of the lost parent, usually strong attachment to a substitute, loss of emotionality, or sudden denial of need for the lost relationship. Premature detachment involves a gross distortion of reality—either of the loss itself, or of the child's need for the lost one. Detachment almost always involves a splitting off of intense emotions. It is the most deceptive system, in that parents so easily overlook the child's underlying pain and react to him as if he were not hurt. Communication is thus blocked and the parents—even assuming they are willing and able to help the child—cannot help. What they say and do is not addressed to the child's pain and thus he finds it irrelevant and frustrating. He concludes—properly—that his parents do not understand him, and so he further detaches himself from what parenting is available. He grows increasingly isolated and lonely.

The only positive aspect of this defense is that the child saves himself from what he perceives as an overwhelming experience. For him, this is a survival maneuver. Indeed, with it he can encapsulate his pain and deal with it at a later time when his ego is stronger and his support system more secure. Thus, we find adults in therapy working through long-buried thoughts and feelings associated with childhood loss (Volkan *et al.*, 1968).

In rejecting the lost parent, the child may also reject those qualities in himself that are like the parent. Such detachment from oneself weakens the child's ego, results in loss of self-esteem and self-awareness, and produces a poor base on which to grow. Some children chose to pattern themselves in any way *but* like the separated parent (they develop a negative identification), and thus severely limit growth potential.

Premature detachment from a separated father is likely to result in a too-close relationship to the mother, providing she is available and nurturing. If she is not, the child may detach from her also, continuing to grow virtually parentless.

Parents of children who so defend themselves feel relieved, naively believing that they have easily adjusted. Only some years later do they realize that the child is disturbed and may trace the difficulty back to the time of divorce. The deceptively benign quality of premature detachment is illustrated by the following cases:

> Betty was four when her parents obtained an amicable divorce. She was told her father preferred to live away from home because it was better for his work. She saw him every Sunday. Normally bright and inquisitive, she asked few questions about the change in her family, was easily satisfied by superficial answers, and made no protest about the loss. Apparently she enjoyed the times with her father. He was rather a quiet man who liked to take her to interesting places. She had little difficulty separating from him when he brought her home and she hardly mentioned him between visits. Apparently not concerned about leaving her father when she left the country with her mother at the age of eight, she was quite disturbed about leaving her cat. Her relationship with her mother is close and not lacking in emotionality though anger has not been acceptable in her family. She functions well at school, has few friends. She now suffers from night terrors.

> Mrs. I., at forty, has difficulties forming dependency relationships. After her parents divorced when she was seven, she seldom saw her father. Though she remembers their post-divorce relationship clearly, she has almost entirely forgotten their earlier relationship. She is told her pre-divorce relationship with him was very close. He was a good father to her. She has few pre-divorce memories of him. She clearly remembers an "embarrassing lack of feeling" when she realized he left home. In later years she came to resent his abandonment, particularly when she was unhappy with her mother. She dislikes those qualities in herself that resemble his. She has difficulty calling him "Daddy," but easily refers to him as "My Father." She abhors men who are like her view of her post-divorce father. She is attracted to men who are like her fantasy of her pre-divorce father, though she cannot form a lasting relationship with them. After the divorce, when her mother had to go to work, she became quite self-sufficient

and absorbed in school work. She became outwardly compliant and inwardly rebellious. Her present rigidly independent stance is a defense against her fear of dependency. She trusts nobody, including herself.

The opposite extreme of premature detachment is *internalization* of the person with the aim of circumventing loss. Internalization may be accomplished by holding a fantasy image of the person or relationship identifying with him (Krupp, 1954) or introjecting all or part of him. (Perls, 1969). At the extreme he may act as if he is the lost person (Deutsch, 1937). The child who internalizes the lost parent accepts the fact of loss, but refuses to allow a new relationship to emerge. He maintains control in a fantasy relationship where in reality his control is strictly limited. He continually hopes for something that cannot be. He thus feels frustrated and angry. Underlying his outward appearance of control is his inner awareness of reality and his actual helpless, hopeless position. Internalization of the whole person with both positive and negative qualities is rare. Few children possess tolerance for inconsistency and ambivalence. Therefore, they retain only selected parts that fit a negative or positive image.

Internalization of negative qualities is more likely to occur if the pre-divorce father was feared. The child then gains power and relieves his own fear. A boy, particularly, may internalize his father's sex-role stereotyped behavior in order to resolve conflicts about his own masculinity. If he is not compatible with his mother, he may accentuate his father's negative qualities as a way of punishing her. He may "become" his father to be sent away like his father. Perhaps he takes on his negative qualities in order to force transfer of his custody to the father. Thus he avoids experiencing the guilt involved in actively rejecting his mother.

Internalization of the negative qualities of a parent lead to feelings of insecurity, anxiety, ambivalence, and poor self-image. The child comes to perceive himself as "negative" just as he perceived the parent internalized. In addition, reactions of others to him are more likely to be negative and thus his self-image is further devalued and his tendency to be fearful, angry, and defensive is increased.

It appears that most children *internalize an idealized positive image* of a separated father, even though he has been cruel or negligent. I recently asked ten adolescent and adult clients from divorced homes: How did maintaining an idealized father-image help you? The replies may be categorized as follows:

1. A denial of the loss. ("I could not accept the fact that we would not be together anymore, so I kept him with me all the time. He was like an imaginary companion." "No one so good could have done such a terrible thing as to leave me, so this way I could pretend it was just temporary and he would be back." "I felt I needed a father, I emphasized the parts of him that I wanted in a father and kept him in my mind that way." "I kept them in my mind as together and happy. That way I didn't have to see them apart. I wanted to have a mother-father unit.")

2. A source of support. ("It really feels good to know that someone always loves you, even if he is 3,000 miles away and you only see him once a year." "He was like a Prince Charming who was coming to rescue me." "I kept hope alive by thinking of him as loving and wanting me." "I felt I always had a haven to turn to— a place to go if things got too bad. Of course, I never tested to find out if he would have had me. Now I can see that he would not have wanted me." "Whenever I had a problem I couldn't solve, I would go to my room and have a fantasy in which he came to me and we talked. I did that until I was sixteen—that is the first time I saw him since I was three. Then, after I saw him, it wasn't so easy because he wasn't like my fantasy. I really felt I had lost something." "I didn't like my mother. This way I had at least one good parent.")

3. A boost to self-esteem. ("I must be OK if someone so nice cares about me." "No one wants to come from bad parents." "When my mother criticized me, I could keep from hearing her by thinking about my father and that at least he really cares so I must not be so bad." "Everybody else had a father. I wanted one too. And mine was better than theirs." "It was like he never left me, so I didn't have to feel guilty about their divorce." "I didn't like myself as a person who thinks bad things about people, especially my father.")

4. An identification model. ("I was afraid that if I carried around a bad image of him, I would get to be like that. So I kept him

'good.'" "I guess I decided what kind of a father I wanted to have, and thought of him that way and then I identified with that image of him." "I don't understand how I got to be so much like him, since I only saw him a few times a year. Well, I am really more like the way I used to imagine him all the time, not the way I see him now." "I didn't like my mother and I didn't want to be like her, so I purposely imitated the good parts of him." "My mother kept telling me I was just like my father. She meant selfish, I didn't want to believe that, so I kept thinking about the good parts of him to be like."

The child who so idealizes the father may considerably distort reality. For example, one girl whose parents divorced when she four and a half often talked about the "tradition" she and her father had of eating breakfast together every morning. Actually, the father never woke up before noon and seldom talked to her at all. Her mother's attempts to "help the child to see reality" were met with considerable resistance. Already viewing her mother as a rejecting person (the divorcer) and as denying her what she wanted, she became increasingly convinced of her mother's "badness" and her father's "goodness." She then clung even more tenaciously to the relationship with her still-distant father. With so little support for her idealized image in reality, she lived more and more in fantasy.

The child who idealizes his father often finds himself at cross-purposes with his mother. The mother wants to let the father go; the child wants to keep him. The mother is uncomfortable with the father's qualities; the child accentuates them. The child may become unacceptable to the mother both as a mate symbol and realistically as a difficult child. The child may define as "good" qualities which are questionable. For example, the child may idealize a father's spend-thrift qualities and strain the mother's limited resources and also clash with her value system.

The most positive aspect of introjection of the idealized image of the lost parent is that the child takes control of satisfying his own support needs when his parents deny him such support. He refuses to be a helpless victim. Furthermore, he surrounds himself with a warm, loving, caring fantasy. He protects himself until he feels strong enough to accept the more harsh reality.

Problems with this defense arise primarily when the ideal and the real father obviously differ considerably. Contrast, for example, the case of the girl who maintained a fantasy relationship for thirteen years with a father who deserted her when she was three. She had full control of the fantasy relationship and was only frustrated when her mother faced her with reality. She had the equivalent to a fantasy playmate or a relationship with Santa Claus. At the other extreme is the case of a girl who saw her father as all-loving and caring and then waited each week for his inconsistent Sunday visit. She often felt betrayed, frustrated, angry, sad and frightened. She had to repress these feelings in order to maintain her fantasy. The negative feelings were instead turned against her mother, who expressed her resentment at the father's lack of concern.

The child's idealization of the father is the defense most disturbing to the mother. This is particularly true if her own ambivalent feelings are resolved by focusing on her husband's negative qualities (Toomim, 1972).

We may assume that the child himself, while holding onto and becoming like the father, is aware that father was unacceptable. To be like father may threaten his security with his mother. This is particularly true for the child who is told he is "just like his father."

It is difficult for a young child to conceive that parents who are different from each other and who reject each other can both be "good." Therefore, if the father is perceived as good the mother is likely to be cast in the "not good" position. Parental attempts to manipulate the child's loyalty, change custody, get more or give less money, and to communicate with each other through the child, serve to increase his tendency to perceive one good and other bad. The roles the divorced parents play also support a dichotomized view. The visiting father takes the child places, goes out for dinner with him, makes up for less time by more gifts and generally sees him only when he wants to and in a relatively good mood. Only the "best" of the visiting father is visible. The mother, on the other hand, increases her role as disciplinarian and has less money to spend than she had when the family was intact. She interacts with the child even when she is tired from working or upset from relationships with other men. She may be seen as rejecting when she pursues her own interests. She is often burdened by her role as single-parent. In addition, he is usually perceived as rejecting or inadequate. The child believes she could have kept Daddy home "if she were better" or "if she wanted to."

Paradoxically, the mother is also a safer person to see as bad, even though rejecting her threatens the child's basic security. The father cannot be taken for granted. He is obviously able to leave and his life is complete in many ways without the child. The child must actively maintain the relationship with him. The child-mother relationship on the other hand is more stable. She has chosen to keep the child, may even have fought for him. Whether she is actually a good or bad mother, she is a consistent external support who, by her role, gives him many opportunities to channel his confused feelings and gain a sense of mastery over his pain by struggling with her. He wants his idealized father but she is there. He wants his needs met by him; he accepts need-gratification from her. Father abandons him weekly; Mother stays—and her presence keeps Father away and thus frustrates the child. It is difficult to express anger to a now giving father; easy to be angry with a controlling mother. However he expresses his distress—through anger, withdrawal, projection, etc.—the person who will be most involved in coping with the distress behavior will be the mother. Her natural reaction to the child's distress may be critical and thus unsupportive. In her own stress, she may not be aware of his deeper needs for security, understanding of his confused feelings, and relief from pain. His distress is generally frustrating to her. Her natural reaction then is likely to further alienate him from her at a time when he needs her most. He is now very likely to react by clinging to her with fear and anger while she reassures him. Still full of hurt and righteous indignation, his ambivalent feelings for her grow and his security is threatened by this interaction.

How Can the Parent Deal With the Child's Defense Behavior?

How the parent deals with the child's defense against the pain of loss is crucial. Confronting the defensive behavior directly tends to make the child *more* defensive. Criticizing his behavior or forcing him to see reality will strengthen the defense structure and build his conflicting and negative self-concept. He will turn against his mother and make meaningful communication with her almost impossible. Yet, it is important that the child accept the reality of his situation. Only as he accepts reality will he be able to effectively integrate his experience and his feelings regarding his changing family and self.

The way in which parents help their children cope with the complexities of divorce changes with the child's age. Children too young to express themselves verbally can be approached through play materials. For example, clay can be used to create a variety of family interactions with an unlimited number of characters. Clay also has the advantage of following the young child, who resists directly confronting his divorce trauma, to deal with it indirectly in third person terms.

Doll play, "dress-up," and role-playing are also good ways of helping the young child work through his feelings of loss.* Snapshots of pre-divorce family life may be compiled into a picture story which can be read repeatedly to keep real memories alive and in perspective. Post-divorce pictures from both parent-lines may also be kept to help integrate the changing relationships that occur as he grows—perhaps as parents find other mates.

Finding substitute need-gratification is a highly personal task. The parent can help explore alternatives; only the child can know what alternative will be acceptable. Many parents mistakenly believe a step-parent will replace a natural parent. For many children a step-parent represents a further loss. He

---

*For more details on play therapy and techniques see Virginia Axline, *Play Therapy* and also *Dibs, in Search of Self.*

may perceive the step-parent as a rival for his natural parent's time and attention; the step-parent may seem to be an intruder into his relationship with his own parents; the new values and new interpersonal structure threaten old accepted and cherished ways. New step-children further erode existing family systems. The problem of integrating such an extended family is a major one.

There is a delicate balance between respecting the child's need to defend against painful reality and helping him confront reality when he is ready. Both parents must work together and with the child to help him see reality as he becomes capable of coping with it.

Divorce never eliminates a parent. It only changes the family structure. For better or for worse a child never loses a parent totally. He has absorbed—introjected—a part of that parent which will always remain with him whether he keeps a fantasy image of him or a real one.

I have focused attention on the basic issue of loss from the viewpoint of the child of divorce. No mention has been made of the child who stays with his father or of the influence of siblings. Too little has been said of the effect of mental age and social maturity and of the quality of parent-parent and parent-child relationships as vital factors affecting the child's divorce adjustment. Unfortunately I know of no research which explores these variables. My hope is that the concepts expressed in this paper will stimulate studies which point the way to effective counseling for children of divorce.

REFERENCES

Axline, V.: *Dibs, in Search of Self*. New York, Ballantine, 1964.

Axline, V.: *Play Therapy*. New York, Ballantine, 1969.

Biller, H.: Father absence and the personality development of the male child. In *Annual Progress in Child Psychiatry and Child Development*. New York, Brunner, Mazel, 1971.

Bowlby, J.: Process of mourning. *Int J Psychoanalysis*, 42:317-340, 1961.

Bowlby, J.: Grief and mourning in infancy and early childhood. *Psycho-Analytic Study of the Child*, 15:6052, 1960.

Despert, L.: *Children of Divorce*, New York, Dolp. Doubleday, 1962.

Deutsch, H.: Absence of grief. *Psychoanalytic Quarterly, 6*:12-22, 1937.

Fenichel, O.: *The Psychoanalytic Theory of Neurosis.* New York, Norton, 1945.

Flavell, J.: *The Developmental Psychology of Jean Piaget.* New York, Van N-Rein, 1963.

Heinicke, C.: *Brief Separations.* New York, Intl Univs Pr, 1965.

Jacobson, E.: *Depression.* New York, Intl Univs Pr, 1971.

Krupp, G.: Identification as a defense against anxiety in coping with loss. *Int J Psychoanal, 46*:303-314, 1965.

McDevitt, J., and Settlage, C.: *Separation-Individuation.* New York, Intl Univs Pr, 1971.

Mahler, S.: How the child separates from the mother. In *The Mental Health of the Child.* Rockville, National Institute of Mental Health, 1971.

Perls, F.: *Ego, Hunger and Aggression.* New York, Random, 1968.

Perls, F.: *Gestalt Therapy Verbatim.* Ogden, Real People, 1969.

Siggin, L.: Mourning: A critical review of the literature. *Int J Psychoanal, 17*:14025, 1963.

Stone, J. L. and Church, J.: *Childhood and Adolescence.* New York, Random, 1968.

Tobin, S.: Saying goodbye in gestalt therapy. *Psychotherapy, 8*:150-155, 1971.

Toomin, M.: Structured separation with counseling: A therapeutic approach for couples in conflict. *Fam Process, 11*:299-310, 1972.

Volkan, V. and Showalter, C.: Known object loss, disturbance in reality testing and "re-grief" work as a method of brief psychotherapy. *Psychiatr Q, 42*:358-374, 1968.

Volkan, V.: Normal and pathological grief reactions—a guide for the family physician. *Va Med Mon, 93*:651-656, 1966.

Volkan, V.: Typical findings in pathological grief. *Psychiatr Q, 44*:231-250, 1970.

Wolff, S.: *Children Under Stress.* London, Penguin Press, 1969.

CHAPTER 6

FUNCTIONAL RETARDATION: A COMPOSITE DEFINITION FOR REHABILITATION SERVICES

JOHN G. CULL AND RICHARD E. HARDY

. . . .

Confusion in Definition

FUNCTIONAL RETARDATION is a disability which is causing great confusion in rehabilitation. Many rehabilitation counselors and state rehabilitation agencies do not recognize functional retardation as a disability. Some agencies designate the condition as a disability which may impose handicapping conditions, but the concept of the condition is hazy. Some rehabilitation professionals view functional retardation as mental retardation. The end result is that few of the unemployed who are handicapped as a result of functional retardation are being provided rehabilitation services. In the opinion of the authors, functional retardation is in existence when an individual is functioning in the retarded range academically and emotionally but not psychometrically. That is, he is at least two or more years behind his age level in academic achievement. He is somewhat immature and tends to prefer a younger group of persons than his chronological age group; or if he identifies with the chronological age group, these individuals tend to be functional retardates themselves. In other words, he is academically retarded, emotionally retarded, and socially retarded; although psychometrically he may be average or above average in intelligence. Therefore, by definition he is not mentally retarded but is functioning as if he were retarded. Rehabilitation requires a clear definition of functional retardation if services are to be properly rendered.

Collecting the Data

In order to make the decision concerning whether or not an individual is functionally retarded, one of the first problems concerns sources of information. How can we establish an information system which can be used to clarify the confusion which exists in the area of making eligible for rehabilitation services persons who are functioning as retardates but scoring in the borderline or higher ranges of normal intelligence on intelligence tests? Information generally comes from several sources: the physician, the educator, the psychologist, and the social worker. These sources and others must be utilized fully if we are to complete a useful composite picture of value which will give us a clear definition of retardation. The rehabilitation counselor needs to have a broader understanding of environmental causes of decreased intellectual functioning in order to help the person overcome as many inhibiting factors as possible.

In dealing with the psychological, social, and educational aspects of retardation, the counselor must remember that persons who are called "normal" or "retarded" in intelligence are relegated to two mutually exclusive groups. We have been too rapid in our efforts to draw a distinct line of differentiation between these two groups, and intelligence tests alone are just not rigorous enough to bear the responsibility of designating individuals as being eligible or ineligible for rehabilitation services on the basis of a specific score.

The rehabilitation counselor needs to have a broad understanding of any condition which impedes the progress of the individual. This concept is particularly important in work with borderline retarded persons because now they are erroneously classified as ineligible (nonretarded) for services in many cases when in fact they are *functioning* on a retarded level. In addition, if the individual is classed as retarded and therefore eligible for rehabilitation services, he must be restored to his fullest potential through the vocational rehabilitation program. The point being stressed here is the importance of using a broadly gauged approach to understanding and interpreting physical, social, educational, and psychological conditions which affect the functional level of the client. The counselor should evaluate medical reports carefully. Pathology, treatment, and prevention approaches should be outlined in the medical report. The combination of medical, psychological, and social data should help the counselor in developing a schema for definition purposes.

Correct and early identification of functional retardation is extremely important in that deprivation in youth adversely affects the ability to achieve in later life. The ideal time to identify, diagnose, and serve the functionally retarded individual is in late adolescence in order that the youngster can develop good adjustment habits. If rehabilitation counselors wait until early adulthood or later to provide rehabilitation services to the individual, the client by that time will have developed a chronic personality pattern which is almost impossible to change. Additionally, the client will be almost devoid of information about jobs and the world of work. For this reason, it is difficult to overemphasize knowing clients well, especially adolescent "functionally retarded" clients. When persons having learning handicaps, a thorough understanding of their background becomes most important. Complete case recording is essential in order to determine the eligibility of a functionally retarded individual. To neglect the full development of information in this complex area of eligibility determination for rehabilitation services is often equivalent to deying the client's eligibility for services.

Activities of Daily Working

Doyle and Seidenfelt (1965) have offered excellent suggestions on the general subject of defining retardation behavioristically as opposed to the traditional psychometric definition. The concepts they discuss have been called Activities of Daily Working (ADW). Activities of Daily Working include:

1) Can the individual adapt to and accept the impact of interpersonal relationships with the people on the job?
2) Can he successfully get to and from work on a regularly available form of transportation?
3) Can he understand and perform all regular activities of the job on which he is placed, and does he have sufficient flexibility to

perform and emotionally tolerate at least two other related jobs to which he may be displaced?

4) Can he understand the importance of carrying out time and attendance obligations of the job?

5) Does he possess sufficient initiative to maintain job performance at acceptable levels with no more supervision than the employer or the supervisor believes feasible?

6) Does he possess sufficient emotional stability to remain on the job until his work merits advancement or until a supervisor can correct annoyances?

7) Does he possess sufficient basic educational skills to manage himself without undue dependence on others to interpret or explain what is expected of him?

8) Does he possess sufficient self-control and social judgment to prevent others from taking advantage of his mental limitations?

9) Does he manage all of his ordinary financial activities without help from others?

The work evaluator's report is of real use in developing a case for or against eligibility for rehabilitation services in that it answers many of the above questions. An individual who is capable of functioning at the average level on a psychometric test, but who is not able to function in these activities of daily working is definitely a functionally retarded individual in that he is behavioristically a retarded person but is psychometrically a nonretarded individual.

An Abbreviated Case Study for Demonstration Purposes

Billy is sixteen years old and is in the tenth grade. He has failed one year in school and has a history of educational problems. Specifically he has had no severe difficulty with authority figures or persons in the school incuding his significant peers. His attendance is irregular, but he is not a seriously disruptive force in the classroom. He has not demonstrated a chronic, maladaptive behavioral pattern which would allow his being diagnosed by vocational rehabilitation workers as having a behavioral disorder.

Psychological tests have been administered and test results are as follows:

WECHSLER ADULT INTELLIGENCE SCALE

Full Scale IQ—   91
Verbal Scale IQ—   90
Performance Scale IQ—   94

Verbal Scale Subtests:		Performance Scale Subtests:	
Information—	7	Picture Completion—	10
Computation—	8	Picture Arrangement—	9
Arithmetic—	6	Block Design—	8
Similarities—	8	Object Assembly—	8
Vocabulary—	7	Digit Symbol—	9
Digit span—	8		

No significant score scatter was observed (normal responses). Intelligence is low normal.

BENDER-GESTALT: On the test essentially normal reproductions were achieved. There was no evidence of disturbance or organicity.

WIDE RANGE ACHIEVEMENT TEST:

Reading Grade Placement	7.8 — 25th percentile	
Spelling Grade Placement	7.9 — 27th percentile	
Arithmetic Grade Placement	7.7 — 25th percentile	

Billy is not mentally retarded according to psychological test scores; and as a result, is ineligible for rehabilitation according to most state agency requirements under retardation. Is he functionally retarded? Through this simple case description and the Activities of Daily Working Scale, we can readily answer that he has difficulty adapting to and accepting the impact of interpersonal relationships in that he is unable to get along well with his fellow students and teachers. He is borderline in attendance in school and probably would be borderline in attendance on the job. We feel that he would have difficulty in performing emotionally in two types of jobs other than the one in which he has been involved—the job of being a student in school. He has no vocational training and there is no way to assume that he would make a positive adjustment on the job without evaluation and prevocational training. In addition, he seems to be poorly adjusted in the school so we might assume that his work adjustment also would be poor. He must not understand the importance of attendance obligations on the job since he is missing substantial time from school.

How many work evaluators and other professional persons would predict that he has the emotional stability to remain on the job until his work would permit advancement or until a supervisor could correct any annoyances which may be making difficulty for him? He certainly does not seem to have sufficient educational skills to manage himself without undue dependence on others. His self-control is in question in terms of adjustment problems in school. The question concerning financial activities is difficult to answer and maybe cannot be answered from the data we have.

According to the Activities of Daily Working Scale, this person is functionally retarded. Since work is one of the main concerns in rehabilitation, it would seem that we are indicating that this person is definitely not educationally, socially, or vocationally adjusted at this time in his development; and yet he is ineligible for vocational rehabilitation services according to an intelligence test score. However, what we would like to stress is that even though he is not mentally retarded, he is functioning as if he were retarded and should be considered seriously for vocational rehabilitation services under the diagnosis of functional retardation.

Summary

In developing and using various types of information in evaluation of retarded persons, counselors and others often do not give enough thought to readily available data which often provide more information than do psychological test results. The mystique surrounding psychological tests has helped move them further down the continuum of "assumed" effectiveness than their actual level of successful prediction. Rehabilitation personnel have put far more emphasis on psychological test results than has been recommended by the test developers.

It should be remembered that although I.Q. scores are most

useful, the measures must not be used as the only indices for educational or vocational diagnosis or predictions. In addition to intellectual capacity, information should be obtained on the client's effectiveness in interpersonal relationships, his feelings about himself, his tolerance of frustration and his motivational level. After the collection of necessary data has been completed, the Activities of Daily Working Scale should be used by the counselor when deciding eligibility for rehabilitation services in cases of suspected functional retardation.

REFERENCE

Doyle, P. J. and Seidenfeld, M. A.: Mental Retardation. In Myers, J. S. (Ed.): *An Orientation of Chronic Disease and Disability.* New York, Macmillan, 1965.

CHAPTER 7

VERBAL DISSIMILARITY AMONG BLACK AND WHITE SUBJECTS: A PRIME CONSIDERATION IN COUNSELING AND COMMUNICATION*

RICHARD E. HARDY AND JOHN G. CULL

LANGUAGE PLAYS an important part in our perception of the feelings of persons toward us and, in general, of the total environment around us (Korzybski, 1933; Whorf, 1956; Jakobovits and Miron, 1967; and Saporta, 1961). Problems stemming from the effects of differences in understanding language which result from verbal destitution and dissimilarities in cultural patterns have been documented (Cadzen, 1968; Ramsey, 1968; Riessman, 1962; Newton, 1960; Record, 1961; Kvaraceus, 1965; and others). According to Orem (1968), language is central to personality development and defects in the language are related to the lower class child's inadequacy feelings concerning his "psychological and social self."

The purpose of this research was to evaluate the meaning of words within the language system to both black and white persons in order to determine whether substantially different meanings exist for people according to racial background. Research results could be of considerable importance to persons who serve as counselors, psychologists, and teachers of black and white persons. Communication between the client and counselor is, of course, the prime vehicle through which success-

---

*Reprinted by permission of the *Journal of Negro Education*, 42:1, 1973.

ful client adjustment can be achieved. If language differences are observed, communication at an effective level may be lacking between counselor and counselee. Attitudes of both the counselor and the counselee are, of course, obviously affected by the effectiveness of the communication process.

Method

Forty-nine black subjects were selected randomly from senior classes at John Marshall High School in Richmond, Virginia. In studying the background of these persons it was noted that a high percentage of them came from low socioeconomic backgrounds. In order to counterbalance this factor and achieve some level of matching for socioeconomic stratum, the thirty white subjects who were selected were chosen from similar classes but from a rural area (Wilson Memorial High School, Fishersville, Virginia). While the matching for socioeconomic status is far from precise, the researchers felt that a bias would be introduced into the study if white subjects from a higher socioeconomic level than black subjects were compared with the blacks on an understanding of common English words. Subjects were generally matched on age, sex, and length of time in school. In addition, all students were in senior English classes.

The Gender Association Survey (Osgood, 1967) which was based on the semantic differential technique was administered to the subjects. The survey consists of fifty English nouns (both abstract and concrete). Examples of words in which there were no differences are love, progress, woman, star, food, peace, girl, anger, tongue, crime, and husband.

Preceding the administration of the survey, no reason for the study was given in order that preconceived ideas about the survey could be held to a minimum. Certain biographical data were collected on age, sex, education, and second languages spoken. None of the subjects in the study used a second language in the home.

Directions for the survey were read to all subjects as follows: "The following is a survey to find the relative gender ascribed to certain English words. Your task is to read each word and then to determine for yourself whether it has a masculine or feminine connotation. For example, if you think the word is very masculine, mark the farthest left-hand space with an X as indicated below:

MAN

MASCULINE   X ___ ___ ___ ___   FEMININE"

Fisher's Exact Probability Test (Siegel, 1956) values for black subjects were then compared with those of white subjects.

Results and Implication

The black and white groups were separated according to sex in order to control for this variable. The standard error of the difference between the two population (sex) means was computed. Both the black and white groups were found to be homogeneous (differences were exactly what could be expected from chance factors alone).

The black group and the white group were then compared on their responses to the masculinity and femininity connotations of certain commonly used English nouns. The standard error of difference between the two population means was evaluated. Significant differences were found.

The most interesting difference noted was a substantial one in the interpretation of meaning of abstract versus concrete words. Abstract words such as guilt, story, work, crowd, hope, fear, respect, money, and theft were the words on which the greatest differences appeared. The following differences may be of interest to the reader: Black subjects rated guilt as significantly more masculine than did white subjects who rated it somewhat feminine. Work was seen by black subjects as a masculine word while white subjects saw it as more feminine. Black subjects saw "crowd" as more masculine than did white subjects. "Hope" was seen by black subjects as more masculine than by white subjects. Black subjects saw "money" as more masculine than did white subjects. In all cases, differences were significant on the words cited at least at the .01 level.

Some implications are as follows: (1) Problems in communication between black and white persons may be more complex than generally believed. These problems may arise in particular when abstract symbolisms are used. Words, of course, are symbols of meaning just as are flags. Recent confrontations on campuses stemming from the hoisting of the Confederate flag represent a good example of the complexity of the communication process. To many black students, the Confederate flag has one definite meaning that is associated with racism, and to some white students it has another definite meaning—that associated with being proud of one's regional heritage. Incidentally, the word flag does not appear on the gender association survey.

(2) It is interesting that sex is not a distinguishing characteristic in terms of how persons assign gender to common English nouns. Male and female subjects seem to be equally distributed in the various responses they make concerning the assignment of values of masculinity or femininity to words. This was a somewhat unexpected result in that role differences are often profound since in most households the male is the bread winner while the female cares for the concerns of the home. This general style of life carries over to teenage boys and girls— the girls often helping their mother while the boys are more often spending considerable time with other male figures mainly of their peer group. It would seem that this cast difference in experience during adolescence would influence results but findings did not reveal a sexual difference.

(3) Persons who are involved in training of counselors at the graduate level should be very much concerned that their students comprehend the differences that seem to exist among black and white persons as they interpret the meaning of words. Results of this study would tend to indicate that many counselors and teachers have not been communicating the exact meanings when they are teaching or counseling either black or white subjects. When questionable, abstract words are used by teachers or counselors it may be most helpful to explore with the individual or group of individuals being counseled or taught the exact meaning of important words as they are being used.

The results of this study definitely indicate that additional, extensive research needs to be completed. At a time when racial tension is elevated (probably due mainly to promises which have not been kept or have been misinterpreted—again problems in communication), the importance of effective written and oral communication cannot be overstressed. If we are to be effective counselors, teachers, community leaders and friends of other people, the first requisite for such involvement is effective communication.

REFERENCES

Cadzen, C. B.: Subcultural differences in child language: An interdisciplinary review. In Hellmuth, J. (Ed.): *Disadvantaged Child.* New York, Bunner-Mazel, 1968.

Jakobovits, L. A. and Miron, M. S. (Eds.): *Readings in the Psychology of Languages.* Englewood Cliffs, P-H, 1967.

Korzybski, A.: *Science and Sanity.* New York, Country Life Pr, 1933.

Kvaraceus, W., et al.: *Negro Self Concept.* New York, McGraw, 1965.

National Council of Teachers of English Task Force on Teaching English to the Disadvantaged: *Language Problems of the Disadvantaged.* Champaign, National Council of Teachers of English, 1965.

Newton, E.: Verbal destitution: The pivotal barrier to learning. *J Negro Educ, 30*:497-499, no. 29, 1960.

Orem, R. C.: Language and the culturally disadvantaged. In Amos, W. E. and Grambs, J. O. (Eds.): *Counseling the Disadvantaged Youth.* Englewood Cliffs, P-H, 1968.

Osgood, C. E., Suci, G. J. and Tannenbaum, P. H.: *The Measurement of Meaning.* Chicago, U of Ill Pr, 1967.

Ramsey, W.: Head Start and first grade reading. In Hellmuth, J.: *Disadvantaged Child.* New York, Bunner-Mazel, 1968.

Record, W.: Counseling and communication. *J Negro Educ, 31*:450-454, no. 30, 1961.

Riessman, F.: *The Culturally Deprived Child.* New York, Har-Row, 1962.

Saporta, S. (Ed.): *Psycholinguistics.* New York, HR&W, 1961.

Siegel, S.: *Nonparametric Statistics for the Behavioral Sciences.* New York, McGraw, 1956.

Whorf, B. L.: *Language, Thought and Reality.* Cambridge, Technology Pr, 1956.

CHAPTER 8

A STUDY OF MANIFEST ANXIETY AMONG BLIND RESIDENTIAL SCHOOL STUDENTS*

RICHARD E. HARDY

B LINDNESS IMPOSES CERTAIN LIMITATIONS upon what might be termed normal human functioning. Long-range effects of such limitations have long been topics of concern. The person with a serious visual defect has unique experiences which often seem to result in anxious feelings, and these feelings, in turn, may substantially affect adjustment to life situations.

Nationwide support for rehabilitation programs indicate that Americans are accepting the responsibility for assuring that mentally, physically, emotionally, and culturally handicapped persons are allowed opportunities for the full development of their capabilities. As a corollary, psychologists feel the responsibility to learn more about their clients in order to help them toward the fullest development of their potentialities. In order to do this, of course, they must depend to some extent upon valid and reliable tests and measurements. Unfortunately, few tests and measurements have been developed specifically for the blind, and no measure of anxiety related to blindness has been constructed.

Research Material on Anxiety Among
Blind Persons Almost Nonexistent

Research material on anxiety among blind persons is almost nonexistent. Bauman (1954) and coworkers claim the first

---

*Reprinted by permission of the *New Outlook for the Blind*, 62:173-180, no. 6 (June, 1968).

scientific writing on adjustment problems of the blind as recently as 1954. In 1957, Dean reported on the evaluation of various tests, including Taylor's Manifest Anxiety Scale (MAS) for use with the blind. He concluded that the blind seemed to differ from both normal and clinical groups on the MAS, and they tend to defend themselves by response distortion. He was unable to differentiate groups of blind persons according to visual acuity, duration of handicap, or adjustment.

Zarlock (1961) found that scores of blind persons on a social adjustment scale were related to high ego strength, low manifest anxiety, and a positive attitude toward blindness. His study concerned magical thinking and associated psychological reactions to total blindness.

The most comprehensive narrative coverage of anxiety as it relates to blindness is offered by Bauman and Yoder (1966) in a recent publication which includes an updating of Bauman's original adjustment to blindness study. The authors have discussed various definitions of anxiety as well as certain research findings and related them to blindness.

The purpose of the research described in this article was the construction and evaluation of an experimental instrument (a scale of manifest anxiety) designed especially for the blind (the partially sighted and the totally blind) and the study of anxiety levels in relation to a blind person's age, amount of vision,* sex, and verbal intelligence. It was believed that a scale of manifest anxiety specifically constructed for blind persons would be more meaningful for them than the commonly used scales. Taylor's Manifest Anxiety Scale (Jones, 1962) was chosen as an example of a commonly used scale and was employed as a general anxiety measure because it is one of the best known. In addition, the MAS was devised to evaluate drive in learning situations and to measure an inner force which makes people competitive. This force may bear a possible special relationship to the effects of blindness in that blind persons must constantly prove them-

---

*Subjects were divided into three groups: (1) the totally blind, (2) those with light perception and projection, and (3) those with relatively useful vision.

selves through competition with the sighted (Bauman and Yoder, 1966).

What Is Anxiety?

In a study of the validity of Taylor's Manifest Anxiety Scale, Kendall (1954) described anxiety as the extent to which an individual

> (a) gave exaggerated and inappropriate reactions on slight provocation, (b) gave general indications of fatigue not attributable to his physical condition, (c) displayed difficulties in elimination not explainable by his physical condition, (d) appeared to be easily upset, (e) showed indications of general restlessness, (f) slept poorly, (g) displayed symptoms of nausea or vomiting not attributable to his physical condition, (h) displayed difficulty in concentration or thinking, and (i) appeared to be generally tremulous.

The Sample: Criteria of Selection

A sample was chosen of all blind* (the partially sighted and the totally blind) students from the residential school population of the Maryland School for the Blind and the Overbrook School for the Blind in Pennsylvania. The sample included 122 males and females, the age levels ranging from thirteen to twenty-two. The study sample consisted of students in regular classes at the residential schools who had no recorded physical or mental handicaps in addition to blindness. All subjects had been blind for at least three years.

Construction of an Anxiety Scale for the Blind

Before writing prospective items for the Anxiety Scale for the Blind (ASB), the following criteria for item selection were established: (1) Each item should be as specific in content as possible; (2) each item should be in language easily understood by blind high school students; (3) each item should relate to anxiety as it is experienced by blind persons; and (4) each item response

---

*Blindness is defined as visual acuity in the better eye with best correction which does not exceed 20/200 or a defect in the visual field so that the widest diameter of vision subtends an angle no greater than 20 degrees (Hardy, 1966).

should contribute to the evaluation of manifest anxiety. Several steps described by Hardy (1965) were taken in the refinement of items. A final step involved the judging of individual items by five clinical experts. Items were judged as good or poor by the five psychologists who were knowledgeable about the problems of blindness. A total of seventy-eight items judged as indicative of manifest anxiety formed the Anxiety Scale for the Blind. A pamphlet explaining and including this scale is available from the Publications Division, American Foundation for the Blind, 15 West 16th Street, New York, N. Y. 10011, for $1.00. Teachers have an opportunity to observe student behavior daily, and their responses to items indicative of manifest anxiety should provide a satisfactory measure of student anxiety external to that measured by other instruments.

Thirty-nine items and true or false answers intended to measure manifest anxiety of students were written, refined, and evaluated by a second group of five independent clinical experts. These judges were asked to evaluate items as excellent, good, fair, poor, or no measure of manifest anxiety. After refinement and evaluation, twenty-three items were chosen to form a scale for teachers to use in rating the manifest anxiety of individual students (Hardy, 1965).

Teachers rated only those students whom they taught. Two teachers rated each student and after three weeks each student was re-rated.

Administration of the ASB and the MAS

The ASB and the MAS were twice administered orally. The first administration was completed in both schools in November 1965 and the second administration was finished the third week in December of the same year.

Rolls of common theater tickets numbered at each end were given to all students. These had been previously rolled to include the exact number of questions for each instrument. In order to assure that each student was answering the correct question, holes were punched in every tenth ticket. True response tickets were placed on the right of the desk and false response tickets were placed on the left.

Students in both schools took the ASB in approximately fifty minutes and the MAS in about forty minutes. Twenty minutes were allowed between tests.

Statistical Procedure

Since the research purposes required investigating the linear relationship between the anxiety scales and also the linear relationship between teacher ratings of students and scores on anxiety tests, the product-moment coefficient of correlation was chosen as a measure of the degree of resemblance between variates in question. A t-test was appropriate for evaluating the significance of observed correlations. Fisher's z statistic (Brownlee, 1961) was used in normalizing correlation coefficients so that comparisons among coefficients could be made. An F statistic was selected to test the significance of differences between any two given correlations.

The split-half method was chosen to evaluate reliability of both anxiety scales, and stability over time was evaluated by a retest reliability coefficient. Average performance on both split-half scores and retest scores were compared through the use of the studentized range statistic (Kendall, 1954).

Teacher rating reliability was tested by correlating the two ratings of each teacher and by correlating the first rating of both teachers and the second rating of both teachers. The first measure indicates the re-rating consistency of teachers, and the second indicates the inter-rater variability. The F-ratio test was used to evaluate the likelihood that teacher ratings between schools differed with regard to variability.

Most of the various statistical techniques were applied by programming the data into a 1620 computer.

Results

The sixty-six students from the Overbrook School for the Blind and the fifty-six from the Maryland School for the Blind were combined to give one large sample rather than two smaller samples. Except in the area of teacher ratings, the two schools did prove to give homogeneous measurements in terms of odd-half splits, retest scores, and verbal intelligence. In the given sample of 122 students, the two anxiety tests correlated significantly for a correlation coefficient of 0.7416. The correlation coefficient between the two anxiety tests was also computed for five subgroupings of the data (see Table 8-I).

TABLE 8-1

CORRELATION COEFFICIENT BETWEEN ASB
AND TAYLOR TEST SCORES

Grouping	Coefficient
Males	0.6915
Females	0.7822
Total blindness	0.6062
Light perception and projection	0.7949
Relatively useful vision	0.7834

A complex pattern of significance emerged when the correlations between anxiety test scores and the teacher ratings were examined. The combined sample of 122 students showed correlation measures of 0.2834 between the ASB score and Teacher A's rating and 0.2891 between the ASB score and Teacher B's rating. A correlation estimate of 0.1942 was found between the Taylor score and Teacher A's rating and a correlation of 0.2253 was indicated between the Taylor score and Teacher B's rating. All were statistically significant at the .05 level of confidence.

The female and totally blind students showed a significant relationship between the test scores and the teacher ratings. Among students with relatively useful vision, there was a significant correlation between the test scores and Teacher B's rating but not between the test scores and Teacher A's rating. Means and standard deviations of all anxiety scales are given in Table 8-II.

On the other hand, the male students and the light perception and projection group indicated no significant correlation between the test scores and the two teacher ratings.

The two halves of the ASB gave a correlation coefficient of

TABLE 8-II

TEST SCORE MEANS AND STANDARD DEVIATIONS

Variable	All Students	Male	Female	Total Blindness	Light Perception and Projection	Relativity Useful Vision
ASB	18.11 (9.60)	17.51 (9.68)	18.65 (9.58)	16.74 (9.23)	20.17 (8.70)	17.84 (9.88)
MAS	15.98 (8.01)	15.10 (7.58)	16.75 (8.35)	13.35 (6.86)	17.55 (8.48)	16.56 (8.14)
Teacher A	4.32 (4.11)	3.65 (3.90)	4.91 (4.22)	4.13 (4.37)	3.79 (4.24)	4.66 (3.94)
Teacher B	4.21 (3.90)	3.79 (3.77)	4.58 (3.99)	4.16 (3.59)	3.24 (3.02)	4.69 (4.35)

0.789 while the two halves of the Taylor test showed 0.717 as their measure of agreement (see Table 8-III). The studentized range statistic gave no indication that means of half scores differed; therefore, there was no reason to believe that either the ASB or the Taylor was internally biased. The retest and studentized range procedures indicated no significant score difference over time.

TABLE 8-III

INTRA- AND INTER-TEST SCORE CORRELATION COEFFICIENTS

Sample Variables	Coefficient of Correlation
ASB/Taylor	0.742
ASB/Teacher A	0.283
Taylor/Teacher A	0.194
ASB/Teacher B	0.289
Taylor/Tacher B	0.225
Two halves: ASB	0.789
Two halves: Taylor	0.717
ASB test/retest	0.746
Taylor test/retest	0.811
Two ratings by Teacher A	0.917
Two ratings by Teacher B	0.929
First ratings of both teachers	0.826
Second ratings of both teachers	0.844

Table 8-IV contains the correlation coefficient obtained be-

tween age and the four anxiety indicators (ASB, MAS, Teacher
A rating and Teacher B rating) for all breakdowns into subgroups of the data. As can be seen, age correlates significantly
with the ASB and the Taylor test results indicating coefficients
of 0.1907 and 0.2532, respectively, for all students. This meant
the older the student, the more likely he was to have a high
ASB or Taylor score. Age for the overall sample was not significantly related to the teacher ratings.

TABLE 8-IV

RELATIONSHIP BETWEEN CHRONOLOGICAL AGE IN YEARS
AND ANXIETY TEST SCORES

Sample	N	Anxiety Scale	Correlation Coefficient
All students	122	ASB	0.1907*
		Taylor	0.2532*
		Teacher A rating	—0.1110
		Teacher B rating	—0.1478
Male students	57	ASB	0.1078
		Taylor	0.1080
		Teacher A rating	—0.2051*
		Teacher B rating	—0.2586*
Female students	65	ASB	0.2859*
		Taylor	0.4077*
		Teacher A rating	0.0442
		Teacher B rating	—0.0348
Totally blind	31	ASB	0.0547
		Taylor	0.1296
		Teacher A rating	—0.0924
		Teacher B rating	—0.2983
Light perception and projection	29	ASB	0.4943*
		Taylor	0.3175*
		Teacher A rating	—0.0165
		Teacher B rating	—0.0082
Relatively useful vision	62	ASB	0.1702
		Taylor	0.2272*
		Teacher A rating	—0.1783
		Teacher B rating	—0.1420

*Significant at the .05 level of confidence.

By breaking the data down according to visual acuity groups, it was shown that the anxiety level of the totally blind student did not vary with his age. Students in the light perception and projection group did show a significant tendency to have higher ASB and Taylor test scores as their age increased. Students with relatively useful vision indicated a positive correlation between age and the Taylor test but not between age and the ASB scale (see Table 8-V).

TABLE 8-V

RELATIONSHIP BETWEEN VISUAL ACUITY AND
ANXIETY TEST SCORES

Sample	N	Anxiety Scale	Correlation Coefficient°
All students	122	ASB	0.0261
		Taylor	0.1444
		Teacher A rating	0.0650
		Teacher B rating	0.0794
Male students	57	ASB	—0.0232
		Taylor	0.1943
		Teacher A rating	0.1206
		Teacher B rating	0.0297
Female students	65	ASB	0.0683
		Taylor	0.0945
		Teacher A rating	0.0034
		Teacher B rating	0.1161

°Not significant at .05 level of confidence.

In examining the sex differences in anxiety scale scores (see Table 8-VI), it was found that females in the light perception and projection group had higher Taylor scale scores than did males in the same group. Sex differences were not candited in any other breakdowns of the data.

According to the results of the correlation analysis, verbal intelligence was significantly inversely related to the ASB and Taylor scores (see Table 8-VII). Female students had an especially high negative correlation between verbal intelligence and all anxiety scores. For male students, verbal intelligence seemed to affect the ASB score only. Verbal intelligence was not significantly related to the anxiety scale scores of the totally blind students, but increased verbal intelligence did vary with the lower ASB and Taylor scores of the light perception and projection group and the group with relatively useful vision.

TABLE 8-VI

RELATIONSHIP BETWEEN SEX AND ANXIETY TEST SCORES

Sample	N	Anxiety Scale	Correlation Coefficient
All students	122	ASB	0.0593
		Taylor	0.1030
		Teacher A rating	0.1535
		Teacher B rating	0.1022
Totally blind	31	ASB	—0.0964
		Taylor	—0.0092
		Teacher A rating	0.2440
		Teacher B rating	0.0870
Light perception and projection	29	ASB	0.1736
		Taylor	0.3588*
		Teacher A rating	0.1489
		Teacher B rating	0.0635
Relatively useful vision	62	ASB	0.0637
		Taylor	—0.0065
		Teacher A rating	0.1172
		Teacher B rating	0.1432

*Significant at the .05 level of confidence.

Conclusion and Discussion

It was concluded that the MAS and the ASB measure somewhat the same properties, and that one instrument seems as useful as the other with blind residential high school students who have no mental or physical handicap in addition to blindness and who have been blind for at least three years.

Results indicate a significant inverse relationship between verbal intelligence and anxiety scores; however, there seems to be no significant relationship between sex category and anxiety scores or visual acuity and anxiety scores. Although visual acuity was found to be a nonsignificant variable, the light perception and projection group scored somewhat consistently higher than

TABLE 8-VII

RELATIONSHIP BETWEEN VERBAL INTELLIGENCE
(WECHSLER-BELLEVUE) AND ANXIETY TEST SCORES

Sample	N	Anxiety Scale	Correlation Coefficient
All students	122	ASB	—0.3326*
		Taylor	—0.3126
		Teacher A rating	—0.1547
		Teacher B rating	—0.1198
Male students	57	ASB	—0.2312*
		Taylor	—0.1422
		Teacher A rating	0.0377
		Teacher B rating	0.0666
Female students	65	ASB	—0.4029*
		Taylor	—0.4070*
		Teacher A rating	—0.2441*
		Teacher B rating	—0.2219*
Totally blind	31	ASB	—0.0953
		Taylor	—0.0211
		Teacher A rating	—0.1584
		Teacher B rating	—0.0676
Light perception and projection	29	ASB	—0.5713*
		Taylor	0.5344*
		Teacher A rating	—0.2301
		Teacher B rating	—0.0655
Relatively useful vision	62	ASB	—0.3644*
		Taylor	—0.2906*
		Teacher A rating	—0.0831
		Teacher B rating	—0.1381

*Significant at the .05 level of confidence.

either the group of the totally blind or the group with relatively useful vision.

It has been shown that manifest anxiety tends to increase with age among blind residential high school students. Researchers may want to consider controlling for the age variable in future studies of this group. Counselors may find it reasonable to expect that older students in residential schools will require more counseling than younger students.

REFERENCES

Bauman, Mary K. (Ed.): *Adjustment to Blindness.* Commonwealth of Pennsylvania, Department of Welfare, 1954.

Bauman, Mary K. and Yoder, Norman M.: *Adjustment to Blindness—Reviewed.* Springfield, 1966.

Brownlee, K. A.: *Statistical Theory and Methodology in Science and Engineering.* New York, 1961.

Dean, Sidney I.: Adjustment testing and personality factors of the blind. *J Consult Psychol,* 21:171-177, no. 2, 1957.

Hardy, Richard E.: Counseling physically handicapped college students. *The New Outlook for the Blind,* 59:182-183, 1965.

Hardy, Richard E.: A Study of Manifest Anxiety Among Blind Residential School Students Using an Experimental Instrument Constructed for the Blind. Unpublished doctoral dissertation, University of Maryland, August, 1966.

Hardy, Richard E.: Prediction of manifest anxiety levels of blind persons through the use of a multiple regression technique. *Int J Educ Blind,* 17:2, December, 1967.

Jones, J. W.: Problems in defining and classifying blindness. *The New Outlook for the Blind,* 56:4, 1962.

Kendall, Edward: The validity of Taylor's Manifest Anxiety Scale. *J Consult Psychol,* 18:6, 1954.

Taylor, Janet, A.: A personality scale of manifest anxiety. *J Abnorm Soc Psychol,* 48:2, 1953.

Winer, B. J.: *Statistical Principles in Experimental Design.* New York, 1962.

Zarlock, Stanley P.: Magical thinking and associated psychological reactions to blindness. *J Counseling Psychol,* 25:155-159, no. 2, 1961.

CHAPTER 9

CASE STUDIES IN DISADVANTAGEMENT
AND DRUG ABUSE

JOHN G. CULL AND RICHARD E. HARDY

R. E. M.
Male—Eighteen years of age
Single
10th Grade Education
Inadequate personality with paranoid tendencies due to drug intoxication

Referral Source

Mr. M. was referred to the Veterans Hospital (VA) by his parents, who were very concerned about their son's drug addiction. Mr. M. began using drugs while in the Army and continued to use drugs since his discharge, two months ago. He has previously lost a job as a salesman with a major tire company, which may or may not be related to drugs. Mr. M. says he realizes the fatal prognosis and wants to get off drugs so he can go to work and make a fresh start.

Social Data

Mr. M. is an eighteen-year-old man who was admitted to a VA Hospital for drug misuse. His parents are a very pleasant and neatly attired couple. His father is in his early forties, his mother is in her late thirties. He was their first child. There are six other children in the family. The parents describe Mr. M.'s early childhood as a very emotional one. He had temper tantrums frequently and often passed out from crying so hard that it caused him to quit breathing. During his adolescent and teenage years he was always quiet and had only a few friends. He also never has been too comfortable with girls. His parents made a point of saying that he did not run around with the "hell raisers" and seemed to think that this was one of the biggest points in his favor. Although he uses drugs, Mr. and Mrs. M. feel their son is not a bad boy.

Mr. M.'s parents related some of their son's guilt feelings over problems with their younger son, Jim. It seems Jim ran away from home just two days before Mr. M. returned home from service. Jim ran away with a 35-year-old woman who Mr. and Mrs. M. feel was manipulating and using him.

He now feels that Jim ran away because of him, although he had been quite close to his younger brother. Jim is still away from the home although his parents have heard that he is well. There are six siblings in the family, sisters age sixteen, fourteen, eight, and five, and brothers aged sixteen and eleven. Mr. M. comes from a family that is described as comfortable with the necessities of life but never with an overabundance of money. His father works regularly and is very strongly committed to the value of work; "the necessity for hard work to get anywhere in life." His mother is a warm supportive person who is greatly distressed over her son's use of drugs and weeps easily on discussing this.

Both parents claim that they knew nothing of his taking drugs until recently when they first noticed a gross change in the patient's behavior. They described him as being normal, outgoing, and happy when he first came home and then overnight he became very depressed and very frightened. Mr. M.'s rapid decompensation was followed by

1. paranoid feelings in regard to people in the back yard laughing at him;

2. attempts made by neighbors to harm his family physically and harm their reputation;

3. his reluctance to get off the bus when he was going downtown to the employment office which caused him to stay

on the bus the entire route and just go right back home and remain in the house, totally afraid to leave.

At this point, Mr. M. and his parents felt the need for hospitalization and very anxiously appeared at the VA office.

He dropped out of school in the tenth grade because he was in constant trouble with the teachers. He enlisted in the Army, thinking that the Army life would be so nice. When he was disappointed and frustrated in the Army, he began taking drugs in order to relieve his depression while in Vietnam. He was taking speed, grass, and LSD. He had thirty trips on LSD in the last two years. Mr. M., a Vietnam veteran, was discharged from the Army with a general discharge under honorable conditions. According to Mr. M.'s information he continued to take drugs until one week prior to being admitted to the VA Hospital.

His girl friend left him because he was on drugs but now because he sought treatment, she has returned to him.

Educational History

Mr. M. completed ten years of school and was described as an average student. He did not participate in extracurricular activities in school. He did enjoy playing basketball around the house but never played it in school. Once he got into high school he could not adjust to the high school routine. His parents were not really sure what it was, if it was that he could not grasp the material or if the classes were too competitive with the other students. During his stay in the VA Hospital, Mr. M. took and passed his General Educational Development (GED) test.

Psychological Data

Mr. M. was referred for psychological evaluation in order to assess possible organic impairment caused by his drug usage. He was given a battery of tests consisting of the Wechsler Adult Intelligence Test, Bender-Gestalt, Projective Drawings and the Rorschach.

Test Behavior

Mr. M. was cooperative, coherent, and relevant throughout the interview and testing. He manifested some interest in and motivation to succeed on the tasks. The major clinical impression of this young man was that of a beaten individual. Although Mr. M. was quiet, soft-spoken and self-denigrating generally, there were occasional sparks of animation.

Test Findings

The measures related to intellectual functioning suggest that this veteran has not suffered organic impairment due to the drug use. His Full Scale on the WAIS I.Q. was 105 indicating that he is currently functioning in the normal range (Verbal I.Q., 106; Performance I.Q., 103). While Mr. M. seems to have the potential for bright normal functioning there are indications that emotional and environmental factors have interferred with his developing adequately. He performs well on tasks that require nonverbal skills, and demonstrates moderately above average ability to concentrate and attend freely to noninterpersonal tasks. His performance decreases on the more academic, verbal, and interpersonal tasks.

Mr. M.'s performance on the projective measures indicate some of the likely sources of his emotional and intellectual difficulties. These are quite consistent with the veteran's description of his family relationship and his schooling.

He has apparently employed denial as a major defense against strong feelings of inadequacy. These inadequate feelings seem to stem from the relationship Mr. M. had with his father. His father is seen as a strong masculine figure who apparently thought little of his son and at least unconsciously made that quite clear. Unable to deal with these feelings and resolve this relationship, Mr. M., as he entered adolescence, apparently took the "easy way out." "If I am nothing, I'll flunk out of school, etc.," at the same time he was a "man" in this flunking subgroup.

Mr. M. appears to be basically bright and a sensitive young man. He seems aware of the raw deal he dealt himself in order to cope with his emotional stress. This has apparently heightened his feelings of inadequacy and lack of self-worth and through the denial there is a fairly strong feeling of depression. In efforts to combat these unacceptable feelings of inadequacy Mr. M. at times comes across as hostile and aggressive. This dynamic picture may help to explain his choice of "uppers" rather than "downers" or any other drugs.

At the present time Mr. M.'s use or denial is sufficiently intact to interfere with his adequately grappling with, and resolving these inter and intrapersonal difficulties himself. It is the clinical psychologist's opinion that, if Mr. M. is, or can be, motivated enough to enter into individual psychotherapy of intensive counseling, he has the capacity for insight and growth. Additionally, when such counseling is undertaken, Mr. M. seems quite capable of furthering his education vocationally, and perhaps, even academically.

Summary

Mr. M.'s current performance indicates that he is in the normal range of intellectual functioning. There is no evidence in the protocol to suggest organic impairment or psychosis. At the present time he may be considered an inadequate personality with paranoid tendencies due to drug intoxication. The records suggest that attitudes within his family have fostered this self-perception. Therapy could prove beneficial and is recommended.

Medical History

Mr. M. has a history of drug usage which led to his military discharge and subsequent admission to the VA Hospital. He has been hearing voices and is in a panic that someone is going to hurt him, although he does not know who this someone is.

Mr. M.'s mental and physical status reveal an eighteen-year-old male, thin, looking utterly in a panic, eyes red from tears, claiming he does not trust anybody and is afraid to be in the building because "the whole world is crazy."

Mr. M. states that he has been in good general health except for these feelings. Smoking, occasional drinking, and use of LSD, speed, and marijuana are Mr. M.'s habits. He has had none of the childhood or adult illnesses and is sensitive to poison oak.

Because he is afraid, Mr. M. claims that "they" think he is a queer, and an addict, and so on. . . . The physician felt that the client was inadequate, immature, and withdrawn, with a flat affect.

Physical Examination

Patient is in no distress, and is well-oriented.
Eyes: negative
Throat: negative
Neck: no adenopathy
Lungs: clear to A and P
Heart: negative
Abdomen: soft, no masses, no area of tenderness
Reflexes, patellar: o.k.
Diagnosis: acute psychosis, paranoid type

Vocational History: Testing and Counseling

Prior to enlisting in the Army Mr. M. worked as an inspector for nine months at D & H, a screw machine company in his hometown. After his discharge from the Army, he worked for a major tire company as a salesman. Mr. M. lost this job due to his drug misuse.

A battery of vocational and interest tests consisting of the Lee Thorpe Occupational Interest Inventory, Minnesota Vocational Interest Inventory, and the Edwards Personal Preference Schedule were administered by a counseling psychologist. According to the Lee Thorpe Occupational Interest Inventory, Mr. M. showed interest in the mechanical field, and he would be satisfied in being an electronic pressman, or a stock clerk. He also stated that he would like to be trained as a steamfitter.

According to the Edwards Personal Preference Schedule, he sees himself as being an aggressive, exhibiting, show-off. However, according to our observation, and other test findings, he is an immature, meek, fragile, and not too adequate person. In reality, he is only eighteen. He could be given some allowance to be immature. We are only glad that he now realizes that he can get along so much better without the effect of drugs.

Mr. James Smith, Mr. M.'s former employer at D & H, was approached about Mr. M.'s reemployment. Information was made concerning Mr. M.'s reemployment with D & H Company, upon Mr. M.'s release from the hospital.

Hospital Summary

Mr. M. on admission was markedly frightened and suspicious. He stated that the whole world looked crazy to him. On the admission ward, he presented himself as a hostile and negative person. He requested his discharge against medical advice. After being coaxed by the staff, he opened his mind and admitted his paranoid feelings and suicidal ideas. While in the hospital Mr. M. continued to suffer from ideas of reference and persecution for quite awhile. IIe is uncooperative and angry, claiming that he was not sick. A urine test proved that he was not taking his medication. He was confronted about this and he agreed to take his medication provided that it would not make him drowsy. Mellaril®, 50 mg q.i.d., was prescribed. Once this medication was increased, Mr. M.'s condition began to improve.

Mr. M. has shown quite a bit of improvement in his condition since being admitted. His affect now seems more appropriate and he is showing more spontaneity. He seems free from psychosis but could have flashbacks in the future from his past experiments with LSD. Mr. M. has been on several passes home and has apparently refrained from taking drugs while there. The hospital staff feels that Mr. M. is ready to go back and resume working as an inspector at D & H Company. This will place him back in a familiar place where he feels he is wanted. And. he knows too where to go and what to do when he is ready for the GI bill training as a steamfitter. He also agreed with us that he will seek supportive therapy and counseling at a mental hygiene clinic. Upon discharge Mr. M. was given a 21-day supply of Mellaril.

B. T. S.
White Male—Nineteen years old
Single
High School Graduate

Drug abuse characterized by an inability to adjust vocationally and socially

Referral Source

Mr. S. is a nineteen-year-old white male. Two years ago, this client was in a vocational rehabilitation school unit. During his senior year he dropped out of school and left town. He has recently returned to Richmond and was referred to this vocational rehabilitation counselor by his former school unit counselor as a client in need of services due to residuals of drug addiction.

Social History

Mr. S. comes from a disrupted family background. This client's mother died when he was very young and he was raised and cared for by various women within the family (2 sisters and an aunt). The client remembers being extremely effeminate and afraid of his peers. His father has been a disabled alcoholic for a long period of time. Mr. S. had interrupted relationships with his father and received no financial support or guidance while growing up. The client stated that he separated completely from his father when he was fifteen years old. Ever since, he has been on his own, searching for his identity and attempting to cope with his emotional problems.

Mr. S. has been a drug user since his high school years. This client was a heavy user of amphetamines and eventually became dependent upon these drugs. He has also used LSD and speed. His leaving high school during his senior year was due primarily to drug abuse. After Mr. S. dropped out of school, he went to Canada, gradually worked his way across the states and finally became a "speed freak" in San Francisco's Haight Ashbury. He lived with a couple and their child. During his stay in Haight Ashbury, Mr. S. was seen by a psychiatrist in a free clinic where he was found to be an extremely depressed youth with homosexual drives and a drug dependency (see Psychological Data below). He was placed in a drug treatment center and withdrew from drug use.

Mr. S. is a seemingly bright young man who is attempting to

work out his problems and his loneliness without family guidance and support. He has been living with friends and acquaintances for the past two years. He is seen by the vocational rehabilitation counselor as cooperative, alert, and quite willing to bend to survive.

Educational History

Mr. S. completed eleven and one-half years of school before dropping out and going to San Francisco. While there he did manage to finish his remaining course work and graduated from a local San Francisco high school. Also while in California, Mr. S. qualified for civil service by passing the Civil Service Examination. He is an intelligent individual who expresses a desire to go to college or to learn a skill or trade.

Vocational History

Mr. S.'s vocational experiences are limited due to his home environment, drug abuse, and age. He never has worked while living in this city. While in San Francisco, he did qualify and passed the Civil Service Examination. He then secured a job with the postal department as a clerk in the concentration center. He earned three dollars per hour. He held this job for two weeks before he was forced to quit due to drugs. This client managed to find odd jobs and eventually worked his way back to this city. He has since been unemployed receiving support from his friends and relatives.

Psychological Data

Psychiatric Abstract From the Haight Ashbury Free Clinic

Mr. S. presents symptoms of anxiety and depression. He is a highly dependent youth and has been placed in a situation with which he is unable to cope—following a failure of a mother substitute relationship. He has been clinging to this relationship for some time as a defense against his very strong homosexual drives. However, he has recently entered into a homosexual relationship with another young man, and as a consequence feels that he has achieved some resolution of his identity conflicts.

This client has been a drug user for many years and has recently become dependent upon amphetamines. It is quite probable that his present emotional state is in part due to wasting effects of continued use of amphetamines, LSD and other psychedelic drugs.

In summary, Mr. S. has an inability to function in the appropriate masculine roles and has resolved his psychosexual conflict through a homosexual adjustment.

Since data was not obtained in regard to Mr. S.'s school cumulative record, the Revised Beta and the Kuder Preference Test were administered by the vocational rehabilitation counselor. The Revised Beta revealed a score of 120 placing Mr. S. in the upper limits of average intelligence. The Kuder Preference Test indicated this client's interests are in the fields of literature and art.

These findings were discussed with Mr. S. He stated he has done considerable writing of poetry and prose and apparently has talents in those areas. Mr. S. intends to further develop these talents in college. But, at the present time he strongly wants to become self-supporting preferably through sales or clerical work. These are his stated goals at the present.

Medical History

Mr. S.'s medical history reveals that he has had no systematic difficulties or apparent illness except the residuals of drug abuse. Mr. S. was sent to a local physician for his general medical examination. On the basis of the following report, no further recommendations were made.

General Basic Medical Examination Record

Frequent headaches: no
Hearing: no
Extreme fatigue: yes
Nervous system: normal
Persistent cough: no
Pain in chest: no
Unusual irritability: yes

Difficult vision: yes
Fainting: no
Asthma: no
Unusual gain or loss of weight: no
Cough producing blood: no
Short breath: no

Swollen ankles: no

Loss of appetite: no

Difficulty in memory: no

TB: no

Hernia: no

Operation: no

Hemorrhoid: no

Diarrhea or constipation: no

Eyes: 20/20 left, and 20/20 right

Nose thorax: negative

Lymphatic: normal

Heart and circulation: normal

Abdomen: normal

Anorectal: normal

Fever: no

Difficulty in thinking: no

Frequent indigestion: no

Rheumatism: no

Convulsions: no

Varicose veins: no

Accident: no

Burning in urine: no

Height: 73″; weight: 129 lbs.

Hearing: o.k.

Mouth and teeth: normal

Chest and lungs: normal

Blood pressure: 100/50

Genitourinary system: normal

Skin: normal

Eligibility

Mr. S.'s primary disability has been diagnosed as an emotional disorder characterized by an inability to stabilize in work. A secondary disability has been diagnosed as residual to drug abuse. Mr. S. expects to later complete his education in college but at this time he needs to gain his independence and self-esteem. Because of his exceptional talents intellectually and his personal insights into his problems along with his withdrawal from drug usage, there is reasonable expectation that he can be gainfully employed.

Plan

A vocational plan was written with sales clerk as the vocational objective. This vocational choice was based on the client's intellectual ability, experiences, and interests. It was felt by the counselor and the client that time was needed for the client to plan his future. A stock clerk position was found with a local department store. The client will earn $50 a week.

Services Rendered

Guidance and Counseling

General Medical Examination

Transportation
Rent for a month
Food bills for a month
Clothing
Job placement
Follow-up

The cost to Vocational Rehabilitation was $250.00. The client's case was closed with status 26 rehabilitation.

Case Reopened

Six months later, Mr. S. came and told his rehabilitation counselor he quit his job after six weeks. The position as a stock clerk was not challenging enough for Mr. S. He stated that he needed to be more deeply involved in some occupation more in line with his self-image.

Mr. S. appeared to be hostile, depressed and lonely to the vocational rehabilitation counselor. He blurted out his feelings in a somewhat philosophical manner. He spoke of moving many times in the past six months. He wanted to talk about the state of the economy and he did not believe there was a job "out there for him." He has been disappointed in not getting a job as a mail clerk.

His Kuder Preference Record Vocational (KPRV) was again interpreted for him. Some effort was made to explore which move would be more in the direction of his long-range goals.

Library assistant and proofreader seemed appropriate jobs for consideration. Local opportunities might include copy editing with a newspaper. Literary and musical interest of a quite professional caliber were also suggested by the KPRV. Mr. S.'s intelligence supports this. An appointment was made for Mr. S. to take the General Aptitude Test Battery (GATB), which will possibly confirm his musical mastery.

It was felt that Mr. S. may have real potential as a composer and arranger if he is willing to go through formal training. At this time he frowns upon formal education and wants to get a job. He does not feel academic discipline is too important since he picks up things very quickly on his own, including some composing of music.

GATB scores indicate Mr. S. is capable in most areas:

G	- 133	Q	- 154
U	- 145	K	- 140
N	- 130	F	- 106
S	- 107	M	- 91
P	- 121		

Mr. S. was informed of the results. The conversation tended to center around music as his long-range area of interest. He has considered music school. The vocational rehabilitation counselor stressed the importance of some concrete long-range planning and the use of his talents. An appointment was made with the chairman of the music department of City University.

Mr. S. would first like to work in the Post Office to prove to himself that he can hold a job for at least half a year. An appointment was made with the Post Office about a job as a clerk.

In his interview with the chairman of the music department, Mr. S. played some of his original compositions. The chairman felt Mr. S. has good potential in the area of music and persuaded him to apply for admission as a music student.

Mr. S. then talked to the personnel director at the Post Office concerning employment. He trimmed his hair and presented a neat appearance for the interview. He mentioned his prior use of drugs to the personnel director. The vocational rehabilitation counselor felt this probably killed any chances of him getting a job.

The client was then urged to search for jobs in the city. He found a job in a medical lab and was hired by a Dr. Hane. Mr. S. discussed the possibility of on-the-job training as a lab assistant under Dr. Hane's direction. It is a thirteen-month training program.

Mr. S.'s GATB reveals that for the vocational profile of the Medical Lab Assistant, he has more than sufficient scores to qualify him for this work. (Requirements are G-110, S-95, P-110; client has G-133, S-107, and P-121.)

The Kuder Performance Test did show a correlation of 79 per cent in scientific computation and the clerical field. He is well motivated to pursue this goal having discussed this with Dr. Hane of the Department of Anatomy—under whom he will be working. This program offers ample opportunities for future employment since a local hospital expects to hire all of these trainees. The client will learn to dissect and prepare specimens for slides, to do all the related jobs and to operate completely with full responsibilities as a medical lab assistant. Tuition will be payable to the Department of Anatomy for this training at a rate of $86 a month. Maintenance to be sought through the Department of Public Welfare and the Training Services Project at a rehabilitation center. Total cost of services was $2,318.

Dr. Hane will be supervising training and totally responsible for all of Mr. S.'s weekly hours, progress and reporting to the counselor.

Job duties include

1. learning the preparation of tissue and various techniques
2. assisting in surgical operation of animals
3. learning the ordering and caring of equipment
4. learning the care and treatment of animals for research
5. learning to use all equipment
6. learning the proper method of mixing and using stain chemicals and dyes.

Mr. S. received a Training Service Project stipend with the stipulation that the money will not be paid if the student has three absences in a week, has been placed on leave for more than one week, has made unsatisfactory progress, or has left the training program.

Mr. S. entered the training program in April. After the first months, he was doing a moderately good job. Dr. Hane felt his main problem was that of being easily offended by any types of critical opinion related to work. Mr. S. knows the techniques on paper but occasionally has a little trouble transposing this knowledge to practice. He attempts to do some things without really thinking carefully about them before doing the task. Dr. Hane has stressed the importance of his appearance and communications with his fellow workers.

The vocational rehabilitation counselor feels that the client is having difficulty in regulating himself to work and personal regimentation but is making progress and is "sticking with it."

Several months later, Mr. S. was again evaluated. Dr. Hane indicated that Mr. S. is learning the proper skills well and does a good job when told what to do. Dr. Hane senses Mr. S. has a feeling of importance to the functioning of the lab. Progress is being made both in technical skills and fellow relationships. The vocational rehabilitation counselor counseled his client about his appearance. He accepted this and changed it sufficiently.

In the last progress report received, Dr. Hane indicated Mr. S. is increasing in skill proficiency. Client is still having trouble in the area of seeing what is to be done. He misses things that should be done without being told. The rehabilitation counselor felt Mr. S. was improving in this motivation, acceptance of responsibility and initiative. He has come a long way form "wandering in the streets."

During the fourth month of on-the-job training, Mr. S. began experiencing a peculiar sensation which he described very vividly as the sensation of "drifting away or being unassociated with reality." He is also aware of occasional, hallucinatory experiences, especially visual perceptions when looking at a blank wall or into a clear sky.

Mr. S. was sent to Dr. Owens, a neurologist. In addition to the above sensations the client has had on occasion some olfactory hallucinations with varying odors each time. He denies headaches, depotopia tenitius and peripheral paratheseas. The neurological examination is entirely within normal limits except for a very slight difficulty walking a tandem.

The EEG is abnormal showing some spontaneous, paroxysmal, dysrhythmic slowing occuring at frequent intervals lasting one to three seconds. These changes are consistent with this symptomatology as his history might suggest. It is difficult to know the etiology of this abnormal EEG. It is likely that this is a residual of some recurrent toxia or anoxic cerebral manifestations occuring in the past.

Interpretation:

The change to a paroxysmal dysrhythmic slowing suggests a diffuse corticoil dysfunction of a chronic nature and the possibility of a lowered seizure threshold to generalize nonconvulsive and/or convulsive seizures without aura. These conditions should be improved with Valium.®

Summary

After six months in the training program Mr. S. terminated himself by leaving and going on the "road" again. It was felt by the Rehabilitation Counselor that the client had begun to take drugs again.

Vocational Rehabilitation could not accept him for services again unless he went to a drug treatment halfway house for therapy. He refused to do this. This case was then closed in Status 28: reason, failure to cooperate.

Case Reopened

After a month, Mr. S. contacted his vocational rehabilitation counselor and asked for drug therapy and a chance to continue in his training. After a month in a drug treatment halfway house, he left. The vocational rehabilitation counselor was unable to locate Mr. S. This case was closed in Status 08.

NOTE: The vocational rehabilitation counselor last heard that Mr. S. was in Belgium traveling from place to place.

J. A. S.
White Female—Eighteen years old
Single
High School Graduate
Drug abuse characterized by an inability to adjust vocationally and socially

Referral Source

Miss S. was referred to the Department of Vocational Rehabilitation by Dr. B. of the Adolescent Clinic City Hospital.

She is presently being followed at the Adolescent Clinic for adjustment reaction to adolescence, characterized by drug abuse. She has been in the methadone program and has received guidance and counseling.

Social Data

Miss S. is an eighteen-year-old white female. Her family background is less than ideal. Her parents have recently divorced, and since then she has been on her own a great deal. Her father is an alcoholic now living out of this state. She is the youngest of three children all of whom have experienced problems in living. She feels that her mother is not very concerned about her actions and cares very little about her. She and her mother argue almost constantly.

Miss S. was arrested for drug abuse. She was caught using heroin. She is presently out on bond and has been referred for a physical examination and evaluation of her drug dependence before she went to court. She was placed on probation with the stipulation that she enter a drug treatment program. Before the arrest, she had been using heroin regularly for six months. She has used a variety of drugs including cocaine, marijuana, LSD, and heroin. She had been exposed to hepatitis two weeks before her arrest. One of the boys she and her friend were sharing their "works" unit with had hepatitis. In spite of all her troubles, she did manage to graduate from high school by going in the summer.

Medical Data

Miss S. was seen by a clinical physician for a general examination and for determination of a physical addiction. She states that she feels fine with no physical complaints. She has been exposed to hepatitis through the use of a friend's dirty needle. She was given 10 cc of gamma globulin as a prophylaxis. Her general appearance is that of a thin, healthy, adolescent female.

General Physical Examination

Height: 64"   Weight: 117½ lbs.
Vision: normal

Skin color: normal

    Eruptions: mild

Hair: oily

Eyes: normal

Nose obstruction: no

Oral hygiene: poor

Gums: caries present

Lymph glands: normal

Thorax: normal

Lungs: clear to auscultation

Hearing: o.k.

Epistaxis: no

Hay fever: no

Toothache: no

Chest pain: no

Cough: mild

Appetite: fair

Abdominal pain: no

Dysuria: no

Blood pressure: 120/70

Heart: RSR normal

Abdomen: soft

Genitalia: stage V of development

Neurological gait: good

              strength: good

              balance: good

              pilonidal sinus: normal

              coordination: good

              reflexes: normal

  Feet: normal

  Femininity

  Personality traits: tense, restless

Pallor: no

Icterus: no

Sinus tenderness: no

Tonsils: normal

Positive findings revealed needle scars on both arms. It is the opinion of this physician that she is physically addicted, needs psychiatric referral and at some time gamma globulin as a prophylaxis for possible hepatitis. The physical impression is that of a young, healthy female with the exception of needle marks. It is also recommended that she be placed in the metha-done program.

Educational Data

Miss S. has not done well in school, especially in high school. Her grades were below average—D's and F's; however, she did manage to graduate from high school by attending summer school to make up for credits lost during the regular year. A transcript of her high school performance indicated that Miss S. was not involved in any extracurricular activities.

Psychological Data

Upon completion of the medical examination, Miss S. was referred to the Guidance Clinic for psychiatric therapy. A battery of tests consisting of the Wechsler Adult Intelligence Scale, Bender-Visual-Motor Gestalt Test, Wide Range Achievement Test-Reading Section, Tree-Person Drawing, and the Rorschach Test were given.

Miss S. is a thin, brown-haired, brown-eyed girl who was pleasant and responsive and who had a tendency to talk in a dunning fashion and to play with her rather greasy, straight hair. She presented a rather dull, uninteresting physical appearance in that she was dressed somewhat sloppily in brown, short culottes, a short brown suede jacket and loafers. However, upon closer inspection, she was actually a rather pretty girl with pretty eyes and a pleasant smile which seemed all too infrequent. Miss S. sat sprawled in her chair and seemed unaware of her bare thighs being exposed, yet she was overly anxious to keep her chest covered up with her jacket; she almost seemed to make a "thing" out of keeping her jacket closed. She appeared to enjoy the testing, and as time went on became more comfortable and was able to laugh; at such times her eyes sparkled and she was a very attractive girl. She talked at length about wanting to leave her mother and go out on her own while at the same time feeling guilty since she was the last child. She thinks her father is a "nice guy" but does not like living with him. She snickered and became evasive while talking about her father; and gave the impression that there is far more involved here than meets the eye. She spoke of her feelings of depression, her having been caught and her sexual experiences with various boys in a curiously detached, depersonalized way. She rationalized having been caught by saying "the vice squad is corrupt," and "this city is too big and unfeeling." She considers the people where her father lives as being "warm," friendly, loving people who judge others for their "inner selves." She further says that people who take drugs because of nothing better to do are much like her.

Miss S. is able to function on the bright normal level of general intelligence according to her full scale I.Q. of 117; her verbal score of 114 and her performance scale of 122. She has difficulty in those areas which require concentration and synthetic ability on visual-motor tasks; her concentration has a tendency to come and go with the result that the quality of her performance fluctuates. On the other hand, she was able to demonstrate superior social comprehension and judgment in a hypothetical situation. Her "gifted" score on the subtest which involved attention to environmental essentials suggests that she is overly concerned with things rather than people. Other areas tested generally fell in the bright normal range. Certainly this is a very bright girl whose intellectual functioning tends to be somewhat erratic because her intellectual energies are being dissipated by emotional concerns. Miss S. is presently reading on the 10.2 grade level, which gives her a standard score of 103 and places her in the 58th percentile for one of her age group. This is considerably below her level of intellectual functioning and is an example of her problem with utilizing her intellectual ability in every day living situations. At this time there does not seem to be any indication of a central nervous system dysfunction. Her test results are those of a bright, sensitive, withdrawn, immature, and somewhat regressed individual who is maintaining a passive-feminine orientation in her approach to her world as a defense against inward strivings toward destructive fighting and sadistic impulses which actually terrify her. She is one who feels depressed, constrained, and trapped and has a sense of not being alive and of watching life pass her by at this time. Actually, she feels unable to participate in life and goes to great lengths to project the blame on other people, circumstances, places, etc. so that she will not be forced to recognize her depressed, inadequate state. She entertains many feelings of inner emptiness and futility.

This is a girl who has much confusion about her sex role and who appears to be experiencing panic over a sexual identity crisis. She is confused about who and what she is, and is frightened and guilty because of her narcissistic and auto erotic urges. She often provokes situations such as seducing the male in order to later resent and blame him for the predicament in which she finds herself. When she deals with the male, it is in terms of her feelings of intense hostility, and her tendency to deal with males as well as people in general in a sneaky, self-centered and manipulatory way. She does have some feelings of panic concerning the male inasmuch as she has a tendency to project on to him her intense sadistic, destructive, aggressive and annihilating impulses.

Miss S. views the female with a sense of anxiety; she feels erratic about the female and has a tendency to be evasive when she deals with the female. She attempts to defend against her sensual impulses toward the female by projecting them on to others. Actually, she remains at the narcissistic level and attempts to cope with her homosexual urges by fleeing to heterosexual involvement in the way of defense. She is one who has intense dependency and oral needs, who is weak and passive, yet has feelings which are too hot to handle and impulses which threaten to be out of control. This is a girl who wants and needs controls and who is presently experiencing panic over an imminent loss of control. She identifies with people on an immature, self-centered level, but has little real sensitivity to, and concern about, people.

It is recommended that she be placed in a living situation which imposes strict controls, such as a school away from home, or if this is not feasible, that she be hospitalized. In any event she should be involved in psychotherapy, preferably of a group therapy nature which will be intensive. It is felt that this girl is experiencing an identity crisis and is fence-sitting at this time;

thus, which way she moves will depend upon the treatment and living situation which she experiences within the next year or two.

Vocational Data

Miss S. has never been employed full time or during the summers. She has expressed an interest in pursuing a career as a social worker and would like to go to college.

Eligibility

Miss S. received a medical evaluation in December, 1971 and was found to be within normal physical limits with no physical restrictions or activities to be avoided. She was noted to be on the methadone program due to drug abuse. Based on a psychiatric and psychological evaluation, she is seen as currently demonstrating numerous characteristics of a behavioral disorder. She has been involved in drug abuse and dropout behavior, and lately has experienced anxiety and depression due to her condition. This condition constitutes a substantial handicap to employment. With the provision of appropriate vocational rehabilitation services a favorable outcome is anticipated for this rehabilitation plan.

Vocational Objective: Social Worker

Since the date of the initial interview this client has received counseling and guidance. Based on the diagnostic information obtained in this rehabilitation program, she has been receiving attention from the Adolescent Clinic at City Hospital and the Guidance Clinic. These institutions have provided the diagnostic infomation which indicates at the current time that this individual is ready for the provision of appropriate rehabilitation services toward the above indicated vocational objective. In order to achieve this goal, she must receive formal vocational academic training within a local facility, tuition, necessary fees, and books. From the psychotherapist in this case, she will receive maintenance, clothes, and transportation in order to participate in the rehabilitation program. At the appropriate time in this individual's rehabilitation plan, she will be placed within competitive employment and follow-up provided in order to insure an adequate vocational adjustment. The estimated duration of this plan at the current time is four years.

Over-all Plan and Financing

Tuition, one semester	$235.00
Activity Fee, one semester	12.00
Health Fee, one semester	20.00
Books, one semester	50.00
Psychotherapy, 15 sessions @ $30.00	450.00
Maintenance, 4 months @ $80.00	320.00
Clothes	75.00
Transportation	45.00
Methadone, 5 months @ $47.00	235.00
TOTAL	$1,442.00

C. W. B.
Black Male—Eighteen years old
Married
Ninth Grade Education
Drug abuse characterized by an inability to adjust vocationally and socially
Character disorder (inadequate personality)

Referral Source

Mr. B. was referred to the Department of Vocational Rehabilitation by the prenatal clinic at City Hospital. He and his wife are currently undergoing family counseling prior to the birth of their child. He had previously been a client of DVR but was closed from a referred status for failing to respond to attempts of counseling or evaluation. He has been in his city's methadone treatment program for the last five years for his heroin addiction.

Social Data

Mr. B. is a seventeen-year-old male. He is married and is expecting his first child. He and his nineteen-year-old wife are presently living with his uncle in the center of the city. They have been drawing general relief for the last two years.

Mr. B. became addicted to heroin at the age of fourteen. His drug abuse began with the use of marijuana at the age of thirteen. He graduated to heroin and after three years his maximum usage was three bags a day. When he was thirteen, he lost his mother upon whom he was extremely dependent, and was left virtually on his own. His father separated from his mother when he was very young. He remembers nothing about his father. It was at this time that he began experimenting with drugs.

Mr. B. presents a pleasant, neat appearance. His dress reflects his constricted economic circumstances. His social life is quite limited, partly due to economic circumstances and his rather narrow range of interest.

Medical Data

Mr. B. stated that his health is good. While he was on drugs, he suffered from malnutrition. But since he has been on the methadone program he has regained his health.

The local physician found Mr. B. to be well oriented in all spheres. On the basis of the General Medical Examination recorded, Mr. B. does not seem to have any overt physical or emotional problems. His drug-seeking behavior is apparently under control by methadone.

General Medical Examination

GENERAL APPEARANCE. This is a seventeen-year-old black male who is well developed and well nourished with no acute distress.
Pulse: 78
Respiration: 18
Blood pressure: 115/75
Skin and hair: normal
Head: normal in size and shape. Eyes: brown. Teeth: good
Neck: normal
Spine: no deformity
Chest: lungs clear
Heart: normal
Abdomen: negative
Extremities: no gross physical abnormalities

Neurological condition: no gross physical abnormalities
Reflexes: present
Weight: 142 lbs. Height: 67″
Impressions: This individual is in normal health.

Educational Data

Mr. B. dropped out of high school in the ninth grade. He stated that his grades while in school were average and below C's and D's. His major reason for leaving school was financial: Being on his own, he felt that he needed to make some money. While in school he did not participate in any extracurricular activity. Overall, he found school to be of little interest or value to him.

Psychiatric Evaluation

The psychiatric evaluation found Mr. B. to be evasive about his psychiatric history and drug history. He presents overt psychiatric symptoms of anxiety and tenseness in normal situations. Episodes of depression were noted but were not considered extremely significant. This particular individual is characterized as having an inadequate personality. It is my impression that Mr. B. is a young man, not greatly endowed intellectually. On top of this, he is passive, inadequate, dependent, and lacking in drive and energy. Certainly a training program within his limits of intellect and emotional stability is in order. However, Mr. B. should not be placed in a situation which would cause frustration. He fears failure a great deal and would take it rather badly.

I would suspect that he has developed sufficient obsessive defenses that will enable him to make a reasonably good employee once he can settle down into a semiskilled "rut."

He has a tremendous amount invested, from an emotional point of view, in his present marriage. He will work hard to achieve stability in this situation.

Psychological Data

A battery of tests consisting of the WAIS, Graves Design Judgment Test, Minnesota Clerical Test, The Crawford Small

Parts Dexterity Test, Wide Range Achievement Test, the Thurston Interest Schedule, the Incomplete Sentence Blank, Draw a Person and the Cornell Index—Form N2. The results are indicated below:

WAIS; norms for a seventeen-year-old group

Verbal Subtest: Scaled Scores

Information-7   Arithmetic-6
Similarities-9   Digit Span-9
Comprehension-6   Vocabulary-5

Performance:

Digit Symbol-12   Picture Design-6
Picture Comp.-8   Object Assembly-10
Block Design-11

Verbal I.Q.-83
Performance I.Q.-95
Full Scale-87

Graves Design Judgment Test

Raw score: 56-85 percentile

Minnesota Clerical Test

Raw score: 149-93 percentile

Crawford Small Parts Dexterity Test

Pins and Collar subtest   40%
Screws subtest   73%

Wide Range Achievement Test

Reading	3.9 grade	2%
Spelling	3.7 grade	2%
Arithmetic	4.9 grade	4%

Thurston Interest Schedule

Of highest interest were the physical science, art, and business areas. Areas of least interest were computational.

Mr. B. is a person in the middle range of dull, normal, verbal intellectual ability and lower in the middle average on the performance scale. His full scale score places him in the upper range of dull normal intelligence. He possesses good skills in the areas of abstract reasoning and short-term memory. Hampered by poor vocabulary and a limited information fund, Mr. B. lacks the ability to deal with tasks requiring social knowledge.

The results of the tests indicated that he possesses adequate manual skills to function in construction areas. He would be hampered in training that required reading skills such as heavy equipment operations.

Personality

Responses on the Incomplete Sentence Blank suggest an immature young individual. He has feelings of hostility directed toward his father. He prizes work highly and is very concerned about his ability to function in competitive physical tasks. Also of great concern to him is his present unemployment situation.

The Cornell Index revealed that Mr. B. has little trouble in relating to those around him. He is troubled about unemployment which affects his feelings of adequacy and self-worth.

It is recommended that Mr. B. avoid any training programs that require a classroom situation. He could function in an on-the-job program in the construction area.

Vocational History

Mr. B. is presently unemployed. His longest period of employment was as a longshoreman. This job lasted for four years. He left because of an apparent lack of demand for his services. He then went to work for a trucking company as a packer. He left this job because of poor pay. The last job he held was as a metal cutter for a bathtub company. This job lasted for a month. He was fired because of absenteeism. Mr. B. stated that his absenteeism was due to his involvement with drugs.

Eligibility

Mr. B. functions at the dull normal intelligence level and has no salable job skills. He has been addicted to heroin and is currently under treatment for his addiction. His previous employment has been sporadic and without any skill value. His inability to obtain stable employment and support his family has caused depression and anxiety. With his inadequate personality and lack of training, he has been unable to maintain permanent employment. His frustration tolerance and self-image are low. He also has difficulty relating to authority figures. These conditions constitute an employment handicap.

Vocational Objective: Carpenter's Helper

Mr. B. has had some previous experience in carpentry handiwork with some success. He wishes to be trained as a carpenter's helper and eventually will advance to apprentice or master carpenter.

This goal is within his capabilities, provided he is adequately prepared for the work task. In order to gain the necessary training and skills the client will have to be helped to prepare for interviews, situations and questioning by prospective Union Apprenticeship programs.

Plans

The client will be given counseling, guidance and help in preparing for apprenticeship program interviews and for training.

R. G. L.

Black Female—Eighteen years of age

Single

High School Graduate

Drug abuse characterized by an inability to adjust vocationally and socially

Character disorder with aggressive and infantile manifestations

Referral Source

Miss L.'s initial referral to vocational rehabilitation was by Dr. Wood of the drug addiction clinic of City Hospital where she was a patient from an overdose attempt. The referral was made for purposes of counseling and support. Miss L. has been unable to adjust due to drug abuse. Drug misuse has handicapped Miss L. both educationally and vocationally. At the time of the suicide attempt it was felt that further treatment was needed and presently it would be unfeasible for Miss L. to receive vocational rehabilitation services. Miss L. was later referred by Mr. Trice of a local drug treatment program.

Social History

Miss L. is an eighteen-year-old, single, black female from the Bronx, New York. She has a three-year history of heroin abuse along with a potpourri of other drugs including cocaine, barbiturates, LSD and methadone. She graduated from Thomas Jefferson High School in New York where she was in the top quarter of her class. After graduation, she came to this city and attended City University before dropping out and going back to New York.

Both of Miss L.'s parents are living and other significant family members include her older sister, Carol, who lives in Washington and her younger sister, Joan, a graduate of a local drug treatment program and currently a staff member.

Miss L. was recently detoxified from heroin addiction in New York via methadone. She then came to this city to visit her sister. On the third day of her visit, she left her sister's home in an apparent daze. She was later found by her sister walking the street in a confused and disorganized state. Miss L. entered her sister's car and within five minutes had a major motor seizure. She was brought to the Emergency Room with a history of having taken 10 to 12 gm of Isoniazid® in a suicide attempt. In the emergency room, she had four more major motor seizures, poorly controlled with 10 mg i.v. Valium doses.

Miss L. was first introduced to drugs while a senior in high school. She stated that her reason for using drugs was to become part of the "in" crowd at school. Her first experience was with soft drugs (marijuana). She gradually progressed to LSD and finally heroin.

Medical History

Miss L. stated that she has been in generally good health since she detoxified from heroin in New York. There is no history of hepatitis or abcess due to her drug use. Physical examination at the time of Miss L.'s suicide attempt revealed a well-developed, well-nourished, black female who was agitated and tachypneic, but awake and responsive to commands. Her blood pressure was 140/90; pulse 98, temperature 101.3; respiration –28. The pupils were equally reactive to light. The examination of the heart showed a normal sinus rhythm without murmurs or gallops at a rate of 95 beats per minute. The neurological examination was given. Miss L. responded to commands and appeared to realize what was going on about her. Her sensory and motor systems were intact. No pathological reflexes were present. She had hyperactive deep tendon reflexes bilaterally. No muscle weakness was evident.

Thirty-six hours after ingestion, the patient was awake and oriented, breathing normally off the nasal oxygen with normal vital signs. At the time of discharge, the patient was alert and oriented.

DISCHARGE DIAGNOSES:
1. isoniazid toxicity
2. seizures secondary to #1
3. metabolic acidosis secondary to #1, resolved

DISPOSITION:
1. appointment in medical follow-up clinic at which time a lateral chest will be done
2. appointment in the psychiatry clinic

Physical examination was given after the client recovered from her overdose.

General Medical Examination Record

Height: 5'5"
Weight: 105 lbs.
Eyes: Normal
Hearing: Good
Nose: Normal
Mouth: Normal
Throat: Normal

Lungs: Chest films show no evidence of aspiration pneumonia.
Abdomen: Normal
Sclerae: Not icteric
Circulatory System: Normal
Nervous System: Normal
Skin: Clear and normal
Orthopedic Impairment: None
Laboratory Data: Blood gases on the Bennett respirator showed
    a PO_2 of 108, pCO_2 of 25, ph of 7.20 and a bicarbonate of 9
Blood Sugar: 199
White Blood Count: 16, 900
Sodium: 150
Potassium: 4.2
Chloride: 102
CO_2: 12
Chest films revealed a right hilar density with no evidence of
    pneumonia
Extremities: No cyanoses, clubbing, or edema; good peripheral
    pulses.

Educational History

Miss L. graduated in the top quarter of her class at school.
While there she was especially interested in the arts, i.e. music
and painting. Although actively involved in the academics and
subjects, she did not participate in extracurricular activities.
She stated that she was a loner and had few friends. There was
no indication that school authorities knew of her drug addiction.

After graduation from high school, Miss L. came to this city
and attended City University. This was due in part to her
sister living here. Her curriculum area was liberal arts with
emphasis in music. During her stay in the city, she became
more involved with drugs especially heroin. Her grades began
to drop and Miss L. finally withdrew and went back to New
York.

Vocational Data

Miss L.'s work experience has been limited to the summer

months between school years. Her principal employment for her summers was as a waitress for a nationally known restaurant chain. This job was temporary in nature. The client has no interest in this area as far as permanent employment is concerned.

Psychological Data

Due to her suicide attempt, Miss L. was referred for psychiatric evaluation. The report stated that this client has no prior history of overt psychiatric systems. Over the past two weeks, Miss L. has had suicidal ruminations, insomnia, sadness or crying. She describes her life as one of loneliness and sadness. She indicated that she was unable to form close relationships with others. It was also felt by the psychiatrist that Miss L. had occasional blurring of ability to organize thinking. With this mild uncontrolled thinking, her affect is flattened. She denied depressive systems at present.

Miss L.'s history suggests early signs of schizophrenia. The possibility exists that the stimulating inclination of the Isoniazid on the central nervous system may be exposing an otherwise subclinical thought disorder.

When Miss L. was asked to reconstruct the night of the suicidal attempt, she was unable to remember any of the night's experiences. She stated that when she recovered from the effects of the drug, she did not realize why she was in the hospital.

Miss L. was seen as an above average person in general ability. The fact that she was a good student in school is indicative of her ability. It was felt that she could best benefit from an intensive drug treatment program. In such a program support and counseling could provide her with the needed tools enabling her to make an adequate adjustment. She will also be provided with constant supervision. The rehabilitation counselor concurred with these recommendations. Due to drug addiction and misuse, she has been functionally limited in that she has been unable to adjust socially and vocationally. In order to learn to live free of drugs in our society, she became an inpatient at a local drug halfway house. It was the opinion of the rehabilitation counselor that Miss L.'s disabling condition presented a definite vocational handicap in that she was unable to maintain herself in society, unable to continue in college and unable to obtain and maintain employment.

The final clinical impression was that she had a definite character disorder with aggressive and infantile manifestations.

Report from the Drug Treatment Center

Upon first entering the program, Miss L. displayed an over-evaluation of herself in terms of an attitude of superiority. She was condescending, arrogant, uncooperative and cynical. She listened to no one and chronically alienated others around her. It was felt that this infantile behavior was a manifestation of severe feelings of inadequacy. She exhibited a rather cavalier attitude toward her own life when she first entered the program. One week prior to coming in as a program participant she attempted suicide by taking a large number of boniazid tablets. When talking to her about this she reacts with unrealistic good humor as if it were some kind of a joke.

After not being able to be handled well in several of the local drug facilities, she was assigned to the North Street Halfway House where she finally responded. The staff members began to see the development of positive attitudes in relationships with others, a friendliness and a development of a definite warmth which was not present before. She also accepts criticism without becoming antagonistic and hostile.

Her improvement was to such a point that it was felt she could stabilize in a work situation. There has not been, on the other hand, a complete resolution of the conflicts she brought with her upon entering the program. With positive support, she has responded greatly and if this is continued in the program and on the job, more growth can be expected. Miss L.'s vocational rehabilitation counselor was notified as to her improvement and her readiness for work.

Eligibility

Miss L.'s primary disability has been diagnosed as drug abuse characterized by an inability to adjust vocationally and socially. A character disorder marked by aggressive and infantile behavior has been diagnosed as the secondary disability. Due to drug addiction, she has been functionally limited in that she has been unable to adjust socially and vocationally. In order for her to live free of drugs in our society, it was necessary for her to become an inpatient at a drug treatment halfway house. It is felt that through the services and support of the drug treatment program, this client will be rendered ready to return to gainful employment.

Plan and Summary

A rehabilitation plan was written with detective (undercover operator) as the vocational objective. This vocational objective was felt to be reasonable and attainable in that this client is well qualified based on her varied drug experience to work undercover to help in identifying drug abusers. This position will be an on-the-job training situation in which she will receive training and experience as a nurses' aide as well as working as an undercover agent.

Summary of Services

Miss L. will enter an on-the-job training situation at no cost to DVR. She will receive the necessary uniforms and transportation needed to begin this employment. She will also receive follow-up services to assure satisfactory adjustment to the job. While involved in the training and employment, she will continue as a halfway house resident where she will receive continued treatment and support. The estimated length of services is four months.

CHAPTER 10

SOCIOCULTURAL FACTORS IN EDUCATING DISADVANTAGED CHILDREN*

PATRICIA G. ADKINS

THERE IS AN INCREASING amount of educational concern for the students who do not fall within the criterion of the middle-of-the-road curriculum designed for monolingual standard-English-speaking, middle-class pupils.

We may use the terms "bilingual," "bidialectal," or "impoverished" to describe these students, but the semantics of the terms fail to encompass the situation.

"Bilingual" may not carry the linguistic connotation of equal proficiency in two languages, as linguists and teachers of English as a Second Language define it. It may describe the student who comes from a Spanish-speaking home, has a Mexican surname, and is culturally and experientially divergent. "Bidialectal" may often mean a single dialect outlawed and rejected by the school environment. "Impoverished" may be applied to black, brown, red and white alike. It is not solely an economic factor but is inextricably woven into the pattern of environment and opportunity. Regardless of label, it is futile to attempt to educate these children in the same manner as their more advantaged counterparts.

Editorials take educators to task for failing to understand the problems of slums, crowded conditions, lack of privacy, insufficient diet, lack of help and interest on the part of the parents,

---

*Reprinted by permission of *Education*, 93:32-35, no. 1 (September-October, 1972).

and lack of understanding of the English language on the part of both the parents and the pupils. "The odds are that such youngsters will drop out of school eight or ten years later with little to show for it but the experience of failure (El Paso *Times,* 1964).

Responsible educators are awakening to the fact that the nation cannot afford to waste the potential productivity of thousands of citizens nor cope with the complex problems that uneducated majorities create.

One of the largest geographic areas of educational concern lies along the border of United States and Mexico. The problematic situation of the student revolves around the sociocultural milieu affecting his learning.

Perhaps the most obvious result of an educational handicap is the economic problem which results. Henry Munoz, an official of the Political Association of Spanish-speaking Organizations, studied the economic conditions of thousands of persons of Mexican descent, concluding in his findings that "illiteracy in English" was causative of the lack of job opportunities (McGown, 1963).

When Mexican-Americans or other ethnic groups seek employment which demands communication in English beyond a minimum, they find themselves vocationally handicapped. They are restricted to such jobs as cooking, cleaning, gardening, or painting because they do not "qualify" for white-collar employment. Regardless of native intelligence or assets of personality, they cannot apply for positions as clerks, office workers, or foremen if they cannot speak the language of the country in which they live.

The University of Texas at Austin, concerned with educational conditions and related income, conducted a study of the economic conditions of "Anglo" families and those with Spanish surnames in Texas. The per capita median annual income of "Anglos" in Texas in 1959 was $4,137, that of Spanish-surname Texans, $2,029. It did not increase appreciably in the intervening ten years to 1969. The figure falls far below the poverty index of $3,000 determined in the federal surveys of low-income disadvantaged.

The economic plight of the parents has a direct influence upon the education of the children in these homes. Welfare workers in the border states frequently report the disappearance of the husband and father when he cannot support his family on his meager wage. This often results in the children dropping out of school and taking odd jobs to contribute to the support of the mother and the younger members (Cline, 1965). Loyalty is strong among Spanish-speaking people; a boy whose mother is working to support the family wants to assist her as soon as he can by dropping out of school and finding a job.

His lack of education leads directly to his continuing poverty, with which the United States government is concerned today. He is likely to be a welfare case, a burden to his community, and a failure in his own estimation and in that of his peers. If he feels inferior and outside the world of the monolingual English-speaking American, then contempt, hate, and unrest are likely to breed. A segregated society is a restless society.

The educational goal of this country must be to fully include all students. This is not always through acculturation and assimilation.

There is a mutual benefit to be gained when cultural exchange is effected. The rich heritage of Mexico is infused in the Mexican-American of the border in the form of art, music, and language. A sense of pride in a Mexican background is not to detract from a good American citizen. Rather, it brings to the United States a warmth of friendship and understanding from Mexico which is highly desirable. If we fail to educate the Mexican-American student to the fullest of his capabilities, we lose the cultural exchange as well as the potential of his thinking and leadership. One of the basic goals of education is to produce an enlightened electorate, able to provide the leaders in a democratic society. One responsibility to the Mexican-American must be that he succeed in this area, for he is often a member of a majority group rather than a minority group and should take his rightful place in the politics of his community.

It seems logical to assume that students with divergent backgrounds have the problem of trying to decide who they are, what they are, and where they actually fit into the scheme in the United States. If they belong to the country, but are still attached to another language, one of the greatest difficulties is the attitude toward the problem. If English is spoken in the home where it is likely to be ridiculed, if peers tease about attempts to be Americanized, if resentment of the American culture is deeply ingrained, resistance may create a psychological barrier which will be a strong deterrent to learning English as a Second Language. A sense of loyalty to culture, family, friends, and first language may be tantamount. This is an American, but he is segregated outside of the realm of the monolingual English-speaking American. His deficiency in the English language may cause him to feel insecure, uneasy, and inferior. He may have misgivings about his own ability. He alienates himself from his family and his friends by speaking a tongue whose native speakers may or may not accept him. He may naturally be confused and filled with doubts concerning the advantage of his new language. Such psychological handicaps unquestionably help to complicate his difficulties. Dr. Horacio Ulibarri, Southern Methodist University, describes the bilingual in the Southwest as a *marginal man.* Dr. Ulibarri explains his term in this manner: "He is marginal because he is neither here nor there, but in between."

The burden rests squarely upon the schools and the teachers to demonstrate to the Mexican-American student that he is not only present, but that he actually belongs. He must be made to feel that his native culture is important; he must recognize the qualities of both Spanish and English, while also recognizing that English is essential for success in the United States.

Dr. Bruce Gaarder, speaking in his private capacity and without official support of the United States Office of Education, states that linguistic, pedagogical, psychological, and social barriers all combine and function in complicated interrelationships to slow and lessen the scholastic achievement of the Spanish-speaking child. He adds that while the linguistic component can be isolated in print and talk, in reality it is inseparable from the others (Gaarder, 1965).

This viewpoint is substantiated by Robert Lado, Dean of Linguistics, Georgetown University, who states that when the bilingual child goes to an English-speaking school, he faces a different set of social and cultural patterns as well as a different language (Lado, 1965).

These factors tend to put the child at a disadvantage with his monolingual English-speaking peers. Few schools have found means to compensate for the social disadvantages of their students and this ever-widening gap becomes more obvious as the child progresses in the school.

The cultural differences in the backgrounds of the Mexican- and Spanish-American and that of the native-born English-speaking American are distinct and varied. Often there is little understanding between the two. Lado stresses the importance of the recognition of cultural differences in bilingual persons. "Because human personality has evolved a variety of ways of life, ways which we call culture; we are constantly misinterpreting each other across cultures" (Lado, 1957).

Language is one key to the solution of the problem. However, if the student accepts the English language as an answer to his immediate and long-range needs, there must come the understanding on the part of teachers and administrators that his social, economic, psychological, and pedagogical problems are all inextricably interwoven. Hunt observes that children of poverty lack many opportunities to develop cognitive skills, they lack especially the circumstances which foster linguistic skills, and the syntax of standard language in which the abstractions of cognitive content are couched (Hunt, 1969).

Teaching must be approached in a different manner. Additional lecture-type instruction is not the key; a change in curriculum may be the remedy. Teachers must be trained to handle the education of the individual. Changes must be effected whereby bilingual pupils may be taught with materials designed for their special needs rather than approaches primarily selected for teaching native English-speaking children. These reflect a middle-class environment and contain little with which the Spanish-speaking pupil can identify. If there is a lack of relevancy in his curriculum, he is not being furnished an equal educational opportunity.

The internalization that exists in the mind of the Spanish-speaking student as to his language, his family, his social position, and his ultimate economic realization provides the incentive that he has to continue his education. Understanding and empathy on the part of his teachers and administrators is a tremendous factor. The teacher is not in the business of failing students. If the educator is successful, the student is successful. There must be continual, free-flowing communication between the student and the teacher. There must be continuous program evaluation and elimination of inadequate program content.

The educational problems of the "culturally divergent" student can be solved by teachers, principals, supervisors, and administrators working together as a team. Such differentiated staffing will produce an awareness of needs and a curriculum designed to insure a successful educational experience for all pupils.

REFERENCES

Cline, Marion, Jr.: Realistic education needed in slum barrios. *Rocky Mt Soc Sci J, II*:222, no. 2, 1965.

Editorial, El Paso *Times,* December 11, 1964.

Gaarder, Bruce: Address to Southwest Council of Foreign Language Teachers, El Paso, 1965.

Hunt, J. McVicker: *The Challenge of Incompetence and Poverty.* Chicago, U of Chicago Pr, 1969, p. 204.

Lado, Robert: *Linguistics Across Cultures.* Ann Arbor, U of Mich Pr, 1957, p. 6.

Lado, Robert: Linguistic and Pedagogical Barriers. In *Our Bilinguals.* El Paso, Second Annual Conference of Foreign Language Teachers, November, 1965, p. 14.

McGown, Tom: San Antonio *Light,* Sunday, November 24, 1963, p. 10-A.

CHAPTER 11

EARLY INTERVENTION FOR
THE DISADVANTAGED*

RUSSELL A. DUSEWICZ

THAT DISADVANTAGED children do not do well in our schools
has become a well-established fact. These children have a
meager environmental foundation upon which to develop cognitive skills and are generally unprepared to cope with the
formal intellectual and learning demands of the school. Typically
entering school with considerably lower language and conceptual abilities relative to their advantaged counterparts, they
maintain this disadvantage and often increase it over time, resulting in what has sometimes been referred to as a "cumulative
deficit." The consequences of this deficit generally lead to educational failure and a disheartening waste of human potential.
Comprehensive efforts at overcoming the early disabilities of
these children must begin at the preschool level.

Although experimental evidence exists in support of the hypothesis that appropriate supplementary experiences at an early
age can result in considerably rapid and significant increases
in development among these children, by far the majority of
such programs have met with only marginal success due to a
variety of reasons principal of which seem to be failure to concentrate on language development and starting too late. The
question remains, however, as to how early in the disadvantaged
child's life intervention should take place in order to maximize
the effectiveness of such a program.

---

*Reprinted by permission of *Education*, 93:54-55, no. 1 (September-October,
1972).

In the present study, thirty-six disadvantaged children nineteen to twenty-eight months of age, were randomly assigned to two groups: a Home Group receiving seventy minutes of tutoring in the home weekly; and a Center Group attending a four-hour per day centrally located cognitive enrichment program. For the Center or Experimental Program, the initial emphasis was on providing an environment of massive stimulation through all sensory channels in a programmed and integrated fashion. The aim was to develop acuteness of perception and discrimination within each of the senses and to then relate perception via one of the senses with perceptions via other senses in an integrative manner. Thus, the child was not only required to distinguish, for example, between two objects such as a bell and a whistle by the way they appear visually, but by the way they sound auditorily. This was later integrated with the way they feel tactually and so on. The infusion of higher-order cognitive materials then followed the establishment of this strong foundation in perceptual-integrative abilities. Assistants were available for specifying the learning tasks for each of the children and for organizing their experiences, providing feedback on performance, and encouraging abstraction of performance into language. The Home Program, on the other hand, served as a control or comparison group.

After 125 program days, analyses of covariance of post-test scores (pre-test scores as covariates) on the Slosson Intelligence Test, The Peabody Picture Vocabulary Test, and the Vineland Social Maturity Scale revealed significant differences favoring the Center Group on the first two measures. Nonsignificance on the Vineland appeared to be artificial.

The relative advances in cognitive development and hearing vocabularly, while as yet inconclusive in the social area, not only demonstrate the effectiveness of a particular program in a particular center but also the potential effectiveness which preschool programs stressing perceptual and cognitive development in general can achieve with disadvantaged children as young as 1½ to 2½ years of age. In addition, the finding of a nonsignificant correlation between gain scores on any of the test measures and the age of subject variable, suggests that for the type of program utilized in the present study a limit has not as yet been reached here as to how young the youngest can be and still demonstrate gains comparable to his older counterparts.

CHAPTER 12

A FURTHER INVESTIGATION OF FACTORS RELATED TO SCHOOL ACHIEVEMENT IN THE CULTURALLY DISADVANTAGED CHILD*

HARVEY R. AUSTRIN AND MILDRED R. BUCK

I N A PREVIOUS REPORT, Buck and Austrin (1971) found that adequate achievers in a sample of eighth-grade, economically disadvantaged black children were significantly more internal in locus of control than a matched sample of underachievers. The finding that individuals who believe that reinforcements are contingent upon their own behavior rather than determined by forces independent of their own action are more likely to be motivated to understand, learn, and develop their skills and knowledge in ways which could assist them in predicting and controlling their futures is a common one in the literature (Rotter, 1966; Lefcourt, 1966; Buck, 1969; Crandall, Katkovsky and Crandall, 1965; Crandall, Katkovsky and Preston, 1962; Coleman et al., 1966; Lao, 1970). A similar concept of personal causation, reported by deCharms (1972), found "origin" rather than "pawn" behavior related to positive achievement and school behavior in a very similar population of inner city youngsters.

The findings of the previous study had provided support for the views of previous investigators (Cohen, 1960; Crandall, 1963;

*The work presented herein was performed pursuant to a grant (No. OEG-6-9-009034-0072(010) from the U. S. Office of Education, Department of Health, Education, and Welfare. However, the opinions expressed herein do not necessarily reflect the position or policy of the U. S. Office of Education, and no official endorsement by the U. S. Office of Education.

Crandall, Dewey, Katkovsky and Preston, 1964; Maccoby, Johnson and Church, 1958; Merton, 1958; Seeman, 1970) that the parental achievement values of the culturally disadvantaged are not significantly different from those of parents in better economic circumstances. However, like Katkovsky, Crandall and Good (1967), the present authors found a supportive positive parental relationship significantly more characteristic of high internal control and adequate achievement in children, adding weight to the importance of the parental role in fostering a child's belief in internal control.

Buck and Austrin (1971) also found that, like the children in the deCharms (1972) study, internal control youngsters were typically rated by classroom teachers as having more positive attitudes toward achievement, behaviors, and personality attributes than those who were more external. In this connection, poor achievers who were more internal tended to be viewed more favorably and rated as less deviant from classroom norms of behavior than externally oriented poor achievers, supporting the contentions of Cronbach (1960) and McGhee and Crandall (1968) that teachers' grades and ratings are strongly influenced, not just by knowledge and skills displayed, but also by pupil attitude and achievement orientation.

One of the more theoretically heuristic of the present authors' previous findings concerned sex differences in internal control. High achieving girls were more internal with respect to both positive and negative consequences than underachieving girls, but this difference was only found for boys in relation to positive reinforcement. Since the Intellectual Achievement Responsibility (IAR) measure used (Crandall *et al.*, 1965) is specific to intellectual-academic situations, the interpretation was made that socioeconomically disadvantaged minority boys as a group, regardless of achievement, tend to view themselves as relatively powerless to control negative academic consequences. This viewpoint may represent appropriate realistic adaptation to a generalized cultural probability estimate in the typical educational situation.

The present study investigated the internal-external control beliefs of disadvantaged minority youngsters, using both the

IAR and the Children's Picture Test of Internal-External Control (Battle, 1963) which is a projective task to measure the attribution of responsibility in a broader situational sample than the academically oriented IAR. The expectation was that, if the previous hypothesis regarding homogeneity of attitudes among the boys had validity, the situational factor was likely to minimize differences between adequate and underachievers on the Battle I-E measure, but would show differences on the educationally more specific IAR measure. Furthermore it was hypothesized that, in view of the item sampling differences between the two measures, differences between sex would be greater on the broader Battle I-E scale than on the IAR.

Method

SUBJECTS.   A sample of fifty matched pairs of black, eighth-grade youngsters from fourteen to sixteen years old were selected from a larger population of disadvantaged inner-city urban school children. Matching was done on I.Q., sex, age, family background and number of siblings.

MEASURES.   The sample subjects were assigned to either of two groups, based on composite scores on the Iowa Tests of Basic Skills. The group of adequate achievers had projected composite scores of 9.2 or above while the underachievers had projected composite scores of 7.1 or below.

For measurement of internal-external control of reinforcements, two measures were used. The first, the IAR questionnaire (Crandall *et al.*, 1965) is a sample of thirty-four forced-choice items each posing one internal and one external choice as the reason for the occurrence of a specific intellectual-academic task or situation. The scale yields two subscores, one for belief in internal responsibility for success (I+) and one for belief in internal responsibility for failure (I−). A summation of the two separate subscores provides a broad measure of internal beliefs for both positive and negative intellectual-academic reinforcements.

The second measure was the Children's Picture Test of Internal-External Control (Battle, 1963), a projective situation requiring the subject to attribute responsibility by indicating "what he would say" in a series of items sampling a broad range of events in a child's life. Scoring is in the external direction, with higher scores indicating greater belief in external control.

Results

The findings, analyzed by t-test, are reported in Table 12-I.

The adequate achievers as a group scored higher in belief in internal control of events on both the Battle I-E and the IAR. Considering the boys and girls separately, the adequate achievers of both sexes were significantly more internal in both total IAR score and belief in internal control of positive reinforcement in academic situations, but this difference did not hold true for internal belief in negative reinforcement. While the adequately achieving girls continued to show greater internality than under-achieving girls in control of failures, there was no significant difference in this area of the IAR for the boys.

On the Battle I-E measure, adequately achieving girls were significantly more internal than underachieving girls, but, as predicted, there was no significant difference between adequately achieving and underachieving boys. The previous significant differences between combined achievement groups appears to be largely a function of the very high externality of the underachieving girls.

As noted in Table 12-II, there are no significant differences between boys and girls, with achievement groups combined. This finding is true for both IAR and Battle I-E measures. Within achievement groups, adequately achieving girls were significantly more internal than adequately achieving boys on both IAR total and IAR negative reinforcement subtotal, but there were no significant differences between them on the Battle I-E. By contrast the differences between sexes in the underachieving group are not significant for any IAR score, but the boys are significantly more internal on the Battle I-E.

Discussion

In general, the findings of the previous group of studies indicated above are supported further by the present findings. Belief in self-responsibility appears to relate strongly to motiva-

TABLE 12-I

BATTLE I-E AND IAR SCORES FOR ADEQUATE ACHIEVER AND UNDERACHIEVER GROUPS

Measures	Boys and Girls Adequate Achievers M S.D.[a]	Boys and Girls Under- achievers M S.D.[a]	t	Boys, Adequate Achievers M S.D.[b]	Boys, Under- achievers M S.D.[b]	t	Girls, Adequate Achievers M S.D.[b]	Girls, Under- achievers M S.D.[b]	t
Battle I-E	14.96 3.87	17.06 4.47	2.51*	15.84 4.37	15.04 4.39	.35	14.08 3.14	19.08 3.61	5.21**
IAR Total Score	27.92 2.53	23.96 3.56	6.40**	27.20 2.94	24.60 3.12	3.03**	28.64 1.84	23.32 3.91	6.15**
IAR Positive I+	13.84 1.69	11.82 2.11	5.28**	13.68 2.08	12.00 1.85	3.02**	14.00 1.22	11.64 2.36	4.44**
IAR Negative I-	14.08 1.56	12.14 2.33	4.88**	13.52 1.61	12.60 2.33	1.63	14.64 1.31	11.68 2.30	5.57**

[a] $N = 50$, $df = 49$
[b] $N = 25$, $df = 24$

* $p < .05$
** $p < .01$

TABLE 12-II

SEX DIFFERENCES FOR ADEQUATE ACHIEVER, UNDERACHIEVER, AND COMBINED GROUPS

	Boys Groups, Combined Achievement Group		Girls Groups, Combined Achievement Group		t-test	Boys, Adequate Achievers		Girls, Adequate Achievers		t-test	Boys, Underachievers		Girls, Underachievers		t-test
	M	S.D.	M	S.D.		M	S.D.	M	S.D.		M	S.D.	M	S.D.	
Battle I-E	15.44	4.36	16.58	4.20	—1.33	15.84	4.37	14.08	3.15	1.63	15.04	4.39	19.08	3.61	—3.55**
IAR Total	25.90	3.28	25.98	4.05	—0.11	27.20	2.94	28.64	1.85	—2.07*	24.60	3.12	23.32	3.91	1.28
IAR Positive I+	12.84	2.12	12.82	2.21	.04	13.68	2.08	14.00	1.22	—0.66	12.00	1.85	11.64	2.36	.60
IAR Negative I—	13.06	2.03	13.16	2.39	—0.23	13.52	1.61	14.64	1.31	—2.69**	12.60	2.33	11.68	2.30	1.40

*p < .05   **p < .01

tion for academic achievement. Poor achievers tend, as a group, to believe that they have little responsibility for their own successes and failures.

From a social learning point of view, there is a differential learning history, with youngsters who make initial successes rewarded by positive responses from reinforcing agents, including teachers and parents, and, in the case of girls in particular, their own peers. Reinforcements include external rewards such as praise, greater acceptance, good grades, promotion, etc. and tend to provide support for the development of a situation-specific, internal belief in control over reinforcements of a positive nature. As this belief system generalizes, occasional failures have only minimal effect in modifying this internal belief structure, and defensiveness and denial in acceptance of internal control of negative consequences are unnecessary.

By contrast, initial underachievers are confronted with an array of negative reinforcements from teachers, parents and, in girls, from their peers, which is most likely to result in the development of an external control belief in academic consequences generally. Thus, the acceptance of external control in this situation may be seen either as a realistic reaction to a perceived, reduced opportunity for intellectual and academic rewards or as a defensive rejection of an internal locus of control.

The significant difference between adequately achieving and underachieving boys on the IAR positive reinforcement subscale is further support for this view. Poor achievers tend to externalize the locus of control of academic successes. However, the degree to which adequate achievers and underachievers report internal control over failures moves closer together, and no significant differences are noted, unlike the findings for girls. While this may represent a "regression to the mean" effect statistically, the increased variability of the underachieving group suggests a tendency to self-blame, a possible factor in the previously noted tendency for the more internal underachievers to be less deviant in classroom behavior (Buck and Austrin, 1971). The lack of a clear differentiation between adequately achieving and under-achieving boys relative to internal control over negative reinforcement suggests also a commonality of outlook for black disadvantaged boys coping with feelings of despair and anomie relative to expected failure in the educational environment.

Like the IAR findings the Battle I-E scores of the girls reveal identical differences between the adequate achievers and underachievers, with the former significantly more internal. However, as predicted, the Battle I-E scores of the two groups of boys are not different, and, even more than the findings on IAR negative subscores, the differences here are minimal. The presumption is made that while there tends to be some differential learning in the overall academic situation, leading to locus of control differences between adequate achievers and underachievers, no such differential learning takes place in the broader range of situations, and cultural similarity of learned expectancies is consequently greater for the black disadvantaged boys regardless of achievement background.

That this distinction is a meaningful one is further supported by the sex differences, with the underachieving boys more internal than underachieving girls on the Battle I-E. This finding seems related to the postulation that general cultural expectations for boys are different from those for girls (Warner, 1949; Winterbottom, 1958; Ausubel, 1963). In real-life situations, boys are expected to take more responsibility in directing their own lives, in planning future goals and in peer group relationships. Thus they tend to develop in the direction of internal orientation more readily than girls, who exist in a more protected environment and are more often in situations with planning and direction provided for them. There appears to be less difference between the educational and general life situation for girls than there is for boys, and they appear to be more invested in and affected by their educational successes and failures.

In addition, in the adequately achieving group, girls are consistently higher in IAR scores than boys, and between sex differences are significant for both the total and negative subtotal scores. Here again the implication is that even the boys who are adequate achievers do not develop the degree of internality characteristic of adequately achieving girls and do not invest themselves in and are not as affected by educational experiences as girls.

Both of the above observations are related to the findings of a previous report (Buck and Austrin, 1971) in which girls were rated by teachers as significantly higher in classroom behavior and attitude than boys. To a great extent, the findings of the present study are in line with the Merton (1958) view that while all groups in society are aware of culturally accepted goals and values, there is considerable variability in the availability of legitimate means to attain these goals. As a function of their experience, black disadvantaged children, particularly the males, tend to develop negative expectancies about the accessibility of legitimate goals through academic-intellectual effort on their part, attitudes which act further to block their efforts and develop further self-defeating motivation.

The present study provides further evidence of the importance, as Rotter (1955) has noted, of taking situational variables into account in making predictions about behavior. The differences in internal-external control beliefs found between the IAR and Battle scales may be attributed in large measure to situational conditions sampled by the items. While some generalizations may be justified from the present study as well as others, relative to internal control and achievement, caution is urged in making a generalization beyond the scope of the measure utilized in the specific study.

REFERENCES

Ausubel, D. P.: Teaching strategy for culturally deprived pupils: Cognitive and motivational considerations. *School Rev, 71*:454-463, 1963.

Battle, E. and Rotter, J. B.: Children's feelings of personal control as related to social class and ethnic group. *J Pers, 31*:482-490, 1963.

Buck, M. R.: Variables related to achievement of disadvantaged children. Doctoral dissertation, Saint Louis University. Ann Arbor, University Microfilms, 1969, no. 70-1843.

Buck, M. R. and Austrin, H. R.: Factors related to school achievement in an economically disadvantaged group. *Child Dev, 42*:1813-1826, 1971.

Cohen, J.: *Chance, Skill, and Luck.* Baltimore, Penguin, 1960.

Coleman, J. S., Campbell, E. Q., Hobson, C. J., McPartland, J., Mood, A. M., Weinfeld, F. D. and York, R. L.: *Equality of Educational Opportunity.* Washington, D. C. Office of Education, U. S. Govt. Printing Office, 1966.

Crandall, V. C.: The reinforcement effects of adult reactions and non-reactions on children's achievement expectations. *Child Dev, 34*:335-354, 1963.

Crandall, V. J., Dewey, R., Katkovsky, W. and Preston, A.: Parents attitudes and behaviors and grade school children's academic achievements. *Genet Psychol, 104*:53-66, 1964.

Crandall, V. C., Katkovsky, W. and Crandall, V. J.: Children's beliefs in their own control of reinforcements in intellectual-academic achievement situations. *Child Dev, 36*:91-109, 1965.

Crandall, V. J., Katkovsky, W. and Preston, A.: Motivational and ability determinants of young children's intellectual achievement behaviors. *Child Dev, 33*:643-661, 1962.

Cronbach, L. J.: *Essentials of Psychological Testing.* New York, Harper & Row, 1960.

deCharms, R.: Personal causation, training in the schools. *J Appl Soc Psychol, 2*:95-113, 1972.

Katkovsky, W., Crandall, V. C. and Good, S.: Parental antecedents of children's beliefs in internal-external control of reinforcements in intellectual achievement situations. *Child Dev, 38*:765-776, 1967.

Lao, R. C.: Internal-external control and competent and innovative behavior among Negro college students. *J Pers Soc Psychol 14*:263-270, 1970.

Lefcourt, H. M.: Internal versus external control of reinforcement: A review. *Psychol Bull, 65*:206-220, 1966.

Maccoby, E. E., Johnson, P. C. and Church, R. M.: Community integration and the social control of juvenile delinquency. *J Soc Issues, 14*: 38-51, 1958.

McGhee, P. E. and Crandall, V. C.: Beliefs in internal-external control of reinforcements and academic performance. *Child Dev, 39*:91-102, 1968.

Merton, R. K.: *Social Theory and Social Structure.* Glencoe, Free Pr, 1958.

Rotter, J. B.: Generalized expectancies of internal versus external control of reinforcement. *Psychol Monogr,* 1966, vol. 80, no. 609.

Rotter, J. B.: The role of the psychological situation in determining the direction of human behavior. In *Nebraska Symposuim on Motivation.* Omaha, U of Nebr Pr, 1955.

Seeman, M.: The Urban Alienation: Some Dubious Theses from Marx to Marcuse. Paper presented at the Annual Meeting of the American Psychological Association, Miami Beach, Florida, September, 1970.

Warner, W. L. et al.: *Social Class in America.* Chicago, Science Research Associates, 1949.

Winterbottom, M.: The relation of need for achievement in learning experiences in independence and mastery. In Atkinson, J. W. (Ed.): *Motives in Fantasy, Action and Society.* New York, Van Nostrand, 1958.

CHAPTER 13

INTERPERSONAL RELATIONS AND MOTIVATION: IMPLICATIONS FOR TEACHERS OF DISADVANTAGED CHILDREN*

Edgar G. Epps

Motivation
Self-concept of Ability
Sense of Personal Adequacy
Implications for Education
References

THIS DISCUSSION FOCUSES on some personality characteristics and attitudes which have been found to be significantly related to school performance. Each of these characteristics has some basis in interpersonal relationships. In this paper, I will describe the relationship between interpersonal relations and the development of personality traits and attitudes which are associated with academic success or failure.

The basic theoretical model of motivation utilized throughout this report is that of achievement motivation. The treatment is based on recent refinements of this theory presented by Atkinson (1964), and Atkinson and Feather (1969). In addition to (1) positive motives of an intrinsic nature, Atkinson postulates that the tendency to approach success is the result of the combined positive and negative effects of (2) fear of failure, (3)

---

*Reprinted by permission of the *Journal of Negro Education*, 39:14-25, no. 1 (Winter, 1970).

perceived probability of success, and (4) the incentive value of the task goal. This paper will focus on two of these factors: fear of failure and perceived probability of success. Considerable attention will be given to self-esteem because it is thought to be relevant to both of these factors. For example, low self-esteem may be symptomatic of both fear of failure tendencies and perceived low probability of success in a valued domain.

MOTIVATION*

McClelland suggests that low achievement motivation is the result of a failure in the socialization process in the home. Negroes as a group, he maintains, are lacking in the achievement motive because of the matricentric structure of the Negro family, and the persistence of child-rearing practices that originated in slavery. He takes for granted that strong mother dependency weakens the development of the achievement motive in sons. (Achievement motivation literature has little to say about girls because the research results with girls have not been very promising.)

If we view need for achievement as "hope for success," we can call it an approach tendency. Atkinson postulates that there is also a general avoidance tendency which he calls "fear of failure." According to this formulation, if the approach tendency is stronger (need for achievement), the individual will strive for success whenever his performance can be evaluated against a standard of excellence, and there is a realistic chance to succeed. But if the avoidant tendency is stronger, an individual experiences anxiety when his performance can be evaluated against a standard of excellence and, although there is a realistic chance to succeed, he would prefer to avoid the situation. When he cannot avoid this kind of situation, e.g. a school test, high levels of anxiety may lead to low performance. The person oriented to fear failure is afraid of competition and evaluation because failure is very painful to him. Behavior which is as-

---

*For this section, the author has borrowed freely from Irwin Katz, "The Socialization of Motivation in Minority Group Children," *Nebraska Symposium of Motivation* (Lincoln: University of Nebraska Press, 1967), pp. 133-191.

sociated with fear of failure includes apathy, reluctance to study, frequent absence, etc. Psychologists have generally concluded that high levels of anxiety produce interfering response patterns which lead to impaired performance. This motive has usually been measured by some version of the Test Anxiety Scale. Examples of the items in this scale are: "During a final exam, I get so nervous I forget facts that I know." (Responses are true or false.) Research results from elementary school, junior high school, senior high school, and college strongly support the statement that children with low anxiety perform better than those with high anxiety on tests and in class, as well as on experimental tasks. Results usually indicate that highly anxious students do well on easy tasks, but perform poorly on complex learning tasks.

My own research with Negro high school students, and the results of Sarason's longitudinal study of white elementary school children, indicate that anxiety scores tend to change with time and new experiences. The elementary school study presented longitudinal data which clearly indicated that children who lower their levels of anxiety during their school years significantly outperform those who experience a rise in level of anxiety.

It is important at this point to look at some of the variables associated with different levels of anxiety or fear of failure in children. Looking first at some ecological variables, my research with elementary and high school children points to significant subcultural differences in levels of anxiety. Lower-class children consistently have higher anxiety scores than middle-class children irrespective of race. Negro children generally have higher anxiety scores than white children. There is evidence from other studies that these differences are probably present in preschool children as manifested by timidity, apathy, etc.

These group differences in anxiety level are probably attributable to differences in socialization practices. The type of interpersonal relationships the child experiences in the family are highly relevant to anxiety formation. If a child grows up in a situation in which there is little reward for successful performance, but where there is punishment for unsuccessful performance, he becomes attuned to guard against situations that may lead to failure and resulting punishment. A recent study in which mothers of highly anxious and not very anxious children were interviewed found that these mothers whose children were relatively high in fear of failure said they do not reward their children for satisfactory behavior in independence and achievement situations, but do punish their children for unsatisfactory behavior in these situations. Evidence from other sources suggests that the same socialization practices that lead to high achievement motivation also lead to low anxiety.

A study of Negro youngsters in Detroit asked pupils to describe the way their mothers and fathers reacted when they were successful or unsuccessful at home and at school. The surprising finding was that the father is the more important parent in the socialization of boys' school behavior. Other research reports that the father's perception of a child's anxious tendencies are more accurate than the mother's. My own research suggests that there are regional differences in the relative importance of parents for socialization among Negro children. There is a tendency for mother's social characteristics (especially amount of education) to be more influential than the father's in a sample of high school students in Jacksonville, Florida, while the tendency for boys in Detroit is for the father's characteristics to exert more influence.

Turning now to the school setting, it seems apparent that next to the parents, teachers are the source of the most important adult-child interpersonal relations. If teachers withhold rewards (positive reinforcements), while dispersing negative reinforcements (punishment and criticism) children's anxiety will in all probability be increased.

Indirect evidence cited by Katz suggests that lower-class children, and especially minority group lower-class children, receive more than their share of classroom exposure to rejecting teachers. A recent study found that *regardless of their scholastic standing,* elementary school pupils from blue-collar homes tended to perceive their teachers as rejecting. Another study found that the race of the teachers seemed to make a difference in how they viewed Negro students. White teachers were more critical of their motivation and ability. Other research indicates that teachers of children with low socioeconomic status are more likely to be dissatisfied with their work and to be critical of the motivation and ability of their children. It is highly probable that negative reactions by whites are more anxiety-producing than negative reactions by Negroes when Negro students are involved.

SELF-CONCEPT OF ABILITY*

One manifestation of a student's perceived probability of success is his self-concept. Academic self-esteem or self-concept of ability has long been thought to be related to school achievement. Recent research has produced results which support this hypothesis in convincing fashion. Work by Brookover and others has demonstrated that, even with ability controlled, self-concept of ability is highly predictive of performance in junior and senior high school. It is not clear, however, which comes first, academic success or academic self-confidence. It is probably a circular development with initial self-confidence of a general sort leading to initial success in school which reinforces self-confidence about learning ability, which in turn leads to additional academic success. Success builds upon success thereby increasing the likelihood that future academic efforts will be successful.

Self-esteem is related to social status as well as to school performance. It is probable that lower-status children enter school with less self-confidence about academic matters than middle-

---

*The pioneer work in this area has been done by Wilbur B. Brookover and others at Michigan State University. Three reports describe the research to date. They are Wilbur Brookover, Ann Paterson, and Shailer Thomas, *Self-Concept of Ability and School Achievement: Final Report of Cooperative Research Project Number 845* (East Lansing, Michigan State University, 1962); W. B. Brookover, Jean M. Lefere, Don E. Hamachek, S. Thomas, and Edsel L. Erickson, *Self-Concept of Ability and School Achievement, II: Final Report of Cooperative Research Project Number 1636* (East Lansing, Michigan State University, 1965); and W. B. Brookover, E. L. Erickson, and Lee M. Joiner, *Self-Concept of Ability and School Achievement, III: Final Report of Cooperative Research Project Number 2831* (East Lansing, Michigan State University, 1967).

class or upper-class children. There is also a strong positive relationship between general self-esteem and that self-esteem which is specific to academic performance. In spite of this strong association between general self-esteem and academic—specific self-esteem, it is only the latter which is closely associated with actual performance in school. The general self-esteem of the child entering school for the first time may, however, be very crucial for his adaptation to the academic setting. If he has high self-esteem, he will in all probability be more self-confident, more persistent in his efforts to meet the demands of the situation, and therefore more likely to receive reinforcement for his efforts early in his school career. This early success reinforces self-confidence and enhances self-esteem in academically relevant behaviors. Thus, the child learns to expect success in school and to associate success with his own achievement-related behavior.

For the child who enters school with low general self-esteem, the process is just the opposite. He is initially less self-confident, therefore approaches new tasks reluctantly, is less persistent in his efforts to meet school demands, and as a result receives fewer rewards for academically relevant behaviors. Thus, his already low self-confidence is further lowered by his inability to meet the requirements of the school situation. The child with low initial self-confidence and self-esteem learns to expect failure in school and to associate school with unpleasant or unrewarding experiences. In addition, lack of self-confidence is highly associated with anxiety, thus leading to an expectation that the school situation will be stressful and anxiety provoking. This encourages a desire to withdraw from the situation which provokes the anxiety. The withdrawal tendency may be characterized by apathy, daydreaming, dependency, absenteeism, disruptive behavior, or some combination of these.

What kind of interpersonal relations produce low self-esteem? It is generally accepted by sociologists and psychologists that self-image is a reflection of the child's perception of the images of himself held by significant others: parents, siblings, peers, teachers, and neighbors. The social status of the child's family determines to a great extent how he will be accepted by others in the community. Parents serve as mediators between the child and the community, interpreting community values and standards for the child and helping the child to evaluate his own status relative to others in the community. Interaction within the family provides the child with direct evidence of his standing on characteristics valued by his immediate family. Interaction with teachers and peers at school provides evidence relative to school and playground social status. If the child perceives a preponderance of low ratings among these evaluations, he is likely to develop a low overall self-evaluation or what we are calling low general self-esteem.

It is quite possible that a child will perceive himself as ranking low on some status-giving traits and high on others. The subjective weighting of his positive status-giving traits against his negative status-giving traits gives him his net self-esteem. Thus, it is possible for a child to have relatively high general self-esteem and relatively low self-esteem relative to specific areas such as school behavior or athletic ability.

The importance of self-esteem in a given area of competence for one's total self-evaluation is to a large extent a reflection of the values held by an individual. These values are, in turn, a reflection of the extent to which specific characteristics are emphasized in a given culture or subculture. In a subculture which places much importance on educational accomplishments, excellence in school carries more weight in total self-esteem than in a subculture which places little importance on educational accomplishments. The child's view of the importance of educational excellence is a reflection of his parents' educational values. If they reward the child more for his academic accomplishments than for his athletic accomplishments, it is probable that he will (at least in the early school years) value his educational skills more than his athletic skills.

The relative value of traits not skill-related such as physical appearance, skin color, stature, and family social status is also determined in the same manner. If such traits are the basis for most status-giving rewards, the relative value of skill is low. If rewards are more closely tied to skills, then the acquisition of skills becomes crucial for self-esteem. Children from minority group homes or lower-class homes are more likely than middle-class children to feel that rewards are based on traits not skill-related. This view may be communicated to them directly or indirectly by their parents who have themselves been unable to acquire the characteristics which denote high status in our society.

Family social status influences the child's perception of the relative importance of various skills in other ways. The availability of specific rewards as perceived by the child is often a reflection of the parents' understanding of the accessibility of specific goals (material possessions, favored occupations, access to higher education). If the child believes that college is out of reach for him even if he succeeds in school, academic skills will have lower value for him than if he thinks college is both accessible and crucial for his future occupational success. If the child believes that academic skills have little value in the real world, that his future rewards depend on excellence in athletic or social skills, or his ability to influence important people, he will tend to develop those skills he perceives as most relevant for future success (while neglecting educational skills). If he feels luck or fate are the primary determinants of future success, he may forego the development of any skills other than those necessary for the enjoyment of the rewards of whatever success comes his way.

In summing up this part of the discussion, it will be apparent that interpersonal interaction is crucial in the process of developing a favorable self-concept of academic ability. We are suggesting that the child learns to value academic skills or not to value them from his parents, siblings, and peers. His values influence the amount of effort he puts into academic pursuits. His efforts are evaluated by parents, teachers, siblings, and peers. Whether he perceives these evaluations to be favorable or unfavorable depends upon the extent to which he is rewarded for his efforts. If rewards are frequent, his net self-evaluation will be favorable; if he is more often unrewarded for his efforts, his net self-evaluation will be unfavorable. Favorable self-concept of academic ability encourages increased effort in school-related pursuits, which leads to more rewards and thus to a reinforcement of the positive academic self-image. In contrast, a poor academic self-image encourages less effort which results in fewer rewards and an increasingly negative self-concept.

How can the circle be broken? There is little evidence available on this point, but Brookover and his associates have experimented with attempts to change the academic self-image by changing the attitudes of significant others toward children with low self-concepts of ability. Attempts to change attitudes of peers and teachers produced no effective change in self-concept of students. There were, however, some positive results from attempts to produce change in students by changing their parents' attitudes toward them. It was found that improving the parents' evaluation of the student's ability resulted in positive changes in student self-concept. Retesting of these students some time after the end of the experiment revealed, however, that the effects were temporary. Whether this implies that the initial favorable results were "Hawthorne effects" rather than real changes in self-image, or that work with parents must be continued throughout the academic career of students with low academic self-image is not known at present. This does, however, appear to be a fruitful area for further experimentation with teachers, peers, and parents.

SENSE OF PERSONAL ADEQUACY

There is a growing body of research which emphasizes the importance for educational performance of a personality characteristic variously known as powerlessness, alienation, locus of control, personal efficacy, internal vs. external control of reinforcements, and anomie.* Although there are a number of instruments for measuring this dimension, many of them quite dissimilar in form, they all appear to be concerned with the same underlying factor: the individual's sense of being able to make things turn out the way he wants them to. To some extent,

---

*The basic reference in this area is the following: Julian B. Rotter, "Generalized Expectancies for Internal Versus External Control of Reinforcement," *Psychological Monographs: General and Applied,* vol. LXXX, no. 1 (1966), whole no. 609.

this notion also encompasses planning ability and ability to delay gratification. In the Atkinson model, this would be a generalized expectancy of a tendency toward success or failure.

The major theoretical framework from which this research stems is social learning theory as developed by Julian Rotter. Experimental studies have repeatedly shown that in situations in which skill is perceived to be responsible for success or failure, 100 per cent reinforcement of correct responses results in more effective learning than partial reinforcement. Experiments have also shown that persons who believe that their own skill, rather than luck or chance, causes success or failure are more persistent in situations which are believed to require skill. This formulation is related to the achievement motivation construct, but is more useful educationally because of more efficient measurement and greater demonstrated educational relevance. The basic idea is that people who have a strong need for achievement also have a strong belief that their own skill or ability will determine the outcome of events in which they are involved. In other words, high motivation for achievement is associated with ability to accept responsibility for one's successes or failures. Rotter postulates that the individual who has a strong belief that he can control his destiny is likely to (a) be more alert to those aspects of the environment which provide useful information for his future behavior; (b) take steps to improve his environmental condition; (c) place greater value on skill or achievement rewards and be generally more concerned with his abiilty, particularly his failures; and (d) be sensitive to subtle (but not necessarily open) attempts to influence him. Rotter's summary is based primarily on results of studies of adults, but many of these generalizations would appear to be relevant for school children.

Research with a children's intellectual achievement responsibility scale has led researchers to conclude that *internality* (the ability to accept responsibility) is definitely related to both school grades and test performance. The internal child sees his own efforts (instrumental behavior) as causing the reinforcement he receives. Thus he should display greater initiative, effort, and persistence in the acquisition of intellectual-academic goals, for he feels that no one else is going to hand him success or prevent him from failing. He should also exhibit greater acquisition of concepts, facts and problem-solving techniques which might subsequently be reflected in performance scores. This is especially true if the teacher bases a part of the grade on effort. Other research, notably the Coleman Report, has shown that sense of control is important in high school as well. The *Equality of Opportunity* survey found this to be the single most important attitude variable for predicting or explaining academic success. Coleman also found that whites have higher control scores than Negroes, and that middle-class students have higher scores than lower-class students. Similar results were found in my high school student study with three separate measures of sense of control.

These findings suggest that socialization for competence takes different forms in different subcultures. The development of a strong sense of personal competence requires a history of interpersonal relationships which reward skill. If parents wish to encourage their children to develop academic competence, they should provide rewards for intellectual skills (Coleman, 1966). Parents' responses to verbal utterances of children, to their efforts to walk, or hit a ball, or imitate a parent all influence the child's sense of control. When the child attempts a skill-related task and is rewarded, he is likely to attempt a similar task in the future. This tendency will also generalize to similar tasks. In other words, a child's sense of personal competence is directly related to the frequency of rewards for efforts to acquire skill. It is very likely that the middle-class child receives more frequent rewarding behavior from parents for intellectually relevant efforts than the lower-class child. He therefore enters school with a much stronger tendency to approach tasks requiring skill than the lower-class child.

Pearl and Reissman state that:

> In school, these tendencies are reinforced. The middle-class student has a virtual monopoly on the rewards of the system. He gets good grades, the teacher expresses pleasure at his performance at

school and his parents express pleasure at home. School affords him dignity, enhances his self-concept, and allows him to feel adequate. . . . In attaining success, the affluent youngster is required to make very few sacrifices and he attains one of life's most precious gratifications—he is allowed to have a feeling of competence. In addition, he participates fully in extracurricular activities and is given the greatest measure of self-determination the system allows.

[In contrast] the disadvantaged youngster receives few rewards because he has none of the attributes to attain rewards. His parents cannot help him. He has few books at home, little space to study, and little stimulation from his peers. He has a language style and a behavior pattern that do not fit easily into the standard classroom situation. He is taught by persons who neither fully understand nor empathize with him (Pearl and Reissman, 1965).

It is not surprising that he feels powerless in the school situation. His sense of inadequacy becomes more intense, his anxiety in the learning situation increases, and his self-esteem in the classroom decreases as he faces continued failure in school.

IMPLICATIONS FOR EDUCATION

If the educational difficulties of disadvantaged children are based on low achievement motivation, high anxiety, low self-concept of ability, and feelings of inadequacy or powerlessness as I have argued, it follows that educational policies should be advocated which have as their goal amelioration of these characteristics. The final section of this paper will describe some general principles which may help educators improve the educational environment for disadvantaged pupils.

The *Equality of Educational Opportunity* survey concludes that the impact of the family on the child has its greatest effect in earliest years, so that family-to-family differences in achievement decline after the beginning of school. This suggests that intervention efforts by the schools should attempt to involve parents as much as possible in the early school years. It was mentioned above that one study has demonstrated that working with parents to change their evaluation of the child's ability yielded positive results. Other research suggests that parents' educational standards (performance standards) are strongly related to student performance. This argues that raising the level of parents' educational (performance) expectations may yield positive results.

One of the central implications of the *Equality of Educational Opportunity* survey is that what the child brings with him to school as strengths or weaknesses determined by his social class is the prime correlate of school achievement. It is influenced—offset or reinforced—most substantially by what other pupils with whom he attends class bring with them as social class-shaped interests and abilities. In other words, as the proportion of advantaged students increases in a school, achievement among disadvantaged students increases. This report implies, then, that racially integrated classes and classes that are heterogeneous in socioeconomic distribution are likely to result in *increased individual academic motivation* for disadvantaged youngsters.

From the results of Sarason's work, it seems clear that we should also concern ourselves with the question of changing anxiety levels from high to low when working with poor school achievers (Sarason, 1966). There is evidence that to some extent anxiety is a function of uncertainty. There is also evidence that it is related to powerlessness. In other words the highly anxious student is uncertain about his ability to do what is necessary to bring about a reward. When parents or teachers are unfair and do not reward correct performance, or when they are negligent and unaware of proper performance, they encourage the child to feel that he is helpless or incompetent. When teachers are vague about what is required of children—what is good performance; what type of behavior will be rewarded; what type of behavior will be punished—they are likely to increase the child's anxiety level.

Even when teacher objectives, instructions and the like are clear to middle-class students, pupils from impoverished backgrounds or different language subcultures may have difficulty understanding what is required or desired of them. One sociolinguistic study reports that middle-class pupils were better than lower-class pupils in understanding teachers' speech. Lower-class pupils with high I.Q. scores did not have this difficulty. The implication seems clear. Teachers must make certain that all of their pupils understand classroom instructions and the nature of the tasks set before them.

A point which is stressed by psychologists who are oriented toward behavior management techniques (operant conditioning), is that there is a great need for teachers to define their goals in behavioral terms. Exactly what behaviors are expected of children in the classroom situation? These must be explained in terms that are understandable to the child as well as the teacher. Stating a goal as "competence in language skills" doesn't help either the teacher or the student. The *behavior must be pinpointed.* It is more effective to say that each child must learn to recite the alphabet; each child must learn to correctly label five colors; each child must learn to repeat sentences exactly as presented by the teacher; each child must learn to use the words, "it," "an," "a," "the," correctly in sentences; each child must learn to sit in his seat in class.

It is not enough to pinpoint the behavior which pupils are expected to acquire in school. It is equally important to make sure that children are rewarded when they attempt to make the desired response. It is especially important for teachers to realize that they must reward every *effort* made by the child to make the desired response. Bereiter and Engelman (1966) state this as their first principle for teachers. *Reward the child who tries.* The primary criterion is not whether the child performs adequately—but whether he *tries.* The child who does not try should have rewards withheld and should be told why. They also suggest that "motherly" coaxing is undesirable. Coaxing simply *invites* the children to have doubts, to wonder if they can do what is required. Most teachers know that they should avoid shaming children. If the teacher demonstrates through her behavior that the children are stupid or that they really cannot be expected to perform a task without coaxing, they will reflect her expectations. The teacher should, therefore, *expect* the children to perform and work hard; she should *expect* them to be "smart"; and she should *expect* to be proud of them most of the time. An educational program based on work motives is designed so that learning is consistently rewarded. This requires providing the child with a realistic definition of success and failure. He should know when his behavior approximates that desired by the teacher. This means giving accurate factual information about correct and incorrect responses. The teacher must base her evaluation on the *manner in which the child works* rather than the outcome. Rules of behavior must be emphasized rather than the child's adequacy. Teachers must be very careful about this because a child's sense of adequacy is as important for scholastic success as fear of failure or anxiety.

Some educators feel that expecting children to work hard in preschool, kindergarten, or first grade will be too stressful for the children. But I remind you that the goal is not to eliminate all stress from the school situation. This could be easily managed by taking the Special Education approach. Research indicates that anxiety does drop sharply when students are sent into special education classes. But there is also a drop in learning. Retarded students in normal classes learn more than those in special classes simply because more is expected of them. Even in the case of the low achiever, it is not the mathematical content that must be diminished, but the ingenuity of the educational technique that must be augmented. To give the low achiever lower goals is but to make the original estimate of him self-fulfilling (Asimov, 1968).

There is some evidence to support the notion that certain types of stress are conducive to good performance. Work with preschool pupils led Bereiter and Engelman to conclude that intensive instruction does not produce excessive stress. Any challenge does induce a certain amount of stress. When we say that a problem or learning task is challenging, we imply that it induces a certain amount of stress in a person, thereby motivating him to strive to solve the problem or execute the task. The child who experiences *no* stress is in trouble educationally as is the child who experiences too much stress. Furthermore, the child whose stress is based on fear of failure, concerns over pleasing the teacher to sheer interpersonal competitiveness is more likely to get into difficulty than the child whose stress is related to curiosity or a desire to achieve competence.

When signs of excessive stress show up in children, they are signals that something has gone wrong in the teaching, that the child has failed to master something he needs in order to handle the task confronting him. Signs of excessive stress usually disappear as soon as the educational lack is made up. Thus *ineffective teaching* which presents tasks beyond the child's capacity produces excessive stress, not hard work.

Finally, it is worth repeating that "success breeds success." It would be advantageous to arrange the reward ration in such a way that the child is rewarded more often for success than he is punished for failure. His sense of competence and his self-concept of academic ability would be enhanced by successful task performances, while the level of anxiety would be lowered. An interesting fact about anxiety has been reported by Katahn (1966). He found that students with high ability relative to their peers perform better when they are anxious while students with average or below average ability suffer performance decrements when they are anxious. It seems, therefore, *that it is more important to avoid anxiety-producing stress* (shaming, threats, etc.) *with average or below average students than with average students.*

This emphasis on providing opportunities for success in school is not intended as a plea for "social promotion." *It is important that rewards be associated with efforts to perform the required tasks.* It is also necessary for students to acquire some skills in order for present success to lead to future success. In order to avoid the stigma of failure in the early years, it would probably be more efficient to utilize some type of ungraded class system. This would permit students to proceed from one level of task difficulty to another at their own speed rather than having to meet rigid grade requirements. Such a procedure would make it possible to avoid presenting students with tasks for which they have had no previous preparation.

I would like to conclude with a statement about teacher expectancies. It is almost a truism in education that pupils learn what teachers expect them to learn. This has been demonstrated recently by the research of Rosenthal and Jacobson (1966). An experiment was tried in elementary school to see if teacher expectations affected pupils' learning. Pupils were tested early in the term with a new I.Q. test. Teachers were then told that some of their pupils (randomly selected by the investigators) "would show unusual intellectual gains during the academic year." Students were tested again at the end of the term (it should be noted that all testing was done by the investigators and the teachers never saw the tests). Those students whom teachers had been led to believe would show unusual gains actually improved significantly more than other students in the same classes. The teachers expected them to learn more and they did. Effects were greatest in grades one and two, and in classes with students of average ability. Effects were smaller for the higher grades and for students in "slow" classes or "honors" classes. It appears that in higher grades and extreme ability groups teachers simply did not believe the evidence which was contrary to previous performance records. There is a suggestion here that in the lower grades and in classes where teachers believe there is room for improvement, it is possible to change teacher expectancies concerning the performance of individual pupils and that this change will result in corresponding changes in pupil performance.

The *Equality of Educational Opportunity* survey points out that good teaching has a stronger relationship to pupil performance among minority group students and lower-class pupils than among middle-class pupils. This argues that teachers may do well to raise their expectancy level when teaching children from disadvantaged backgrounds. Raising teacher expectancies may do much to compensate for the lack of educational encouragement these children get at home. It is also important, however, to raise parental expectancies if long-term improvement is desired.

Throughout this paper it has been implicitly assumed that the goal of education is to prepare young people to be useful citizens. This assumption implies that certain minimum skills such as reading, writing, and basic arithmetic are necessary. It also implies that these basic skills can be taught to everyone who is not severely handicapped. It is hoped that more and more teachers will come to accept the belief that nearly all school children can learn these basic skills. It may be true, as Coles argues, that "the poor don't want to be middle class" (Coles, 1965), but it is also true that the poor place a high value on education and believe that better education is necessary if they are to improve their condition and provide a better future for their children. This desire for better education for their children should be channeled into effective ways of raising the educational standards of parents in "low performance" school districts or systems with the aid of universities and federal programs.

REFERENCES

Asimov, Isaac: Third R. updated. *New York Times Book Review*, October 27, 1968, p. 22.

Atkinson, John W.: *An Introduction to Motivation*. Princeton, D. Van-Nostrand, 1964, Ch. 9.

Atkinson, John W. and Feather, Norman T. (Eds.): *A Theory of Achievement Motivation*. New York, Wiley, 1966, Ch. 20.

Bereiter, Carl and Engleman, Siegfried: *Teaching Disadvantaged Children in the Preschool*. Englewood Cliffs, P-H, 1966, pp. 81-85.

Coleman, James S., et al.: *Equality of Educational Opportunity*. Washington, D. C., U. S. Government Printing Office, 1966.

Coles, Robert: The poor don't want to be middle-class. *New York Times Magazine*, December 19, 1965, p. 7.

Katahn, Martin: Interaction of anxiety and ability in complex learning situations. *J Pers Soc Psychol*, 111:475-479, 1966.

Pearl, Arthur and Riessman, Frank (Eds.): *New Careers for the Poor*. New York, Free Pr, 1965, pp. 71-72.

Rosenthal, Robert and Jacobson, L.: Teachers' expectancies and children's IQ's. *Psychol Rep*, XIX:115-118, 1966.

Sarason, Seymour B.: The Measurement of Anxiety in Children: Some Questions and Problems. In Spielberger, Charles D. (Ed.): *Anxiety and Behavior*. New York, Acad Pr, 1966, pp. 63-79.

CHAPTER 14

AN ATTACK ON IMPEDIMENTS TO EFFECTIVE CROSS-CULTURAL TEACHING*

LAMORE J. CARTER AND OLIVER D. HENSLEY

A LITTLE OVER A YEAR AGO, a ten-year-old black, deaf child in Monroe, La., had never attended school, had never played group games with other children, had seldom ventured from his home, and could not utter a distinguishable sound. Today, however, he speaks haltingly, "hears" through lip-reading techniques, shares the excitement of classroom games, and is engaged in learning activities that allow him to achieve continued academic progress and self-satisfaction.

What accounts for this change? The answer, in a sense, is simply, "He was given the opportunity to learn." But the question still remains: How did that happen? Of course, forces may promote immediate change and it is often difficult to identify the exact source that initiated the changing process. However, certain college and public school people in Arkansas, Louisiana, and Mississippi think that at least part of the answer to this question lies in a model for in-service training devised at Northeast Louisiana University. The success of Project LIFT (Laboratory Institute to Facilitate Teaching), a significant departure from traditional in-service training programs, leads these educators to believe that they can gain acceptance of and support for educational changes by the whole community if they train

---

*Reprinted by permission of the Office of Child Development, Department of Health, Education, and Welfare, *Children Today* (formerly *Children*), January-February, 1971, vol. 18, no. 1, pp. 19-22.

action research committees to devise and install preplanned changes in the public schools.

Project Development

LIFT initiated a long series of unprecedented activities in the early part of 1968, when black educators and white educators from the Ark-La-Miss region met to formulate plans to produce biracial cadres of professional educators who would attempt to bring better educational programs for all children to their local communities.

The multistate and biracial approach to solving problems was a new and exciting experience for these educators. Sometimes the initial meetings of the principals for planning activities were awkward and filled with suspicion. In some instances, administrators of colleges less than fifty miles apart had never received an official visit from each other to discuss the pooling of resources to solve critical regional problems. The cooperative planning of many colleges, both black and white, with public school officials opened a whole new communication system based on interpersonal patterns that are now used with increasing frequency.

The goal of these early designers of LIFT was to retrain ninety-six teachers who had been assigned to racially integrated schools to use new teaching strategies and to innovate curriculum projects for improving instruction for every disadvantaged child. The project was funded by the U. S. Office of Education under the Education Professions Development Act in the latter part of 1968. It started the first of its four distinct stages of development in January, 1969.

The first step, the awareness stage, was designed to sensitize the participants to the special needs of the disadvantaged child in their schools and to acquaint them with the resources that could help them meet his needs.

The second step, the design stage, was planned to encourage local civic leaders, action research committees, consultants, and neighborhood school representatives to design special programs needed in their own specific areas.

The third step, the laboratory stage, was designed for trying out the plans. The participants spent six weeks in a pilot school where their plans were given a trial run in classes attended by disadvantaged children. After assessing the effectiveness of their designs, the action research committees revised their programs and applied them in their local schools during a semester of extensive field testing.

The last step, the demonstration stage, gave educators and lay people in the area an opportunity to see selected new programs operating successfully in integrated schools in their home district. The Project LIFT participants conducted tours of their new programs for parents and teachers when school was in regular session.

During the eighteen-month operation of LIFT, the participants and staff shared many successes. They also suffered a number of frustrations as they ran head long into a long-established way of life.

Some Problems

One of the first problems encountered by LIFT was the antagonistic attitude of news media and conservative politicians. After the first LIFT meeting, the local newspaper printed the inflammatory headline, "Plight of Negro Blamed on Whites," over a story of an interview with a LIFT speaker. This created a great deal of controversy in the community and provoked numerous hostile phone calls to the college by persons bent on finding out who was "stirring up trouble." Politicians misquoted LIFT speakers and distorted the philosophy of the program in the newspaper, on radio and TV, and at meetings of business, civic, and social organizations. They continuously condemned the project and asked for "public repudiation of insidious statements" and "an end to this outrage." Political pressure was applied to state commissioners and school officials "to end the misappropriation of the taxpayers' money to such ill-advised projects."

Quickly LIFT's staff and participants started for the first time to work for a change of the news media's attitude toward the project. Black and white editors, radio and television personalities, and politicians were brought as guests to LIFT seminars where they became involved in helping the participants devise strategies to enlist the aid of journalists in promoting educational change.

After several exposures to LIFT's philosophy, participants, and additional information about the project, the attitudes of key people in the news media changed from negative to very positive. Feature stories, TV specials, and radio interviews highly supportive of LIFT began to attack the basic reasons that new programs were not being developed in the schools. While LIFT did not drastically change the beliefs, attitudes, and values of all news people in this area, it did convince the influencers that the program would benefit the community and that they should support needed local educational programs and LIFT activities. As the news media became more supportive, the community at large became more receptive to proposed educational changes.

The most persistent problem for Project LIFT was racial prejudice. In almost every suggestion for change in the local schools, the often unspoken, but unyielding, resistance that prevented change was directly connected with opposition to promoting further racial integration. This resistance was evident in the awareness phase of LIFT as some of the participants openly opposed the program's basic philosophy of upgrading education for disadvantaged children in integrated schools. The concept of biracial teams working on common tasks was also repugnant to some of the participants, and some dropped out of the program after the first two meetings because they could not work with people of the opposite race.

Perception Deficits

One of the authors of this article, Lamore Carter, functioned as LIFT's consulting psychologist. He identified the major problem in the area of attitude change for teachers working in an integrated school as the "Thing" and "Halo" phenomena, which he defines as follows:

1. The "Thing" phenomenon is the relative inability of most

white Americans to perceive and accept black Americans without some prejudice based on imagined deficits.

2. The "Halo" phenomenon is the relative inability of most black Americans to perceive and accept white Americans except as persons fundamentally competent, better, more knowing, and less likely to have faults.

In an address to the ninety-six LIFT participants, Dr. Carter described how these phenomena impede teaching.

"It is the 'Thing' phenomenon that makes it difficult or impossible for a white teacher, pupil, or school administrator in traditional educational environments to view and accept a black teacher, pupil, or school administrator as a person with no more than the usual human frailties. There is the constant and forceful expectation on the part of the white educators that some significant deficit of professional competence, personality, or character will be discerned in the black educator. Under such circumstances, the expectation is almost always confirmed, because the white teacher, administrator, or pupil is subconsciously searching for negative factors and has a limitless range of choices.

"It is the 'Halo' phenomenon that makes black teachers, pupils, and school administrators look for more competence, perfection of personality and character in white teachers, pupils, and school administrators and find it when it is not there."

The discrepancy in perception represented by the "Thing" and "Halo" phenomena is due primarily to the cultural experiences that condition both blacks and whites to regard a wide range of behavior of whites as acceptable and natural in whites, and, at the same time, to regard similar behavior in blacks as artificial and imitative.

At first, participants tended to divide along racial lines and to come to the LIFT meetings as separate black or white units from their schools although their superintendents had told them to function as a single unit. Several months later, after they had been immersed in biracial work-study tasks and exposed to seminar leaders from various races, disciplines, and nations who specifically planned programs to make the participants more openminded, they voluntarily began to ride together and had apparently shed much of their traditional bias. These cognitive-affective deficits in LIFT participants were reduced by having black teachers and white teachers work together on practical problems existing in their schools.

Project LIFT assaulted another misconception. Prior to 1969, no summer school for elementary children had operated in the Ark-La-Miss area. The excuse for not supplying such opportunities was that disadvantaged children did not like school and would not attend if a school were opened. LIFT, with the excellent assistance of a courageous superintendent, opened a laboratory school that accommodated 200 disadvantaged students for six weeks. Many more children applied for admittance but had to be refused because of the lack of facilities. In 1970, several school districts on their own opened summer school programs for disadvantaged students and for the first time provided remedial programs for children with severe learning handicaps.

Demonstration Stage

The shedding of myths and misconceptions, a major goal in the awareness and laboratory stages of Project LIFT, was in a sense actually a means to another end—bringing about educational progress in the schools.

The laboratory phase of Project LIFT provided the resources for teachers and community leaders to plan an attack on specific problems in their local areas. The effectiveness of their planning activities was tested in the demonstration stage. At this stage LIFT's staff and participants had the obligation to establish in local integrated schools demonstrations of innovative educational programs.

Bobbie Bowie, a teacher in Monroe, La., fulfilled her obligation by developing a program for teaching deaf children to lip read, to learn to speak through the EFI (Electronic Futures Incorporated) training system, and to work with materials and participate in social activities specifically designed to help them. Benjamin Boyte, a teacher in Concordia Parish, designed and conducted a course in drama to effect better verbal communication between students in an integrated all-boys high school.

Last spring, his course was adopted in several schools in Arkansas.

A new approach to teaching science was initiated by Madolyn Abraham in Bossier City, La. She used the discovery method of teaching, relying on field exercises instead of textbooks or workbooks. She also helped black students and white students adjust to one another by assigning research projects to racially integrated groups as well as to individuals.

Elsie Warnock, a junior high school teacher in El Dorado, Ark., attacked the problem of apathy and absenteeism in poor readers of both races. She gave both individual and small group assignments, using books and other kinds of materials, reading machines, pacers, and tachistoscopes (a mechanical device that flashes a specific number of words on a screen for a governed period of time). Her students increased their academic achievement significantly, and as a result she found that their attitudes toward school had improved.

Two administrators, Ernest Choyce and Loyce Nute, initiated a special program for retraining thirty-eight elementary school teachers in Morehouse Parish, La. They also converted a traditional academic program into an individualized program that rewards students for achievement.

Linda Bourgeois, a special education teacher in Vicksburg, Miss., initiated a success-oriented program to produce positive self-concepts in handicapped students by demonstrating techniques for teaching students to acquire feelings of pride of accomplishment and heightened aspiration levels. She was particularly successful in changing the attitudes of her colleagues toward children needing special education.

The Action Research Committee in Lake Village, Ark., consisting of several LIFT participants, instituted for all the teachers in the public school system an elaborate in-service training program to investigate problems related to school desegregation.

Joan Minor, language arts teacher in Vicksburg, Miss., constructed a black studies program for the sixth grade that provided special packets of materials to help black students and white students learn about Negro culture. In addition to using materials she prepared herself, she assigned her class group projects to collect contemporary information about Negro culture.

Sue Breland, a special education teacher at J. B. Cooley Hospital in West Monroe, La., instituted a special program for mentally handicapped children from economically disadvantaged families. The fifteen children in her class practiced basic social, academic, and physical skills and thereby improved both their emotional and physical fitness.

Each of these demonstration projects has its own story. Each participant approached a problem differently and planned a unique attack. Each program now stands on its own base and is vigorously engaged in promoting better education for the disadvantaged. Project LIFT is no longer in existence, but through such demonstrations, the scope of its influence has widened and its spirit is continuing.

Major Outcomes

Behind each of the purposes of Projects LIFT was the necessity for changing the way black and white teachers, pupils, administrators, and nonschool people look upon one another. Faulty interpersonal perception generates negative interpersonal interaction. Such a project starts with candid acknowledgment that the pressing needs of our time demand that each person (teacher, administrator, pupil, parent, or citizen) cooperate to produce a learning environment free of impediments for all America's children.

Today, a significant number of black teachers and white teachers are effectively teaching black children and white children together, and experiencing commendably harmonious relationships in schools of the Ark-La-Miss region. Some say it is a "great pretense" that will soon blow up in the form of interracial squabbles. However, some very fruitful results have already accrued. It is now the responsibility of the participants to continue the promotion of good teaching in integrated schools.

CHAPTER 15

TEACHING WORD RECOGNITION
TO DISADVANTAGED BOYS
WITH DIFFERENCES IN AUDITORY
AND VISUAL SKILLS*

ROBERT H. BRUININKS

• •

Method
Subjects
Instructional Program
Results
Supplementary Analyses
Discussion
Implications for Research
References

• •

M ANY CHILDREN ENCOUNTER great difficulty in reading under prevailing methods of teaching. Surveys of large school populations indicate that the prevalence of children with a reading difficulty ranges between 10 and 30 per cent (Malmquist, 1958). The problem of reading retardation among disadvantaged children is particularly acute; reading failure among children of lower socioeconomic status is abut four to ten times the rate reported for the rest of the school population (Chandler, 1966).

---

*The research reported herein was supported by grants to George Peabody College for Teachers from the National Institute of Child Health and Human Development (HD-973) and the Ford Foundation under the auspices of the Nashville Educational Improvement Project. The article is a partial summary of a doctoral dissertation completed under the direction of Professor Lloyd M. Dunn at George Peabody College for Teachers. The author also wishes to acknowledge the many helpful suggestions of Professor Raymond C. Norris.

Attempts to identify the factors related to early reading failure in children have been numerous. Among the more persistently mentioned causes of reading problems are deficiencies in auditory and visual perceptual skills. Many studies report significant correlations between these skills and measures of reading in the primary grades (Smith and Dechant, 1961). Moreover, on measures of auditory and visual perception, the evidence indicates also that poor readers are often inferior to good readers of comparable mental ability (Bruininks, 1969).

In comparison to more advantaged peers, children of low socioeconomic status are inferior in a variety of auditory and visual perceptual skills (Buktenica, 1966; Deutsch, 1964). Since the evidence consistently reveals the coexistence of a high prevalence of perceptual problems and reading problems among the disadvantaged, the difficulty they experience in learning to read may develop as a consequence of pronounced deficits in one or both of the critical sensory modes required for the normal acquisition of language skills.

Methods of teaching which ignore the perceptual strengths or deficits of disadvantaged children are likely to magnify the difficulty they encounter in attempting to develop reading skills. Yet current reading instruction ignores the perceptual abilities of children, while continuing to place an inordinate emphasis upon global differences in verbal ability. Although a few educators have given attention recently to the matter of teaching reading to children with different perceptual aptitudes, much confusion still remains concerning the efficacy and implementation of this approach. Bannatyne (1967), for example, recommends for certain types of reading problems that instruction be tailored to the child's sense modality weakness (e.g. auditory weakness/ Gillingham Method, Color Phonics). Conversely, others advise that initial reading instruction be matched to the child's perceptual strengths and combined with supportive training on skills in the weak sense modality (Johnson and Myklebust, 1967).

In a few retrospective studies evidence has been obtained which suggests the presence of an interaction between perceptual strengths and approaches to teaching reading (Bond, 1935; Fendrick, 1935; de Hirsch, Jansky and Langford, 1966). More direct, prospective investigations dealing with this question have found that no appreciable advantage accrues from matching methods of teaching to auditory and visual perceptual aptitudes of children (Bateman, 1967; Harris, 1965; Robinson, 1968). Unfortunately, past studies have contained a number of methodological limitations, including (1) very limited assessment of perceptual skills; (2) use of groups with average and/or above average intelligence with inconsequential differences in perceptual abilities; (3) insufficient control for differences in teacher effectiveness; and (4) employment of teaching approaches which did not differ enough in instructional emphasis to test adequately the relationship of matching teaching methods to the perceptual characteristics of children.

From a consideration of research on perception and reading, it would seem efficacious to group children for early reading instruction according to their perceptual aptitudes. If a student is deficient in visual perception and memory skills, for example, the teacher might use either instructional techniques which stimulate this deficit, or ignore it by building upon auditory perceptual strengths. Such grouping might especially facilitate the development of reading skills among children from disadvantaged environments—a group which is particularly predisposed to develop perceptual and reading deficiencies.

In order to adequately assess the efficacy of matching teaching procedures to the perceptual aptitudes of children, it is necessary to alter the methodological approaches employed in past research studies. Taking into account the limitations of past investigations, the present study employed (1) a comprehensive battery of tests to identify subjects with differing auditory or visual perceptual abilities; (2) a sample comprised of educationally disadvantaged boys (a group with a propensity to develop significant perceptual and reading difficulties); and (3) teaching procedures in which the subjects were taught to recognize lists of unknown words under controlled teaching conditions. It was predicted that providing reading approaches consistent with the auditory or visual perceptual strengths of

disadvantaged boys would facilitate their learning to recognize
and retain a list of unknown words.

TABLE 15-I

TESTS MEASURING PERCEPTUAL COMPONENTS OF EARLY READING

Perceptual Abilities Measured	*Names of Tests*	
	VISUAL	AUDITORY
Fine discrimination of likenesses and differences	Perceptual Speed (Primary Mental Abilities)	Wepman Auditory Discrimination Test (signal only)
Perception of figure from ground; freedom from distraction	Children's Embedded Figures Test	Wepman Auditory Discrimination Test (signal plus noise)
Sequential memory for discrete units	Visual-Motor Sequencing (Illinois Test of Psycholinguistic Abilities)	Digit Span (Wechsler Intelligence Scale for Children)
(a) Blending—ability to synthesize discrete units into a perceptual gestalt; or (b) Closure—ability to predict a whole from a part	Visual Automatic	Roswell-Chall Auditory Blending Test
Ability to retain a perceptual gestalt (whole), or meaningful material	Memory-For-Designs	Auditory Attention Span for Related Syllables (Detroit Tests of Learning Aptitude)
Ability to match auditory or visual temporal stimuli with visual stimuli arranged spatially	Visual Integration Test	Auditory Integration Test

METHOD*

Instruments for Measuring Perception: Each subject was administered a comprehensive battery of six auditory and six visual
perception tests. On the basis of research and theory in the
area of early reading instruction, the tests selected were those

---

*A more detailed description of the subjects, procedures and rationale underlying the choice of tests can be obtained from the author or the Institute on Mental Retardation, George Peabody College for Teachers, Nashville, Tennessee.

which measured auditory and visual perceptual abilities considered essential to the development of early reading skills. Moreover, an attempt was made to match the tests across modalities so that they measured the same, or similar perceptual attributes (see Table 15-I). The tests were administered to each subject in the order discussed below.

Visual-Motor Sequencing (McCarthy and Kirk, 1961): This assesses the subject's ability to reproduce a sequence of visual stimuli from memory.

Perceptual Speed (Thurstone and Thurstone, 1963): This measures the rapid visual recognition of likenesses and differences between objects and symbols.

Auditory Attention Span for Related Syllables (Baker and Leland, 1967): This test measures short-term memory for sentences.

Visual Automatic (Kass, 1962): This is a measure of visual perceptual closure.

Memory-For-Designs (Graham and Kendall, 1960): This test measures visual-motor memory.

Children's Embedded Figures Test (Karp and Kornstadt, 1963): This measures the ability involved in perceiving a simple geometric figure embedded in a complex one.

Digit Span (Wechsler, 1949): This test is an auditory measure of short-term memory of digits presented sequentially.

Wepman Auditory Discrimination Test (Wepman, 1958): This is designed to measure the ability to distinguish between the fine differences that exist among the phonemes used in English speech. For this test each subject received two alternate test forms on a Wollensak Model T-1500 tape recorder—one under a "signal only" condition, and the other under a "signal plus noise" condition. The signal plus noise condition was administered to assess the subject's ability to discriminate between speech sounds in the presence of distracting background noise which consisted of voices recorded in a college cafeteria.

Roswell-Chall Auditory Blending Test (Roswell and Chall, 1963:) This assesses the ability to synthesize separate speech sounds into whole words.

Perceptual Integration Tests (Sterritt and Rudnick, 1966): These measure the ability to match a temporal code received via the sense modalities of audition or vision with a visual and spatially arranged dot pattern. On the Auditory Integration Test, temporal code patterns consisted of pure tones; in the Visual Integration Test, the temporal patterns were presented in the form of light flashes. Following the presentation of a temporal code, the subject was instructed to choose a configuration from three sets of visual-spatial dot sequences which looked like the pattern that had just been presented. Each test was preceded by detailed instructions and six practice exercises.

SUBJECTS

The total subject pool consisted of 105 boys, with a mean Stanford-Binet I.Q. of 90 ($s = 10.25$) and a range of 70 to 110. All subjects were reported to have possessed adequate auditory and visual acuity, according to Head Start medical examinations, school records, or teacher reports. The subjects had a mean chronological age of eight years, seven months, and a mean grade equivalent score of 2.74 ($s = .82$) on the three reading subtests of the Metropolitan Achievement Tests, Elementary Battery. The sample was selected from among thirty-two classrooms in eight schools of the Public Schools of Metropolitan Nashville-Davidson County, Tennessee. The subjects had participated recently in a two-year experimental reading and language development project designed to assess the efficacy of three phonically oriented reading approaches and an oral language stimulation program in the first two elementary grades. According to indices of socioeconomic status and ratings by school personnel, the subjects were considered to be economically disadvantaged.

Auditory and visual perceptual dominance groups were established by administering to each subject the perceptual tests listed in Table 15-I. To identify subjects with auditory or visual perceptual strengths, the raw scores of each test were converted into standard scores. Negative scores were eliminated by applying a linear transformation to each standard score, using a mean of fifty and standard deviation of ten. The sum of standard scores for the auditory tests was subtracted from the sum of standard scores for the visual tests (i.e. V-A). Subjects whose difference scores were in the upper 25 per cent of the distribution were designated as subjects with *visual perceptual dominance,* while those whose differences were in the lower 25 per cent were classified as subjects with *auditory perceptual dominance.* Following this procedure, groups were established which had (1) strengths in visual perception and weaknesses in auditory perception, or (2) strengths in auditory perception and weaknesses in visual perception. The original visual and auditory perceptual dominance groups each contained twenty-six subjects. Six auditory and two visual perceptual dominance subjects were eliminated from the study because they did not miss enough words to undertake the word learning task. A further deletion of subjects was made in the visual dominance group in order to satisfy the criterion of proportionality for the analysis of variance. The final sample size in each perceptual dominance group was twenty subjects.

Tests of significance between the perceptual dominance groups indicated that the two groups did not differ significantly on mean reading grade equivalent scores of the Metropolitan Achievement Tests, Stanford-Binet I.Q. or CA. As anticipated, both groups were significantly inferior on the perception test performance in their weak sense modality. Moreover, the visual dominance subjects were significantly superior to those in the auditory group on visual perception test score ($p < .001$), while auditory dominance subjects obtained significantly higher auditory perception test scores ($p < .001$).

INSTRUCTIONAL PROGRAM

Each subject was taught to recognize fifteen unknown words by a visual or sight-word teaching procedure, and fifteen unknown words by an auditory or phonic method. The teaching procedures were taken primarily from the Mills Learning Methods Test (Mills, 1964). The Mills Test consists of four sets of 2-by-4-inch picture-word cards (nouns)—one set each for the primer, first, second, and third grade reading levels. Ordinarily the words within only one grade level are administered to the child in order to identify a specified number of unknown words. The child is then taught to recognize a subset of these words according to four different standardized teaching approaches.

Two alterations were made in the standardized procedures of the Mills Test as a result of a pilot study and extensive field testing. First, certain steps were deleted from the Auditory and Visual Methods: The final teaching procedures for these two methods each included five different steps. Under the visual teaching method, each subject was taught to recognize fifteen unknown words according to procedures which emphasized association of the word with a picture, configurational outline of the word, and other visual characteristics such as length, and so forth. In the auditory method, subjects were taught to recognize a set of fifteen unknown words according to teaching procedures which stressed sounds of the individual letters, and to blend the individual sounds into a whole word. The second procedural change involved increasing the difficulty level of the Mills Test for third grade boys by increasing the number of words taught in each approach from ten to fifteen. This change in procedure necessitated the addition of a number of words (nouns) from the Thorndike and Lorge 30,000 Word List (Thorndike and Lorge, 1944).

Two female instructors were trained to administer the modified Mills Learning Methods Test. Both instructors had some experience in teaching as well as in the administration of psychometric tests. Instructors saw each modality strength subject for a total of three or four sessions. On the first session, a pretest was administered to each subject to identify between thirty and forty unknown words out of a possible total of 205 words. The unknown words were then shuffled and a minimum of fifteen to twenty words were assigned randomly to each of the two teaching approaches. Subjects were taught to recognize each list in a 23-minute lesson, spending approximately one and a half minutes on each word. Following the teaching lessons, the amount of learning was assessed by an immediate recall test.

The second session took place one week later when a measure

of delayed recall was secured by testing again the ability of each pupil to read aloud the same list of fifteen study words. Following the recall test, the second list of fifteen words was then taught to the child using the second teaching procedure. (In a few instances, it was impossible to administer the second teaching lesson immediately following the administration of the delayed recall measure. Thus, it was necessary in these cases to administer the second teaching lesson within a few days of the recall test.) The amount of learning for the second teaching session was also assessed by the administration of an immediate and delayed recall test on the study words. On both of the tests, the fifteen study words were administered in random order among twenty distractors selected at random from the original list of 205 words. The learning criteria consisted of the number of study words recognized correctly on the immediate and delayed recall tests under each teaching method.

The order of the teaching methods was randomized across subjects with the restriction that both orders were represented equally within each perceptual dominance group (i.e. A to V and V to A). Whenever it was feasible, the instructors were assigned randomly to schools with the restriction that they had to teach the same number of subjects within each order of presentation and teaching method combination.

RESULTS

Statistical analyses on the immediate and delayed recall scores were conducted by an analysis of variance (perceptual dominance x length of retention x teaching method x order of teaching presentation). Means and standard deviations on Mills Test scores for the perceptual dominance groups appear in Table 15-II. Descriptive statistics for the immediate and delayed recall measures and the methods of teaching for the total group of forty subjects appear in Table 15-III.

The analysis of variance on Mills Test scores for the auditory and visual perceptual dominance groups is in Table 15-IV. Examination of Table 15-IV indicates the presence of a sig-

TABLE 15-II

DESCRIPTIVE STATISTICS ON MILLS TEST SCORES FOR THE
PERCEPTUAL DOMINANCE GROUPS

Source	Visually Dominant (N = 20)		Auditorily Dominant (N = 20)		Mean Difference
	X	s	X	s	
Visual Method					
Immediate Recall[a]	7.10	5.17	9.00	4.60	—1.90
Delayed Recall[b]	5.65	5.59	7.95	4.70	—2.30
Total	6.38	5.25	8.48	4.57	—2.10
Auditory Method					
Immediate Recall[a]	6.65	5.29	8.30	4.31	—1.65
Delayed Recall[b]	5.50	4.88	7.25	4.44	—1.75
Total	6.08	5.02	7.78	4.27	—1.70
Totals	6.22	5.18	8.12	4.47	—1.90

[a]Recognition of unknown words immediately following instruction
[b]Recognition of unknown words exactly one week after instruction

TABLE 15-III

DESCRIPTIVE STATISTICS FOR RETENTION INTERVALS
AND METHODS OF TEACHING

Source	N	X	s
Immediate Recall[a]	40	7.76	4.86
Delayed Recall[a]	40	6.59	4.94
Visual Method[b]	40	7.42	4.97
Auditory Method[b]	40	6.93	4.68

[a]Computed over both methods of teaching
[b]Computed over both retention intervals

nificant effect only for length of retention. The mean of the
immediate recall test scores was significantly higher than that
obtained on the one-week delayed recall test ($p < .001$). The
other comparisons involving perceptual dominance groups,
methods of teaching, and order of teaching presentation failed
to reach statistical significance. The mean difference between the
auditory, and visual methods, however, approached statistical
significance ($p = .06$). Table 15-III reveals that the visual
method of teaching resulted in higher performance scores over

TABLE 15-IV

ANALYSIS OF VARIANCE ON MILLS TEST SCORES FOR THE
PERCEPTUAL DOMINANT GROUPS

Source	N	Sum of Square	Mean Square	F-ratio	F.95
Between Subjects	39	3457.600			
Perceptual Dominance (A)	1	144.400	144.400	1.58	4.11
CD	1	15.625	15.625	.17	4.11
ACD	1	15.625	15.625	.17	4.11
Error Between Groups	36	3281.950	91.165		
Within Subjects	120	389.500			
Retention (B)	1	55.225	55.225	18.86*	3.94
Method (C)	1	10.000	10.000	3.42	3.94
Order (D)	1	0.900	0.900	.31	3.94
AB	1	1.600	1.600	.55	3.94
AC	1	0.625	0.625	.21	3.94
AD	1	1.600	1.600	.55	3.94
BC	1	0.225	0.225	.08	3.94
BD	1	0.000	0.000	.00	3.94
ABC	1	0.225	0.225	.08	3.94
ABD	1	1.600	1.600	.55	3.94
BCD	1	1.225	1.225	.42	3.94
ABCD	1	0.025	0.025	.01	3.94
Error Within Groups	108	316.250	2.928		
Total	159	3847.100			

*$p < .001$

both retention intervals. Contrary to prediction, the interaction
between perceptual dominance and method of teaching did not
reach statistical significance. Finally, none of the other interactions involving the attributes of perceptual dominance, methods
of teaching, length of retention interval, or order of presentation
attained statistical significance.

SUPPLEMENTARY ANALYSES

Post hoc analyses were conducted on the Mills Test scores
of the ten auditory and ten visual dominance subjects with
more extreme differences in auditory and visual perception test
scores. In this analysis, the attributes of order of presentation
and length of retention interval were ignored. (The perceptual
dominance groups did contain the same proportion of subjects in

each of the two orders of presentation.) This analysis again confirmed the earlier one in that no significant difference in performance was obtained between the two perceptual dominance groups, and the interaction between perceptual dominance and methods of teaching was not significant. However, the auditory and visual dominance subjects combined had significantly higher scores under the visual method of teaching, in contrast to those obtained under the auditory or phonic approach ($p < .01$).

DISCUSSION

The results of the present study failed to support the prediction that the use of teaching methods consistent with the auditory and visual perceptual strengths of disadvantaged boys would facilitate their learning to recognize and retain a list of unknown words. The findings revealed that the subjects learned to recognize unknown words equally well under teaching procedures which matched either their perceptual strengths or their perceptual weaknesses.

This suggests that the matching of visually or auditorily oriented methods of teaching to the perceptual abilities of disadvantaged children in the *upper primary grades* has limited utility as an approach to corrective or remedial reading. Support for this generalization also comes from supplementary correlational analyses (Bruininks, 1969). Correlations between the auditory and visual perception tests and reading achievement were low to moderate in magnitude, suggesting that the influence of perceptual abilities upon the development of reading skills *at this age level* may not be of sufficient importance to predict learning under different approaches to instruction. Failure to obtain an interaction between perceptual dominance and teaching approaches, however, was consistent with the results of previous studies by Bateman (1967), Harris (1965), and Robinson (1968) with first-grade children. Evidence suggests that reading methods which teach to the perceptual strengths or weaknesses of children neither facilitate nor deter the development of word recognition skills.

Contrary to prediction, perceptual dominance groups in both

the primary and supplementary analyses demonstrated greater learning under the visual teaching method. Evidence of superior performance under this approach was obtained in the supplementary anlysis on subjects with more extreme differences in auditory and visual perception scores; the difference between the two teaching methods in the primary analysis only approached statistical significance.

In an attempt to account for the seemingly inconsistent results between the two analyses, additional comparisons were made between the more extreme perceptual dominance group and those subjects with less discrepant perceptual scores on I.Q., reading achievement, and socioeconomic status. While the two groups were comparable in I.Q. and in reading ability, subjects with more extreme perception test scores rated significantly lower with regard to the educational level of the better educated parent (10.35 vs. 11.42 grades; $p < .05$). No significant differences were obtained between groups on income level or quality of housing, however. Since educational level is probably a more sensitive index of socioeconomic status for this sample, subjects in the more extreme perceptual dominance groups may have been more educationally disadvantaged. Possibly subtle effects of past experiential history (i.e. amount of environmental enrichment) were more important than perceptual abilities in influencing performance under the two methods of instruction. However, the findings represented in the supplementary analyses may merely represent statistical artifacts attributable to the non-normal distribution of the learning scores or the use of multiple analyses on the same subjects.

Superior performance under the visual teaching approach is particularly noteworthy, in light of the fact that the subjects had been exposed to systematic training in phonics during the first and second grades. These results are congruent, however, with the findings of recent studies dealing with the perceptual and learning characteristics of disadvantaged children. On a serial learning task, Katz and Deutsch (1964) found a visual presentation superior to both an auditory and an alternating auditory-visual presentation for disadvantaged Negro boys. Hill and

Hecker (1966) found no significant differences in learning performance under auditory and visual modes of presentation with a group composed largely of middle-class children. The findings of these studies are supported by an increasing accumulation of evidence indicating the existence of pronounced auditory perceptual deficits among disadvantaged children (Deutsch, 1964). It appears that the weight of reported evidence suggests that the disadvantaged learn more efficiently when verbal material is presented visually. Development of visual strengths among disadvantaged children probably evolves from long-term exposure to an environmental milieu in which the signal-to-noise ratio is nearly equal (Deutsch, 1964). Excessive background noise of many lower class homes may encourage an orientation toward developing structure and order through concentration upon visual experiences. However, poorer performance of disadvantaged children as measures of auditory perceptual functioning may be in part a result of differences in dialect patterns between child and examiner, rather than any factors inherent in their perceptual abilities or style.

IMPLICATIONS FOR RESEARCH

Although the present study instituted improvements in methodology over similar studies, it was nevertheless subject to a number of limitations. First, the subjects may have possessed confirmed reading habits after three years of school experience which were more influential than perceptual characteristics in determining performance on the criterion task. Past reading experience, moreover, undoubtedly served to reduce original auditory and visual perceptual differences among subjects, thereby obfuscating any potential relationship between methods of teaching and sense modality dominance. Second, groups were selected on the basis of discrepancies on composite auditory and visual perceptual test scores. The selection criteria might have been made more stringent by requiring *consistent* superiority on tests reflecting modality strength and inferiority on those indicative of perceptual weakness. Finally, the instructional program was found to be too short in duration for some subjects. Inspection of the immediate and delayed recall scores revealed a sizable proportion of the subjects attained either very high or very low scores in both methods of teaching. The foregoing methodological limitations suggest the need to replicate the present study with an extended instructional program among nonreading disadvantaged children at the kindergarten and first-grade levels.

In recent years, the diagnostic model of teaching has been recommended for the amelioration of learning difficulties. The validity of the clinical teaching model rests upon the questionable premise that the diagnostic devices truly reflect critical correlates of reading performance. Unless diagnostic devices possess demonstrated validity, fundamental changes in reading performance will seldom accompany the remediation of deficit areas of functioning. Well-controlled investigations are urgently needed to assess the value of clinical teaching approaches in amelioration of learning difficulties, along with parallel efforts to develop specific diagnostic aptitude tests.

Future research should also endeavor to determine the effects of differential environmental backgrounds upon the development of linguistic and perceptual abilities in disadvantaged children. Efforts to eradicate any identifiable perceptual and linguistic deficits of the disadvantaged through systematic training and studies of the effects of such training on the development of early reading abilities should continue to receive emphasis in compensatory education programs. Perhaps careful sequencing of reading experiences and training in deficit areas of behavioral functioning will lead to an appreciable reduction in the prevalence of reading failure among the "one in three" who are considered educationally disadvantaged.

REFERENCES

Baker, H. J. and Leland, B.: *Detroit Tests of Learning Aptitude. Examiner's Handbook.* Indianapolis: Bobbs, 1967.

Bannatyne, A.: Matching Remedial Methods with Specific Deficits. Paper presented at the 1967 International Convention on Children and Young Adults with Learning Disabilities. Pittsburgh Home for Crippled Children, 1967.

Bateman, B.: The efficacy of an auditory and a visual method of first-grade reading instruction with auditory and visual learners. *Curriculum Bulletin,* 23:6-14, 1967 (Publ. at Eugene, University of Oregon, the School of Education).

Bond, G. L.: The auditory and speech characteristics of poor readers. *Teachers College Contributions to Education,* 1935, no. 657.

Bruininks, R. H.: Auditory and visual perceptual skills related to the reading performance of disadvantaged boys. *Percept Mot Skills,* 29:179-186, 1969.

Buktenica, N. A.: Relative contributions of auditory and visual perception to first-grade language learning. Unpublished doctoral dissertation, University of Chicago, 1966.

Chandler, T. A.: Reading disability and socioeconomic status. *J Reading,* 10:5-21, 1966.

de Hirsch, K., Jansky, J. J. and Langford, W. S.: *Predicting Reading Failure, a Preliminary Study.* New York, Har-Row, 1966.

Deutsch, C. P.: Auditory discrimination and learning: Social factors. *Merrill-Palmer Quarterly,* 10:277-296, 1964.

Fendrick, P.: Visual characteristics of poor readers. *Teachers College Contributions to Education,* 1935, no. 656.

Graham, F. F. and Kendall, B. S.: Memory-For-Designs Test: Revised general manual. *Percept Mot Skills,* 11:147-188, 1960.

Harris, A. J.: Individualizing first-grade reading according to specific learning aptitudes. Research Report. Office of Research and Evaluation, City University of New York, 1965.

Hill, S. D. and Hecker, E.: Auditory and visual learning of a paired-associate task by second grade children. *Percept Mot Skills,* 23:814, 1966.

Johnson, D. J. and Myklebust, H. R.: *Learning Disabilities: Educational Principles and Practices.* New York, Grune, 1967.

Karp, S. A. and Kornstadt, N. L.: *Manual for the Children's Embedded Figures Test.* New York, Cognitive Test, 1963.

Kass, C.: Some psychological correlates of severe reading disability. Unpublished doctoral dissertation, Urbana, University of Illinois, 1962.

Katz, P. A. and Deutsch, M.: Modality of stimulus presentation in serial learning for retarded and normal readers. *Percept Mot Skills,* 19:627-633, 1964.

Malmquist, E.: *Factors Related to Reading Disabilities in the First Grade of the Elementary School.* Stockholm, Sweden, Almqvist and Wiksell, 1958.

McCarthy, J. J. and Kirk, S. A.: *The Illinois Test of Psycholinguistic Abilities.* Experimental Edition. Urbana, Institute for Research on Exceptional Children, University of Illinois, 1961.

Mills, R. E.: The teaching of word recognition, including the manual of directions for the Learning Methods Test. Fort Lauderdale, The Mills Center, 1964.

Robinson, H. M.:, Visual and auditory modalities related to two methods for beginning reading. In Hausdorff, H. (Ed.): *A.E.R.A. Paper Abstracts.* Washington, D. C., American Educational Research Association, 1968.

Roswell, F. G. and Chall, J. A.: *Roswell-Chall Auditory Blending Test* New York, Essay Press, 1963.

Smith, H. P. and Dechant, E. V.: *Psychology in Teaching Reading.* Englewood Cliffs. P-H, 1961.

Sterritt, G. M. and Rudnick, M.: Auditory and visual rhythm perception in relation to reading ability in fourth grade boys. *Percept Mot Skills,* 22:859-864, 1966.

Thorndike, E. L. and Lorge, I.: *The Teacher's Word Book of 30,000 Words.* New York, Bureau of Publications, Teachers College, Columbia University, 1944.

Thurstone, L. L. and Thurstone, T. G.: *Examiner's Manual, PMA, Primary Mental Abilities, for Grades 2-4.* Chicago, Science Research Associates, 1963.

Wechsler, D.: *Wechsler Intelligence Scale for Children,* WISC manual. New York, Psychological Corporation, 1949.

Wepman, J. M.: *Auditory Discrimination Test.* Chicago, University of Chicago, 1958.

CHAPTER 16

PHILADELPHIA SCHOOL-WORK PROGRAM FOR DISADVANTAGED YOUTH*

Saul S. Leshner

I T IS LIKELY that the youngster reared in an urban black ghetto will spend much of his school career in trying to cope with an education that is unrelated to life as he knows it. These young people are beset by, and endure, poverty, inferior housing, dependency, crime, illegitimacy, and poor nutrition. They usually find little meaning in reading, writing, and arithmetic, the basis of all modern vocational education and training. School may thus be viewed as irrelevant and of little value in dealing with day-to-day problems of survival.

Furthermore, a limited background of experience, no less than that available in the rural areas and back country, equips the ghetto resident poorly for formal learning of middle-class material. His "cultural alienation" leads to continuing low achievement or failure. And if his behavior is disruptive, his learning slow, or his interests mainly outside the school, he may be classed as retarded, a behavior problem, or unmotivated, and his education oriented accordingly.

This was the dilemma that concerned the Philadelphia public school system when, in 1965, it joined the Jewish Employment and Vocational Service in a three-year study of disadvantaged and disabled high school students, under an SRS grant.

The main purposes of the study were to determine the nature

---

*Reprinted by permission of the *Rehabilitation Record*, September-October, 1969, vol. 10, no. 5, pp. 31-33.

of the educational disabilities manifested by disabled and disadvantaged pupils, and to devise possible remedies. From the study could be developed revisions in school curricula and instructional methods which, if applied early, would prevent or at least reduce these problems.

The magnitude and urgency of the problem of maladjusted youth, however, demanded that the study incorporate practical rehabilitation objectives. The project therefore also undertook to help the students to continue in school with better success or, if dropping out seemed inevitable, to prepare them for entering and maintaining training and employment.

A total of 276 students (176 boys and 100 girls) were referred from both special classes and regular grades. They ranged from sixteen to eighteen years of age and had been classified by the schools as mentally retarded, emotionally disturbed, or as having a personality disorder. Their "disadvantaged" status was reflected in the fact that over 95 per cent lived in Negro ghettos in North Philadelphia. About 55 per cent of the families received public assistance; half had no male adult in the home. Over 40 per cent of the project students had court records and 34 per cent were members of fighting gangs.

The procedure was to assign groups of forty pupils to school for half a day and to the JEVS Work Adjustment Center for half a day, for a full school year. The three schools which participated in the program were Thomas Edison, Benjamin Franklin, and Simon Gratz high schools. Counselors selected the students on the basis of overt learning and behavior problems, high truancy rate, and probability of dropping out of school.

In the home school two types of special instruction were given the pupils. They attended remedial classes staffed by special teachers and, in addition, received individual tutoring in English, arithmetic, and spelling. Effort was made to improve the realism of school subjects by linking reading and arithmetic to work processes; geography, history, and social studies to work products, distribution, the labor force, the consumer, technical factors, and so on.

School coordinators divided their time between the high schools and the JEVS Work Adjustment Center so as to maintain common effort between both institutions and assure attention to the individual pupil's needs. They met daily with each pupil to review progress and to provide tutoring and educational guidance. They also arranged for part-time work certificates for those who needed after-school or weekend work.

School coordinators also visited the pupil's homes occasionally to secure understanding and support. From the beginning, parents were actively involved in helping their children stay in school, and active solicitation of their participation produced a parents' organization that included many who had never joined the PTA.

At the JEVS center a variety of services were provided. It was considered that a systematic, organized work experience would improve behavior and work patterns. The pupils would not only learn through directed activity and experience to harness their energies, but would also form a sense of identity with work they could perform successfully, and thus would begin to establish vocational goals. Further, they would learn from experience that if they wanted to stay in the program they had to conform to basic rules and regulations, account for every lateness or absence from school or the center, and otherwise exhibit effort to adjust to program requirements.

The first three weeks were devoted mainly to educational and vocational evaluation of each student. Again using activity as the basic method, evaluation was achieved through use of work samples and an exploratory production situation. Educational and psychological tests were used selectively, since many of the pupils had negative reactions to formal testing. Evaluation was aimed at assessing abilities, interests, and problem areas and also at trying to determine the extent to which various personal and social traits could be modified or reversed, or ways in which the behavior and performance of the pupil could be improved. From this kind of evaluation, a plan of redeveloping behavior and achievement capability could be formulated. During the evaluation the pupil was confronted with a variety of real experiences which permitted observation by the evaluator of his responsiveness and adjustability and also offered insight to himself as well.

It was immediately observed that most of the students had been misclassified by the schools. For example, 64 per cent had been assessed as mentally retarded, but JEVS evaluation revealed retardation in only 27 per cent of the cases. Most of the youth had greater latent intellectual power than they had exhibited in schools, but functioning was impaired by varied personality disorders.

Evaluation was followed by a guided work experience on live production, for which piece rate wages were paid. This phase of the program was primarily concerned with developing acceptable attitudes for work and systematic work patterns. Under supervision of industrial foremen, work assignments were initially simple and dealt with uncomplicated processes such as packaging, folding, and stamping.

Progressively the work became more difficult and complex, demanding greater coordination, dexterity, discrimination, and judgment related to qualitative output. At the same time, other pressures were gradually introduced to increase tolerance for the personal and social stresses of work. More emphasis was put upon personal grooming, punctuality in attendance, observations of rest breaks and schedules, and production efficiency.

During the production period, behavior and performance were observed by a counseling psychologist. He met with the students who presented special problems, in an office away from the production area. The counselor was able to help the pupil to express his difficulties and the meaning of his experiences and to re-address himself more effectively to the work situation.

Individual and group counseling were also available to each individual. Counseling dealt initially with personal and social adjustment; later, it was geared to more concrete vocational issues such as work performance and occupational planning. Case-work services involved help on such personal matters as grooming and personal hygiene, and related to problems of a social and parental nature.

Toward the end of the school year the vocational experience was sharpened by placing the students in a specialized work setting under a vocational trainer. The purpose of this phase of training was to enable the individual to become more intensely aware of the nature and requirements of work in such fields as the metal industries, warehousing, woodworking, tailoring, service stations, institutional maintenance, and services. This vocational training offered possibilities for occupational identification and also represented typical jobs the youngster might expect to enter when he left school.

It has been observed that many disadvantaged and handicapped youngsters tend to be unorganized in their behavior. These tendencies are sometimes described as impulsive, unstable, present-oriented, or unmotivated response patterns. It was to deal with these difficulties that close and continuing surveillance and consistent, prompt direction of each pupil were maintained.

Much of the learning of the disadvantaged is impaired because of a limited background, which results in vague perceptions or a lack of meaning of educational and vocational material. All of our remedial effort was designed for the individual at his level of ability and readiness for change. Also, staff members and VISTA volunteers would visit the home of the pupil who was absent without "calling in," to reengage him with the program.

The results of the project were generally effective in keeping the students in school. Two hundred seventy-six youths entered the program, but thirty-two were evaluated as not needing it and returned to school full time. Of the 241 actual cases, 191 completed the project, and of these, 112 continued in school. The seventy-nine who left school either were placed in employment (35) or entered vocational training programs (44). Teachers and counselors in the referring schools reported heightened motivation and achievement and lower truancy among the pupils in the JEVS program.

A follow-up of the fifty cases regarded as program failures showed that only three had actually obtained a full-time job. Most of them seemed unable to relate to authority or associates in their school or the work center, to tolerate structured activity, or to cope with work and study pressures. Perhaps more significant were their prevailing and unchanged low cultural values and low aspirations, attended by profound feelings of low worth and mistrust of official or helping agencies. It would seem that rehabilitation processes are yet to be devised for meeting these problems.

A number of implications and conclusions are derived from the JEVS experience:

— Intensive and systematic rehabilitation effort can help a large proportion of disabled ghetto youth to continue in school, benefit from education, and develop the personal and vocational identities needed for adjustment.

— Ghetto parents, properly approached, can and will participate in their child's rehabilitation.

— Incentives for educational and vocational development are inherent in successful achievement; money or economic need seem less motivating than they are commonly regarded, as attested by the fact that most of the pupils might have opted for the Neighborhood Youth Corps or other antipoverty programs where earnings were considerably higher than in our program.

It has become commonplace to observe that schools need more relevant curricula and pupil-centered instruction with flexibility in individual programing. This point was clearly reinforced by the project findings, particularly where community resources can be more fully incorporated in the educational process. Early identification of pupil problems, support in the form of remediation and counseling, and a realistic approach to learning in which adjustive behaviors are cultivated (as contrasted with primarily verbal or symbolic communication), are basic requirements for preventive as well as corrective rehabilitation.

In brief, it is considered that the depth of the problems presented by disabled and disadvantaged youth requires rehabilitative and educational procedures which embrace the efforts of a number of disciplines and supportive measures. We continue to need solutions for an array of problems, among them a clearer definition of the role of the school and rehabilitation counselor, a sharper specification of the physical facilities that house combined educational and rehabilitation programs, a reordered curriculum for primary grades that prepares the pupil to meet later educational and vocational standards, and—perhaps most important—a functional classification system that articulates the problems of individuals who may be educationally and vocationally handicapped in more than one way.

CHAPTER 17

HANDICAPPED YOUTHS LEARN
CHILD CARE*

Robert M. Hanson, Harriet Burger, and Robert Phillips

IN THE PAST TWO YEARS, 112 handicapped high school students—both boys and girls—in New York's Westchester County special education classes have benefited markedly from a course in infant care. So have the nine infants and toddlers who have received care in the course. So have the parents of the babies.

Child care is one of nine prevocational courses which were developed in 1968 by the Board of Cooperative Educational Services (BOCES). These courses are offered in half-day sessions each school day at the Fairview Center, a 12,000-square-foot facility at Elmsford, a northern suburb of New York City. The students spend the other half of the school day in special education classwork in their separate schools.

BOCES has been running special education programs for handicapped high school students for more than ten years, and it has been paying close attention to the interests and the needs of these special students. A few years ago, it became apparent that more occupationally oriented work was needed to maintain the interest of the special education students while they were in school and to give them a start toward employment after they finished school.

The Fairview Center came out of that conclusion. The center is staffed by teachers and aides, a social worker, psychologist,

---

*Reprinted by permission of *Rehabilitation Record,* 11:24-26, no. 6, November-December, 1970.

school nurse-teacher, and a vocational rehabilitation counselor. It accommodates an average of 150 exceptional students from seven high schools in its nine areas of training.

As one of its work-oriented courses, the child care program was developed at the center to help students to acquire the skills and concepts necessary for the proper care of infants in a family setting. The plan was that, in the process of giving this care, the students would learn about the stages in early child development. Traits of patience, attention to detail, and responsibility would be encouraged. A knowledge of good nutrition would be gained. Through practical experience, the students would learn to keep themselves well-groomed and to maintain cleanliness in the home.

These accomplishments would serve them personally and as a basis for possible future employment in the field of child care. They would experience success at each evidence of the babies' progress, since they would have contributed to it. It was hoped that the understanding and self-confidence that each student would gain through caring for an infant, would enrich not only the baby's life, but his own.

The students are selected from the general population of exceptional adolescent children served by BOCES. These are youngsters who are in special programs because of physical, mental, or emotional handicaps. Although comprehensive and sequential records are available on each child, no attempt is made to group them according to the nature of their problems. Classes for girls are formed solely on the basis of chronological age, and for boys on the basis of their interest.

The program is staffed by a school nurse-teacher and a teacher's aide. Its facilities are located on the first floor of the building and consist of a nursery, a bathroom, and a combination kitchen and classroom. There is a private entrance, which eliminates the necessity of bringing the babies in and out through the school.

Three babies are chosen each year from the community, with preference given to the youngest. It is preferable to have them as close as possible to six weeks old at the beginning of the term so that the students gain the widest range of experience.

We try to include both male and female babies. Total care, without charge, is offered to the infant during school hours. The parents' only responsibility is to provide transportation for the baby to and from school. In cases where the parents are unable to do this, arrangements can sometimes be made to have this service performed by community volunteers.

The course is planned to be eight weeks in length, but it is flexible and can be adjusted according to the needs of a particular group. The general plan, however, is to keep the same three babies for the entire school year and to change the groups of students every eight weeks. There are two sessions a day, one in the morning and one in the afternoon, with six students in each group. This ratio makes it possible to assign two students in each session to one particular baby. It has been found that in this way, the student develops a closer relationship with the infant and the baby is protected from indiscriminate handling.

The curriculum has evolved from the original goals and from the expressed interest of the students. It grows like an amoeba, by assimilating questions which are raised frequently. Still, it is only a guide; discussions branch off in many directions.

The course begins with theory and concepts. Here the students concern themselves with purposes and goals of the course, conception, pregnancy and delivery, adjustments and responsibilities involved in adding a new baby to the family, abnormal terminations of pregnancy, birth control, normal infant growth and development, nutrition, illness in babies, safety, and accident prevention. These subjects are dealt with formally in each session's half-hour class period and informally whenever appropriate to the activity in progress.

The development of practical skills is the focus of the second unit of study. Each student has an opportunity to become proficient at the myriad tasks involved in the daily care of an infant. Every procedure is first demonstrated by the teacher, followed by a return demonstration by each member of the group. Each student must practice with a doll until enough dexterity and confidence is developed to progress to the babies.

All tasks are performed under the close supervision of the nurse-teacher. The tasks include handling, carrying, dressing, feeding, and bathing babies, formula-making by use of the terminal sterilization method, reading thermometers, giving alcohol sponge baths, ordering groceries, maintaining cleanliness and sanitary conditions, making up cribs, folding diapers, care of the laundry, making a schedule, and keeping records.

The most important benefit the students derive from the program is the development of positive attitudes toward infants and infant raising, which will enrich their relationships with children.

Our approach involves encouraging development without forcing it, recognizing that self-discipline is a prerequisite to disciplining children, planning for discipline that will be constructive rather than punitive, realizing the sacrifices required for conscientious child-raising, respecting the uniqueness of every child, and appreciating that raising a child is a joyful and rewarding experience.

The program has had a noticeably favorable effect on the babies, their parents, and our students. The babies have thrived. Their physical improvements have been startling. Conditions such as chronic bronchitis, hypospadias, inguinal hernia, and blocked tear ducts have been corrected by having the school physician make the proper referrals. Such other problems as malnourishment, diaper rash, and cradle cap have been eliminated by working with the parents. The babies have responded well and have developed into alert, confident, and outgoing toddlers.

The parents appear to be pleased and appreciative of the care given to their children. They come to the nurse-teacher more and more freely for advice and suggestions. In its efforts to help the parents, the center develops closer ties with the various public and private service agencies and in this way becomes a more integral part of the community.

Most gratifying has been the effect the program has had on the students. The school's clinical staff—coordinators, psychiatrists, psychologists, and social workers—has reported that the students become less hostile to authority and more receptive to learning while in this program. In many cases, negative behavioral symptoms which a student has previously exhibited disappear in this course.

Motivation is very strong on the part of the students to acquire learning and skills, to control their behavior, and to accept responsibility for the infant assigned to them. One reason for this may be that the rewards are immediate, both in the responses of the infant and in the approval of peers and teachers.

The reactions of the boys have been most dramatic, as the babies have elicited from them uninhibited expressions of affection and tenderness. These relationships have been mutually beneficial, particularly for those babies who do not have a father living in the home and have not previously received any male attention.

Several of the students have subsequently been employed as teacher's aides in classes for young children, as attendants in the pediatrics wards of hospitals, as candy-stripers, and as mothers' helpers. Many more have shown an interest in working with children as a career. All the students have enjoyed the opportunity of doing for someone else.

One of the boys stated the consensus of the students succinctly. He said, "This course got to my feelings."

CHAPTER 18

A THERAPEUTIC APPROACH TO THE REHABILITATION OF THE YOUTHFUL DRUG ABUSER: THE SEED

JOHN G. CULL AND RICHARD E. HARDY

APPROXIMATELY TWO YEARS AGO, the SEED was founded in Fort Lauderdale, Florida, by Art and Shelly Barker. The basic design of the program is the general treatment model developed by Alcoholics Anonymous; however, there are several modalities which are peculiar to the SEED. The description which follows is basically an outline of the goals and methods of the program; however, certain intangibles which are difficult to describe exist in the program.

The SEED was developed because of a desperate need for help which existed for young people in the Fort Lauderdale area as a result of the heightened incidence of drug abuse. It was felt that new approaches to the problem were needed; therefore, the SEED concept evolved. The SEED program's concept was based on the premise that man can change his behavior and can live and cope in his environment. The young people who seek help from the SEED program learn that they can no longer *cop out* with drugs; but that they have daily problems and must learn to live with them. At the SEED, they obtain a sense of belonging to something meaningful along with the knowledge that they can find purpose in their lives with the extra ingredient—a sense of dedication toward helping themselves and helping others to help themselves. The primary function of the SEED program is to provide rehabilitative services for the young person who has become a drug experimenter, user, abuser, or addict.

204

Application Criteria

The SEED is made available to anyone needing help. The addict who must have some sort of maintenance—such as methadone—to assist him in achieving detoxification will not be accepted by the SEED until such time as he is able to tolerate a truly *cold turkey* program of abstinence. Since its main program is not detoxification, the aim is to work with the experimenter, user, abuser, or addict who has used drugs less than ten years. Because of the age range—nine years to early twenties—parental consent of the majority of applicants is needed.

Anyone in need of detoxification treatment and seeking help from the SEED is referred to the appropriate facilities. Those applicants who are in need of medical attention are referred to appropriate hospitals and/or their private physicians. These young people then come back to the SEED program once they are considered to be in sound medical health. Other than these selected criteria, the SEED makes no distinction concerning participation in the program.

Physical discomfort of *withdrawal* is at a minimum among participants. Even those young people who have used heroin for two or more years and have $200-a-day habits (this is equivalent to $60 to $65 in New York) take only approximately three days to pass through the withdrawal symptoms.

Background of the Program Participants

A unique factor of the SEED program is that it reaches into the schools. In this community, estimates show that between 70 and 85 per cent of the children are experimenting with, using, or abusing drugs. The SEED has been successful in reaching young people through referrals made by principals, teachers, and counselors of the various schools in Broward County. The apparent change in students using drugs such as the decline of grades, failures, and dropouts, along with attitude change has added to the frustration and dilemma of educators. Due to the referrals made by educators to the SEED program, the majority of the young people destined to become delinquents and burdens on society have been able to continue in school education and to aid teachers in understanding the drug problems of the young. The young abuser is of considerable help in helping other drug abusers since he understands not only the values but also the language of the drug culture (Hardy and Cull, 1972).

Many young people, no matter how well they progress, have environmental backgrounds which are quite impossible for them in terms of adjustment. If there is no reinforcement from the family, the young person will constantly meet with disappointment and discouragement. For those young people in this particular situation, the SEED has been able to assist with the cooperation of either the courts and/or various agencies (vocational rehabilitation, family services, etc.) in obtaining foster homes and has been successful in continuing to work with them in their new environments.

Service Delivery System

The first phase of the SEED's program consists, in most cases, of a two-week program of intensive group discussions but is expandable when needed. During this two-week period, the group discussion sessions average approximately twelve hours per day. In these sessions, the participant is aided in gaining insight into what he is and what he has done to his life by taking drugs; but more importantly, he learns what his life can be for him and the impact he can have on others if he is *straight*. These two weeks represent the equivalent in time of the participant's going to a psychologist and/or psychiatrist for a period of three years on a one-hour, once-a-week basis. The fourteen-day intensive group sessions provide a radical and comprehensive change which facilitates the learning process of the participant. The SEED is operated on a continuous seven-day basis. The participant in this fourteen-day program is at the SEED from 10 a.m. to 10 p.m., during which time he is involvel constantly in *rap* sessions under the supervision of staff. These rap sessions are carefully guided and the intensity is maintained at a controlled, effective level. When necessary for certain individual needs, *rap* sessions also are held on a one-to-one basis with a staff member.

Upon successful completion of this first phase, an additional three-month period ensues which requires the participant to attend four group sessions a week. This phase of the program offers practical application of his learning processes. He learns to function and cope in his environment while returning to the group involvement. The criteria of success of this program are based not only on the fact that the young person is drug free, but also on his attitude change toward life; that is, there is a love of self and others, community and country, and a sense of dedication to help his fellowman.

Due to the age of participants, they can adjust well to change. The amount of attitude change in the individual seems to indicate that the three-month period is quite effective. In some instances, individuals require either an extension of the two-week period or an extension of the three-month program. Periodic follow-up is done to see how the participants are doing.

If the participant learns well and grasps the meaning of honesty, love, respect, discipline, and affection, there is no need for him to go back to drugs. For the young people who are found to have deep-rooted psychological, or serious physical problems, the SEED makes referrals to medical doctors, psychologists, and/or other community programs. This is true particularly during the individual's participation in the two-week intensive program.

Up until his introduction to the SEED, the *druggie's* best, most reliable friend has been the lie that he speaks and lives in order to mislead his parents and his teachers. This same lie directed to a staff member at the SEED is guaranteed to trigger a *choicely worded* verbal barrage not soon to be forgotten. Why? Because the staff member is a former *druggie* himself and can *smell* a lie that you or I would accept as fact!

Because it is tough to lose an old friend—and the lie has been his *best* friend—it must be replaced with something of at least equal value. This is where the SEED asserts its true strength and individuality. Just after the above-described verbal barrage, the staff member will close the one-on-one session by saying to the thoroughly deflated recreant, "I love you." No one who has heard this shopworn phrase as it is spoken at the SEED can fail to be deeply moved by the sincerity and purpose behind its use. The reinforcing effect of true concern (love) is quite awesome.

The success of the SEED program also depends largely on family participation. The families are encouraged to attend two meetings a week to participate with the young people. Through this participation, the parents can get an overall picture of what the SEED is about and can see the gradual improvement of not only their own children but also those of other parents. They also can acquaint themselves with these other parents.

The group participation of parents and children, particularly those parents who are deeply involved with the program, has produced remarkable results in that the family unit is brought closer together and gains a better understanding of the dynamics of its problems. Also, with the family, it has been observed that a greater level of love and compassion evolves within the family.

Fundamental to the continuing success of the SEED's program —especially during the period immediately following the two-week initial phase—is a highly effective intelligence network put together by Art Barker which is composed of ex-druggies, teachers, police and concerned friends. If an apparently rehabilitated participant is seen even talking with an unreconstructed acquaintance, Art knows about it in a matter of minutes and is able to get to the offender for further therapy before recidivism sets in.

Staffing and Training

The SEED has been able to train group leaders and help them develop talents of leadership. It also has been successful in encouraging these group leaders to continue more intensively in all endeavors to help combat the drug problem in the Fort Lauderdale area.

The SEED is strictly a paraprofessional organization with its group leaders and staff coming from the program. Because of its uniqueness, the quality of staffing can be maintained only on this basis. Art Barker is responsible for the overall operation of the program and for seeing that the outline and guidelines which have been developed are followed and the objectives fulfilled. He is also responsible for seeing that the other personnel maintain a high level of proficiency in meeting their obligations and fulfilling job requirements. Additionally, he is a liaison officer with other agencies in the community to effect cooperation and coordinate efforts that benefit the community maximally without duplicating existing services.

There are four senior group leaders whose responsibility it is to maintain group supervision when groups are in session. They assist in training new group leaders and junior group leaders. The junior group leaders are individuals who have gained some insight into the workings of the SEED program, but as yet have not developed the maturity or had experience which would prepare them to take a major responsibility for the conduct of either the initial intensive group sessions or the latter therapeutic group sessions. As they gain responsibility, they move on to being senior group leaders and assume a role of deeper responsibility. The staff of the SEED program, twenty-five paid workers and fifteen volunteers, can effectively handle the approximately three hundred active participants in the program.

Impact and Results

The SEED has had a demonstrable impact in the Fort Lauderdale area. Its program has reached into the courts, the jails, the minority ghetto areas, and the schools of Broward County. The Broward County Personnel Association officially adopted the SEED as its 1971 drug project and assisted in obtaining employment for the successful young people while in, as well as when leaving, the SEED program. The district supervisor of the Florida Parole and Probation Office and his staff have performed a vital role in the rehabilitation of these people during and after their participation in the SEED program. The SEED also uses resources such Broward General Hospital, Henderson Clinic, Family Services, Community Services, Vocational Rehabilitation, and adult education on an emergency and a referral basis. The SEED recently became a member of the Cooperative Area Manpower Planning System (CAMPS) which is sponsored by the local city governments of Fort Lauderdale and Broward County. CAMPS is attempting to create a force of local agencies to effectively coordinate and cooperate in employment-developing opportunities. One role of the SEED is that of rehabilitating young people to enable them to become employable and constructive members of society and their community; therefore, involvement with these other social action agencies is essential.

It is interesting that the professionals who visit the SEED to observe the program seem to elevate different factors to prominence. One man might be struck by the obvious affection which permeates relationships between staff and participants; another by the sense of discipline displayed; and a third by the basic honesty of the program.

We feel the most effective factor influencing the youthful drug abuser at the SEED is peer pressure. The youthful ex-druggie is a potent influence in exerting conformity behavior. Cull (1971) has shown that peer pressure is influential even among schizophrenics who have rejected interaction with the social world in a manner somewhat similar to the members of the drug culture. Social roles are changing rapidly. No longer do the elders in our culture exert the impact on behavior and judgment they did in the past (Cull, 1970); consequently, the SEED has turned to the group which can exert sufficient social pressure to change behavior—the youthful "ex-druggies."

The drug dependence problem is one of the most pressing in the country, and Broward County is no exception. This is evidenced primarily by arrests, particularly of the youth between ages thirteen and twenty. The SEED's records substantiate this age span and document the fact that many youths start on drugs at an early age and advance from marijuana to hard narcotics within one year. In an effort to combat the drug problem, the SEED was founded approximately two years ago. The basic model for the program is the general tratment program developed by Alcoholics Anonymous, with some very important modifications.

The counselors or staff members are rehabilitated drug offenders. After having gone through the program themselves, they have been judged to have the necessary skills and motivations to assist in helping others. These skills consist basically of the ability to develop an empathic relationship with others, the presence of strong desires and a dedication to help others and themselves, and finally, the ability to become skillful and succesful group leaders.

The group sessions may be categorized loosely with the more formal Guided Group Interaction and Transactional Analysis type groups. In the sessions of the SEED, both formal and informal group pressures are brought to bear upon the individual members by other members and leaders. As may be expected, it takes a very skillful leader to know when and how to apply pressure to any particular member or any particular segment of the group. This leader also must know how to channel the group's pressures to effective and fruitful endeavors. The group leaders are extremely adept at reading the character of each member and then applying or halting the pressures. Having once been drug offenders themselves, they are able to pierce the protective shell which each drug offender throws about himself. The group leaders refuse to fall into the verbal and the cognitive traps which the drug offender erects. In the language of "Transactional Analysis," the leaders see the games drug abusers may be playing and refuse to play them. They then point out to the individual how false ideas have led him to his present state of affairs.

The atmosphere where this guided group interaction takes place contains simply *affection, empathy, discipline,* and *love.* This love is a powerful tool in the hands of skilled leaders. In social power terms, the leader has been endowed referent power by the other members of the group. While at no time will he deny any group member, he does, however, skillfully manage the application of power. He uses his power to maintain motivation by reassuring those members who may have just received the brunt of a group session.

The above-described atmosphere of love has been coupled with the skillful handling of guided group interactions to form the SEED's unique and highly successful program. A new member attends two full weeks of twelve-hour sessions. If he has not made adequate progress, he may continue for two more weeks. Once a member has shown that he is responding, he is then allowed to return home. Prior to this he has stayed in the home of another participant and has gone to school or work from that home. After finishing this period, he returns to SEED for further group sessions every night for three hours and all day Saturday. This process lasts for three months. The member is then *straight* and attends only once or twice a week from then on.

During the day, there are two separate groups—one for males, the other for females. Particular problems are discussed and solutions found. In the evening, there is a general session which every member attends. The staff members take turns leading the discussion and help each other whenever necessary. Twice a week there is an open session in which parents, friends, teachers, probation and parole officers, and concerned others participate. At the open meetings, there are usually about 250 members and up to 400 visitors.

An essential element in the success of the SEED is the amount of community participation and aid. Referrals to the SEED program come through many channels. Some are self-referrals, others come because of parental or peer pressure. The various courts are probating individuals to the SEED and sometimes send an individual to it for a pre-sentence diagnostic type study. Many individuals, of course, come because of the attention of concerned adults such as relatives, teachers and police officials. The SEED, because of its unique method and unequaled success ratio (now claimed to be over 90%), has managed to gather full community support.

Summary

In summary, the SEED is an organization of former drug offenders who are dedicated to helping others. Its president, Art Barker, is a truly rare individual who has somehow combined great skill and genuine concern with the ability to teach and treat drug offenders. Its program of guided group interaction, honesty, concern, and understanding seems to have meshed into a workable method. The testimony of parents, doctors, friends, teachers, prison officials, members of school boards, and others all point to the fact that the SEED is a viable, dynamic program.

REFERENCES

Berne, Eric: *Transactional Analysis in Psychotherapy.* New York, Grove, 1961.

Cull, J. G.: Age as a factor in achieving conformity behavior. *Journal of Industrial Gerontology*, Spring, 1970.

Cull, J. G.: Conformity behavior in schizophrenics. *Journal of Social Psychology*, vol. 117, July, 1971.

Hardy, R. E. and Cull, J. G.: Language of the drug abuser. In Hardy, R. E. and Cull, J. G.: *Drug Dependence and Rehabilitation*. Springfield, Thomas, 1972.

Urbanik, Richard: Report on the SEED: A working drug treatment program in Fort Lauderdale, Florida. North Carolina, Department of Correction, 1971 (unpublished).

CHAPTER 19

VOLUNTEERING TO HELP INDIANS HELP THEMSELVES*

EDMUND DIMOCK AND BARBARA RIEGEL

DISCONTENT OVER the plight of a neglected Indian tribe has prompted the authors and a group of social workers in San Diego County, California, to organize their own volunteer project to do something about it. Aided by other volunteers, we have developed a number of activities to resolve some of the educational and economic problems of the Indians who live on the Viejas Reservation in a rural area of the county thirty miles east of San Diego. The activities—at first resisted by the Indians themselves, but now enthusiastically welcomed—consist of a tutoring project for school-age children, delivery of food commodities to the elderly and handicapped, and improvement of communication between the Indian and the white communities. We think that through our project we have demonstrated the considerable impact on social problems that professionals can make by volunteering their skills.

The Viejas Reservation is one of nineteen Indian reservations in the county. In common with other reservations, its water supply and sewer facilities are inadequate, its housing is substandard, and it is not served by public transportation. Indians were moved to the Viejas Reservation in the 1930's when their original lands were sold to San Diego for a reservoir. Most of

---

*Reprinted by permission of the Office of Child Development, Department of Health, Education, and Welfare, *Children Today* (formerly *Children*), 18:23-27, no. 1, January-February, 1971.

the small, unpainted wooden houses were built at that time; now they are in disrepair. However, there is electricity in most of the houses.

About thirty families with fifty children live on the Viejas Reservation. The younger children attend elementary school five miles away in Alpine; it has eight grades and an enrollment of 700. The high school, with an enrollment of 1,800 students, is fifteen miles away in Lakeside. For many years these schools made little attempt to interest or retain the Indian students; they did not teach Indian culture until 1970-71. The dropout rate among the Indians who enter high school in this area is more than 80 per cent.

A number of adults from the reservation work in San Diego or in nearby communities because there are no jobs on the reservation. The reservation church offers no social or cultural activities for the Indians, but some integrated cultural and recreational groups in Alpine are open to them.

The deplorable housing conditions on the Viejas Reservation and the others in the county are a result of many years of inadequate budgets for the Bureau of Indian Affairs. Moreover, BIA does not provide social or health services on these small reservations. The only social services are provided by social workers from the county department of public welfare who maintain regular contact with recipients of public assistance, and the school nurses who provide health services for children at the elementary and high schools. The nurses seldom visit the reservation, however.

Our involvement with the Indians started in April, 1969 when twelve of us, members of the California Social Workers Organization, formed an ad hoc committee to help the people of Viejas Reservation deal with problems that we had become aware of through our experiences with Indian recipients of public assistance.

We realized that we could not satisfy such major needs as housing and sanitation. All of us felt, however, that we could play a significant role in easing two situations that the Indians particularly resented—lack of awareness on the part of the schools regarding the needs of Indian students and a general lack of communication between Indians and other residents of the community.

Overcoming Resistance

Initially, we had difficulty convincing the Indians that we really wanted to help them. Our committee offered its services to the Intertribal Council, an OEO-funded organization designed to help the Indians on reservations improve their living conditions, but nothing came of this. Finally, when the Intertribal Council sponsored a meeting on housing problems, one of the social workers assigned to the Viejas Reservation obtained an invitation for several members of our committee to attend. Specifically, we were asked to furnish a speaker to describe the provision in California's public welfare program for funds for special housing needs. We shared the platform with representatives from the Intertribal Council of California, the Indian community action program, the Bureau of Indian Affairs, and the Department of Housing and Urban Development.

The committee members who attended this meeting observed the Indians' ambivalence toward "outsiders." On one hand, the Indians appeared to want help; on the other, they tended to reject proffered assistance because they did not trust non-Indians. More than once during the discussion, Indian leaders angrily spoke of white men who had offered to assist them but who never had returned with the help. They also pointed out that some white "helpers" had had ulterior motives—motives that resulted in exploitation of the Indians.

The meeting, although marked by "friendly suspicion," proved the starting point for our committee's subsequent work. That night the Indians asked one of our members to write an article for the newsletter of a statewide Indian organization about how persons receiving public assistance could obtain funds for housing repair.

Knowing that these Indians' experiences with white men have been characterized by broken promises, our committee members resolved that we would follow through on every project we initiated.

At one point during the meeting, the Indians discussed the U. S. Department of Agriculture's commodity distribution program, a Federal plan that makes staple foods available to low-income families. In San Diego County, the welfare department administers this program and volunteer agencies distribute the commodities from centers to which the recipients must come. One speaker said that Indians who qualify for the program had to travel from fifteen to sixty miles to reach a distribution center. Clarence Brown, the spokesman from the Viejas Reservation, described the difficulties that the older Indians had in obtaining commodities. With no public transportation available, many had no way to get to a distribution center. Others, after traveling long distances, sometimes found the distribution center unable to provide commodities. To remedy this situation, the Intertribal Council planned to set up its own commodity distribution center.

We learned later that the Indians' distribution center would be located sixty miles away and would not be able to serve the Viejas and other Indian tribes in our part of the county. We then found a distribution center thirty miles from the Viejas Reservation that agreed to cooperate with us. The tribal spokesman and the tribal council helped us set up a commodity delivery service for eighteen families on the reservation. Volunteers from the committee spent one evening each month working on this project.

From the first we realized that the Indians would not permit us to help them in meaningful ways until we gained their trust. The commodity project offered concrete evidence of our desire to help. However, because we did not involve the Indians in the actual pickup and delivery of food, we were not as successful with this project as we had originally hoped. Also, because of heavy demands on our time in providing services to the Viejas Reservation, we were unable to develop food distribution projects on any of the other reservations in need of similar services. However, we helped representatives from two smaller reservations arrange to get commodities from a nearby distribution center that had not previously been open to their people.

As an outgrowth of our demonstration of the need for a county-wide food delivery service, last fall the Intertribal Council obtained a truck, and hired a food commodity coordinator and a driver. These positions are both staffed by Indians. When the Indian delivery service began in September, 1970, we discontinued that part of our activities because there was no longer a need for our volunteers to deliver food.

Interesting Others

During our activities on behalf of the Indians, we found that as a segment of the county population they were an almost invisible minority; the average white resident of our county was unaware of the number, location, and population of the reservations. This was true even in the small city where the Viejas Reservation Indians shopped. Moreover, the white residents who did know about the Indians were not particularly concerned. Their idea of help was to donate their discards—broken toys, wornout appliances, and clothing with buttons and zippers removed. Both the adults and children who received the items were disgusted; one Indian parent said "I don't know *anyone* I would give old things like that to."

To date we have been unable to change this pattern of giving, undoubtedly because the givers have a stereotyped image of the Indian and a general lack of information about his needs. Those of us who work with Indians know that their needs are no different from the needs of other minorities—better education, jobs, and housing. Most of all they need to be recognized as individuals who have a contribution to make to society.

In the eastern part of the county, a group of merchants, public officials, and school administrators was working to modify the community's white, middle-class attitudes toward minorities. Although blacks and chicanos were represented in this group, there were no Indians. Our committee sent a speaker to describe our commodity distribution project to this group, which showed a great deal of interest in local Indians and their problems.

After the meeting a local newspaperman interviewed several of us about our committee's work. We convinced him that the Indians' plight was much more newsworthy than our small efforts, and arranged for him to meet Mr. Brown, the spokesman for the reservation. Since that time the daily newspaper has published several articles and editorials about the Indians' problems.

The community group promptly took up the Indian cause with fervor. Devoting many meetings to the subject, the group heard speakers from the Public Health Service and the Bureau of Indian Affairs discuss the water problem, which was different for each reservation. Its members arranged tours of local reservations, led by tribal leaders and Bureau of Indian Affairs staff. Next the group held an open house at a local high school to enable interested white citizens to meet and talk with Indians about their needs, including an adequate water supply. As a result, its members solicited funds and materials from businesses to improve conditions on the reservations. They obtained pipes through the Sears Foundation to use in replacing the waterline to the Viejas Reservation. The work is now being done by Mr. Brown and some volunteers. The community group also sponsored a Human Rights Day that honored racial and ethnic minorities residing within the community.

Tutoring

Our committee has also been involved in tutoring school-age Viejas children. We proposed this tutoring project during a meeting of the Viejas tribal council. The council members cordially received our offer and told us that they were willing to provide the clubhouse and utilities at their expense. Mr. Brown, the tribal spokesman, assumed overall charge of the project, as he does for all reservation matters.

Neither the elementary nor the high school offered a balanced presentation of Indian history in its curriculum. Textbooks contained only the cowboy-and-Indian type of reference. Moreover, Indian parents had keen memories of the slights they experienced over the years at the hands of teachers, administrators, and school nurses. For example, although the Indian children were meticulously groomed, the nurses frequently asked the children about personal hygiene and bathing. Ironically, the California Indians have had a long tradition of daily bathing, in the belief that it makes them stronger and healthier. Teachers described Indian children as withdrawn in the classroom and prone to fighting on the playground. The fights frequently stemmed from the racial slurs that the children experienced—such as "dirty black Indian" or "nigger."

Because of our own observations of the high dropout rate of Indians in the ninth or tenth grades, members of our committee considered the tutoring project vital for helping these Indians achieve expertise in asserting their rights. The views of the parents coincided with ours, and most of them have received this project with enthusiasm. The tribal spokesman delegated to his sister, Florence Barrett, secretary of the council, the task of assisting us in establishing the tutoring project. She contacted parents, gave us information on each child on the reservation, and made arrangements for all the preliminary meetings and tutoring sessions at the clubhouse. A consultant on Indian languages to the linguistics department of the University of California at San Diego, Mrs. Barrett has a keen interest in seeing her own four children complete college. It is doubtful the project could have been sustained without her dedication and help.

Some tutors volunteered after reading newspaper stories about the project; others were recruited by friends. The tutoring group eventually included thirty-five people, including twelve public welfare workers, a number of college students, and several housewives. Each volunteer tutor donated a minimum of three hours a week. Generally, the initial group has remained active, except for two social workers who returned to graduate school. Although most of the tutors worked or lived within twenty miles of the Viejas Reservation, few of them had had any knowledge of Indian problems before joining the project.

The tutoring school began operation in June, 1969. It now has thirty-five elementary school children attending. We have emphasized reading and mathematics, although we have helped students in all their school subjects. Because of the limited time any one tutor could devote to this project, we planned only one two-hour tutoring session a week for each child. A measure of the school's success is the large number of children who drop in without appointments to obtain help with homework. Some evenings when we are swamped with drop-ins, we utilize older students to help younger ones.

From the beginning the tutors noticed an overwhelming, almost immobilizing, lack of self-confidence in the younger children. By the time they had passed the sixth grade, the children had developed a hostility toward school and an attitude of not caring about their progress. This might be called the pre-dropout syndrome.

In addition to academic help, we arranged special activities for the Indian children, such as picnics, trips to the zoo and beach, a tour of the college that several tutors attend, a Halloween party, and a Games Day on Labor Day.

Public school teachers told us that most of the children who were tutored showed improvement during the last school year. These children seem to be most interested in music and art, while arithmetic and reading remain rather tedious subjects for them. In several of the readers that the schools donated to us, we found prejudicial stories perpetuating the image of the primitive Indian. Eventually we discontinued using such books.

We were unable to reach the Indian high school students on a sustained basis. Of the six we know of, two were good students and did not need us, while four who needed a considerable amount of help were too embarrassed to admit it. They remained interested bystanders and enjoyed the social contacts with several tutors. By the end of the year, three of the marginal students had dropped out of school.

Stimulated by the interest of Indian parents in educational courses for themselves, the adult division of the high school initiated an adult school at a convenient location on the Viejas Reservation in April, 1970. Establishment of this school was a most gratifying result of our contacts with the tribe. High school level courses were taught from April through June. The first class included seven adults and five recent high school dropouts, three of whom we had persuaded to enroll. Funds have not been available to continue classes in 1970-71.

Changing Attitudes

Although our tutoring project brought no direct improvement

in the teenagers' school performance, we made some progress in changing attitudes of teachers and administrators toward the Indians. Committee members held numerous meetings with the school guidance staff to try to establish communication between them and the parents and to foster a more understanding approach on the part of the school toward the students. The high school responded by requesting funds to employ an Indian teacher-counselor to develop more relevant materials and methods for the Indian student. This special project began in September, 1970, under the direction of a Sioux Indian as teacher-counselor. A former volunteer in our tutoring project, she is admired by the Indian residents for her talents and her pride in her cultural background.

A junior college scholarship program for students of minority groups, including Indians, was scheduled to get underway in September, 1971. When funded and implemented, the program was to offer courses on the reservation to anyone over eighteen years of age. Indians were to participate in formulating the courses of study.

After several meetings at the reservation clubhouse, communication between the Indian parents and the school improved. The parents, who had previously withdrawn from contact with school personnel, were surprisingly outspoken in their criticisms of past and present injustices occurring in the school. Voicing their belief that the white schools did not want their children, the parents cited many incidents arising from misunderstandings as proof of this. They told of insulting remarks made by white students or teachers, which they viewed as part of a general pattern to discredit Indian children. Furthermore, they said that whenever fights erupted at school, Indian children were automatically blamed as the instigators. They charged that their children were treated as slow learners. As children these parents had attended the Alpine grammar school during the 1930's and 1940's when there were separate restrooms for "Indians and colored." Many problems remain in relation to the public schools, but the initial steps toward greater understanding are taking place.

Although the people on the reservation have no outstanding

artifacts or commercial products, they have preserved certain elements of their culture. Most of the middle-aged and all of the elderly Indians know the Diegueno language, but they have made no formalized attempt to teach it to the children. After listening to some members of the tribe express concern that their culture and language are dying, we decided to initiate a course on their culture for the children with the aid of parents and a local anthropology professor. So far, however, we have not had an opportunity to work on this project.

At the beginning of our volunteer work on the Viejas Reservation, we were bombarded with attitudes of hopelessness, even on the part of very young children. "It won't work" was the standard response to our efforts. We now hear parents say indignantly that the school owes their children a decent education. In spite of a tradition of never expressing anger, these Indians have begun to do so. It seems to us that they are aware of changes in the white society's attitudes toward minorities that will inevitably lead to improvement in all areas of their lives.

One by-product of our committee's project is the education we have received from our association with the Indians. We have had the rare opportunity of learning directly from the Viejas Indians themselves about their values and life styles. These encounters have been uniquely enriching experiences for us.

CHAPTER 20

A COMPREHENSIVE CONSULTATION
PROGRAM FOR CHILDREN
IN A DAY-CARE CENTER

Martin A. Silverman and Eva Wolfson

• • • • • • • • • • • • • • • • • • • •

• • • • • • • • • • • • • • • • • • • •

THE JOINT COMMISSION on Mental Health of Children (1969) has demonstrated that children in the lowest socioeconomic groups are handicapped by multiple problems affecting their physical, emotional, and cognitive development. Since the problems appear early and grow steadily worse with the passage of time, it follows that intervention should take place early in the children's lives if it is to be maximally effective.

The preschool period in some ways is an ideal time at which to intervene. Early socialization is taking place and school attitudes and learning patterns are just beginning to be laid down. Children in day-care centers and neighborhood nursery schools are still young enough to respond to outside influences. Maladaptive patterns in most instances have not yet become so ingrained as to resist modification. Children at such early developmental levels benefit greatly from changes in child-rearing patterns effected at that time and their parents are more receptive to outside opinions when their children are still little.

In this chapter, the authors would like to report upon a program of early intervention which developed out of six years' work at a day-care center in New York City. Our work was carried out as part of a larger project, administered by the Child Development Center of the Jewish Board of Guardians, under the overall direction of Dr. Peter B. Neubauer. The project has been in existence for ten years at the time of preparation of this report. In addition to providing consultation services to a number of day-care centers and community nursery schools in several disadvantaged neighborhoods on Manhattan's West Side, it also has included a pre-nursery school program for two- to three-year-olds, an infant care program, and a program for children in families temporarily displaced to "welfare hotels."

The day-care center intervention program which we will describe took several years to evolve into its final form. It developed empirically out of our attempts to meet the total needs of the center's staff and the children they served. There are three main branches to our program. Initially, it consisted of classroom observation and consultation with the director and his staff. As we proceeded in our work, we saw that there were some situations and problems which went beyond the professional competence of the center personnel. We found that in many such instances, it was not feasible to refer the family elsewhere for assistance. Therefore, we provided direct diagnostic and therapeutic assistance, to the extent permitted by our own staff limitations, to those children and families who could not otherwise obtain it. The third arm of our program grew out of the request of certain members of the teaching staff for direct help in developing classroom techniques geared to the specific needs of the children with whom they were working. We put together several small classes through which we might study the children's learning problems more closely. We thought at first of turning them into demonstration classes for the teaching staff, but that did not prove feasible. We gradually recognized, however, that the small groups we had put together constituted a valuable supplementary educational and therapeutic resource that facilitated the children's progress in the classroom.

THE DAY-CARE CENTER POPULATION AND
THE PROBLEMS OF ITS STAFF

Before we describe our assistance program and trace its development, we should like to present a picture of the children and the special problems which they brought with them to the center. There were eighty children altogether, ranging from three to six years of age. The day-care center was located in an urban renewal area with a very high rate of crime and drug use. A variety of ethnic and cultural backgrounds were represented, but most of the children came from southern black, Latin-American, or Haitian families living close to or at a minimum subsistence level. Most of the children came to the center because their mothers had given up welfare assistance and had taken jobs, or had joined job-training programs leading in that direction. The majority of the children lived in one-parent families and many had been raised within socially disorganized and fragmented family circumstances. Some of the children had been passed from one surrogate parent to another. Many had been exposed repeatedly to scenes of adult sexual behavior and cruelty.

Their parents tended to be anxious, at times depressed, overburdened people who either had little energy left over from struggling with the demands of their everyday life or were overwhelmed by the task of rearing children. The stimulation they provided tended to be uneven and unfocused. They maintained discipline by demanding blind compliance with unexplained, externally imposed rules rather than encouraging the progressive internalization of inner controls. They neither rewarded nor encouraged investigation or experimentation.

The children had responded to their environmental experiences by developing pragmatic techniques which suited their lives at home, but which had ill prepared them for the social and learning experience which they found at the day-care center. They were highly distractible. They reacted to their teachers' friendliness and attempts to stimulate their curiosity and intellectual interest with excitement and disorganized behavior. They were reluctant to exercise their skills or to venture into new areas of activity. They had had little experience with toys or sophisticated playthings. Their anxious vigilance lest their possessions be taken away from them interfered with their ability to explore the manipulative possibilities of the educational materials made available to them. Sharing was difficult; they had little self-confidence and they tended to give up rather than risk failure. Defensive patterns were organized around avoiding change and restricting experience to a narrow range. They depended upon external rules and regulations to maintain order and tolerated changes in routine very poorly. The children's range of intellectual potential seemed no different from that of other groups of children their age, but their language development, fund of information, judgment, concept development, and reasoning skills were too deficient to permit them to fully avail themselves of the nursery school materials which were available to them. They lacked confidence in themselves and did not expect to be rewarded even if they did somehow achieve success. Although they were hungering for emotional contact, they could accept it only when they felt that they were in control of the interchange. They insisted on attention when *they* demanded it, but were distrustful of unsolicited friendliness or offers of assistance. They would not permit the teachers to get too close to them.

It is not surprising that the teachers felt frustrated and helpless. When they reached out to the children, their overtures were rebuffed. When they tried to stimulate the children's curiosity and promote investigation and intellectual development, they found that they responded with excitement which they could neither regulate nor channel into constructive activity. In such instances, the children forced the adults to provide stringent measures to discipline and control them from outside. The most enthusiastic teachers soon found themselves acceding to the children's insistence that excitement and stimulation be avoided in favor of maintaining calm, order, and the status quo.

CONSULTATION WITH THE DIRECTOR AND HIS STAFF

When we arrived at the center, we found that morale was low. The teachers felt frustrated, helpless, and defensive. They bickered among themselves and there was a high rate of teacher absence. Except for a few who were content with spending year after year doing little more than keeping order in the classroom, they did not stay on for very long. No more than a few of the ten teaching positions were filled by the same person for any length of time.

The director welcomed our offer of assistance. Regular meetings were set up with the teachers. The director, the day care counselor (who worked with the parents), and, at times, the pediatrician, attended as well. At the staff's request, we started out by discussing individual problem children. At first they were hesitant about accepting our recommendations. This turned out to stem from two sources. On the one hand, they seemed to have a need to prove that the difficulties in the classroom were caused by a few incorrigible bad apples among the children rather than (as they secretly feared) by lack of ability on their part to cope with the problems and meet the children's needs. They eventually told us that they also had feared that our intervention program would serve our own needs rather than theirs, as had occurred elsewhere with intervention by other groups who not only had not been helpful, but had left additional problems in their wake.

We gradually demonstrated that we were both interested and capable of using our understanding of child development *to help them carry out the job that they wished to carry out* and that we had no ulterior motives. Although they were still quite sensitive about requiring help from outsiders and expressed resentment at times when our views conflicted with certain of their pragmatically acquired beliefs, the teaching staff could not help but appreciate the welcome changes that had taken place when they had adopted some of our suggestions. First the director and day-care counselor and eventually the teachers and their aides began to consult us about general procedures which went beyond the special needs of a few individual children. We helped them revamp their method of assessing new children. We also helped them to improve the way in which they assisted new children and their parents to make a good initial adjustment to the center. We provided a developmental point of view and assistance in understanding certain dynamic aspects of the children's behavior to supplement the training in preschool education and intuitive methods of handling children which were already at their disposal.

Considerations of individual problem children served as the principal springboard for these more general discussions. We were unable for a long time, for example, to convince the teachers that many of the children would be unable to make use of the cognitive training which they were offering them unless they first corrected certain emotional and cognitive deficiencies. They scoffed when we suggested that they either teach English to those who did not understand, or address the children in their native language. They insisted that children of that age "pick up English quickly on their own." A fortunate experience led them to reconsider this view. Julio was a four-year-old boy who refused to take part in activities, clowned, and hit out continually at other children. The teachers thought he might be retarded and asked us for an opinion. When we watched him carefully, we discovered that he was a very bright but also very proud little boy to whom it was very important that he do well at the things in which he was engaged. Unable to understand more than a few words of what was being said around him, he was feeling frustrated, defeated, and angry. His behavior served to ward off these feelings by enabling him to avoid the source of his distress and by granting him a semblance of strength through fighting. A crash program to teach him English led to a dramatic transformation. This helped convince the teachers that we may have been right in suggesting that they assess each child's development and fill in the gaps in order to facilitate their ability to make use of the educational program.

Another child was a bully who could not tolerate correction

or criticism and repeatedly got into fights with other children. When we looked into his background, we found that he lived alone with his mother in a fatherless household in which he was being treated in essence as the man of the house. His classroom behavior stemmed in large part from his attempt to fill the inappropriate role in which he was being cast and from the enormous oedipal anxiety that was generated. When the teachers adapted their approach to him to take this factor into consideration, they began to find him much easier to manage. This experience and others like it stirred the teachers' interest in learning more about the children's lives and in giving consideration to the emotional factors influencing their behavior. The information which the day-care counselor was able to provide began to assume more importance to them and they became increasingly interested in getting to know the parents. Eventually, we were able to help them set up regular meetings with the parents, in which they could discuss the children and facilitate each other's attempts to foster their optimal development.

One of our most difficult tasks was to convince the day-care center staff that among the children whom they considered to be well-adjusted, were a number of very troubled youngsters whose coping mechanisms actually were hindering their development. This was a group of emotionally starved girls who had developed a facade of pseudo-competence and pseudo-independence that was very convincing on the surface. Their good behavior, apparent self-sufficiency, and eagerness to help maintain order and discipline made them favorites of the teachers. From our vantage point as observers in the classroom, however, we could see that, although they desperately wanted to be taken care of, they were vigorously denying it and playing the role of little adults to maintain the fiction that they were self-sufficient. Since they were unable to allow themselves to be little children, dependent upon the teachers for instruction and help, they were unable to make effective use of the nursery school program. They were always busy in the doll corner and dress-up areas playing out their defensive fantasies rather than engaging in activities which would promote cognitive growth. It was not until the facade began to crumble in one or two of them, in response to deteriorating conditions at home, that their problems began to be appreciated.

DIAGNOSIS AND TREATMENT WITHIN A DAY-CARE CENTER

We became aware early in our work at the center that even with help the teachers could not be expected to meet the special needs of all the children. Their obligations to their classes as a whole limited their ability to give individual attention to every child who required it. Some of the children were too anxious, apathetic and withdrawn, disorganized, or emotionally hyperactive to function adequately within a large group. There were some children who required help that was beyond the teachers' professional training. At times, we were able to refer children to existing facilities in the community, but our efforts were often defeated by long waiting lists and bureaucratic red tape. We also worked with the director of the day-care center to recruit high school students and adult volunteers to work with some of the children.

To meet the need of the remaining children, we decided to offer diagnostic and treatment services directly at the center, insofar as our resources allowed (our team consisted of a child psychiatrist, a psychiatric social worker, and an educational consultant with specialized training in child development, who were available on a limited, part-time basis). We will summarize our experiences, a more detailed description of which has been published elsewhere (Silverman and Wolfson, 1971). To begin with, we found that the behavioral characteristics of children growing up in the unevenly stimulating and partially disorganizing environment from which many of our children had come (see Malone, *et al.*, 1967, for an excellent description) sometimes masked such disorders as minimal brain dysfunction and childhood psychosis.

We saw graphically that in working with disadvantaged communities it is necessary to distinguish carefully between characteristics of the population at large and manifestations of individual differences among its members. The expressivity of certain disorders varies in different populations (Hollingshead and Redlich, 1958; Harrison, *et al.*, 1965; McDermott, *et al.*, 1967). Although poor children differ from one another as much as those from more advantaged communities, workers in the field tend to fall prey to certain myths and generalizations about the poor (Herzog and Lewis, 1970) which interfere with their capacity for objective observation.

These professional biases also affect decisions about whether and how to treat children from lower socioeconomic communities. Sophisticated techniques tend to be withheld from them, either because they are not expected to make good use of them, because of the cost in time and manpower, or because of the personal preferences of therapists for patients with a socioeconomic background similar to their own (Gordon, 1965; Schneiderman, 1965). We have found, however, that when we have adjusted our approach to the individual characteristics of the population involved, we have been able to make successful use of a variety of treatment techniques, ranging from brief, crisis-oriented intervention to intensive, long-term, psychoanalytically oriented psychotherapy. Although certain of the modalities we have employed are indeed time-consuming, it would not be realistic to expect that more superficial methods would have sufficed (Hersch, 1966; Spurlock and Cohen, 1969; Mayer and Schamess, 1968; Marmor, 1970). Space limitations preclude our presenting the extensive clinical data which would be required to demonstrate this; those who are interested will find such material in our 1971 paper.

We found that the parents were much more able to understand and support their children's treatment than the literature would have led us to believe, although they often were too beleaguered by their everyday problems to take part in collateral treatment or casework for themselves. A great deal of tact and thoughtfulness was required from us to dispel the mistrust which had accumulated in the parents during years of insensitive treatment by people at certain public agencies. We also found that we had to be very thoughtful of the hurt pride that was involved in their accepting unsolicited help from us for their children.

In addition to the more usual diagnostic considerations, we found that it made sense to pay careful consideration to logistical practicalities in our selection process. Attendance records and stability of family residence became important factors. Through sad experience, we learned that it would be extremely difficult to refer any of the children for further treatment elsewhere after they left the center. In addition to starting as early as possible, we obtained parental permission, in advance, for the children to continue their treatment with us after they had gone on to elementary school (either walking to the center or being transported by volunteers), in case their treatment was not completed by the time they would leave for first grade.

We learned a great deal about special aspects of conducting psychotherapy with children from this particular background. Our treatment techniques were dictated in part by the inconsistent parenting, repeated loss of important objects of affection, lack of privacy, material deprivation, lack of protection against real dangers, etc., which many of them had experienced. Space limitations prevent us from presenting an adequate explication here.

It was not easy to work with this particular group of patients. The children often tried to push the therapist away for long periods of time. They tested the therapist's devotion, interest, and self-control quite severely. It was necessary to refrain from "giving" too much to the children to make up for their emotional and material deprivations. We also had to struggle with resentment of their extreme demands and the frustration of relatively long periods of seeming lack of progress. The children often resorted to the mechanism of identification with the aggressor (A. Freud, 1939) to frustrate, deprive, and bully the therapist as had been done to them in their lives. The fact that we were able to speak to each other about these experiences helped us to be able to tolerate them. It was distressing not to be able to provide assistance for more than a fraction of the many deserving children at the center (which we suspect is one source of the well rationalized decision by many professionals working with poor children not to offer treatment to any of them).

The results more than made up for the difficulties encountered along the way, however. It was extremely gratifying to watch children whose development had been severely retarded in major areas and who had shown serious behavior or learning disorders develop into more confident, capable youngsters who appreciated their worth, coped with the exigencies of their lives and progressed in their overall development. Several of the children we treated for serious behavior and learning problems went on to win awards for academic achievement by the time they reached the third or fourth grade.

SMALL EDUCATIONAL-THERAPEUTIC GROUPS AS A MEANS OF FACILITATING COGNITIVE AND EMOTIONAL DEVELOPMENT

As the teachers began to see that the assistance we gave them yielded practical results, they became interested in our opinions about general classroom procedures. We discussed teaching methods, materials, room arrangements, behavior management, etc. To study the children's learning problems more closely, our educational consultant began to meet twice a week with a group of five children from the oldest group who were performing far below their capacity and would not nearly be ready for first grade by the time they left the center. She provided an enriched program of cognitive training aimed at improving their verbal skills, attention and concentration spans, concept development, reasoning, judgment, and fund of knowledge.

We were able to work with them for six months before they left the center. During that time, we saw that their emotional handicaps seriously hindered them from making good use of the learning experience we had offered them. They were so fearful of failure, for example, that they became anxious and abandoned projects upon which they were working whenever they ran into any difficulty. It was clear that they needed to develop greater self-confidence and had to learn how to tolerate temporary setbacks (by progressing slowly with encouragement, support, and frequent praise through tasks of gradually increasing complexity) before they would be able to make good use of the cognitive stimulation and training.

We also saw that they were extremely hungry for attention and warmth, but when it was provided, it stimulated them to pitches of excitement which they could not handle. Their contacts with the special teacher in the small group stirred up their dependent wishes and provoked sexual excitement and aggressive impulses which quickly were translated into boisterous, disruptive behavior or into flight from the source of stimulation. It followed that activities and materials needed to be chosen very carefully, and that they would require help with their self-control and their ability to deal with excitement.

When the pilot group left the center to go on to first grade, we decided to make some changes in our approach. Although our aim would remain fundamentally educational, the pilot group had taught us that in the future we would have to pay attention not only to cognitive deficiencies but to the emotional factors interfering with the children's learning as well.

At the beginning of the following school year, we set up three groups of seriously underachieving children aged three, four, and five years respectively. Since each group contained five or six children, this meant that a fifth of all the children at the center were taking part. Each group would meet twice a week until its members graduated, whereupon a new group of three-year-olds would be formed to take its place.

We studied each child's history, home environment, personality characteristics, and classroom performance before we started. We tried to maintain a balance in each group between children who were overactive and boisterous and others who were quiet and withdrawn. The sessions were gradually increased from forty-five to ninety minutes. The child psychiatrist on the team sat in once a week, after which the session was discussed at length.

We will briefly describe our experience with the groups. A more thorough report is available elsewhere (Silverman and Wolfson, 1970). Although each session was carefully planned, we often made major changes in deference to the children's shifting emotional availability. We used simple materials and made a point of weaving familiar details from the children's everyday lives into the educational content. Games, songs, trips and similar activities were used to foster the children's *active* participation in the learning process (Inhelder and Piaget, 1969; Piaget, 1970).

The children in each group were cooperative, well-behaved,

and enthusiastic at first. Within a month or two, however, they grew restless and fidgety. They became demanding, hyperactive, and oppositional. They were increasingly excited (sexually in the older groups) and aggressive. The disruptive behavior which emerged seemed to be aimed both at discharging the feelings being stirred up within them and at forcing the teacher to pay attention to them and provide the controls which they could not impose upon themselves.

A pattern developed in which the first part of each session was devoted to helping the children control their excitement, settle down, and organize themselves so that they could engage in learning activity for the rest of the session. At first, external limits had to be set and enforced. The children tried hard to follow the rules and gradually learned to regulate first one another and then themselves. We used trial and error and attempted whenever possible to reinforce and strengthen each child's own preferred method of settling himself down. The time spent during the sessions on facilitating self-control gradually diminished so that more and more time and energy could be devoted to learning.

We had to be careful for a long time to avoid competition and minimize experiences of failure out of consideration for the children's low frustration tolerance and shaky self-esteem. We made sure to be as consistent and reliable as possible to overcome the distrust which they felt towards adults. We noted absences and sent cards when a child was out for a long time due to illness or vacation. Successes were rewarded with praise and admiration. Material rewards and gifts were never utilized and food was provided only during birthday parties. We kept track of what was occurring at home and did what we could to help the children, individually or in a group, to master traumatic occurences which periodically drained away their attention and mental energy.

The following vignette illustrates our approach. In order to promote categorization, logical organization of experiential details, and hierarchical classification, we were working on the distribution of furniture in the various rooms of an apartment.

In the midst of this, one of the children began to regress to whiny, petulant, babyish behavior when he was put out of his mother's bed into one of his own for the first time. Two others, whose positions at home were being threatened by the arrival of another sibling, began to regress into similar behavior, although they struggled against it. We responded by shifting the focus of the sessions to a library book about a new baby. The discussion shifted back and forth between the book and the feelings of the children in the group who felt impelled to act like babies to capture their mothers' attention. When the children seemed to be recovering from their regressive shift, we switched to another library book, about the different rooms of a baby's house, as a transitional way of returning to the original lesson plan.

We followed the progress of the small group participants while they were at the center and followed two of the groups through the second grade. During the first year with us, they improved significantly in confidence, initiative, interest in learning, and relations with their peers. By the second year, they began to stand out as the most alert, inquisitive, knowledgeable, and conceptually advanced children in their classrooms. Their personality problems improved much less than their learning ability, however. Although they were no longer the disorganized, aggressive, or withdrawn children they had been before their small group experience, they still had significant characterological problems, which had been modified but were still relatively prominent.

A rough test of basic nursery school skills devised by Dr. Helen Robinson of the City College of New York was administered to two groups before and after a year of participation (maximum possible score 68.0). The results indicated a good deal of improvement (Table 20-I), although lack of standardization and the absence of a control group limit the conclusions which can be drawn.

A more important indication of the success of the small groups was the report we received from the first and second grade teachers of the children we followed into elementary school. Almost all the children were near the top of their classes academically, although most of them were showing behavioral

TABLE 20-I

BASIC NURSERY SKILLS BEFORE AND AFTER
PARTICIPATION IN SMALL GROUPS

	Range Before	Range After
4-year-old Group	24.0 to 53.5	49.5 to 67.0
5-year-old Group	37.5 to 55.0	57.0 to 64.5

disturbances. The latter took the form of restlessness, shyness, excessive dependence upon objects from home, hypersensitivity, or intermittent disruptiveness.

We are aware that the children may need further assistance as they move on through school, but we are pleased nevertheless with the gains they made while at the day-care center. We agree with Wilhelms (1970) that it is unrealistic to expect intervention at the preschool level to do the job alone and that ongoing assistance at successive levels is probably indicated.

Several of the elementary school teachers we interviewed made an observation which we found interesting. They told us that the children who had been in our small groups had attached themselves upon entry into first grade to a subgroup of intelligent, academically superior children in the classroom and had continued to associate with them thereafter. Our impression is that this represented an attempt by the children to recreate for themselves in first grade something similar to the small group experience which had been so helpful to them at the day-care center.

SUMMARY AND CONCLUSIONS

We have described a program of assistance at the day-care center for children in lower socioeconomic communities. We provided consultation to the director and his staff to facilitate communication and share our knowledge of the developmental and dynamic forces at play in the classroom. We provided a range of diagnostic and treatment services for some of the children and worked with a number of them in educational-therapeutic small groups. The results were extremely gratifying. Children who had been floundering emotionally and cognitively became able to learn and, in some instances, went on to become superior students. Aided by the perspective we provided in our conferences with them, as well as by the improvement in the classroom behavior of the children to whom we gave direct assistance, the teachers achieved increasing success in their work in the classroom.

Staff morale improved markedly. The teacher absence rate declined and the turnover rate among the staff dropped sharply. The latter can be attributed in part to a significant increase in salary and fringe benefits which was granted during the latter half of the period covered by this report, but the trend was clearly under way well before the first raise was received. The center acquired a reputation as one of the best in the city, a fact of which the staff members were justly proud.

It is our firm conviction that the results we were able to obtain would not have been forthcoming had we been unidirectional in our approach. By this we mean two things. First of all, what we have seen indicates to us that to facilitate the learning of children who are socioeconomically disadvantaged, it is not enough to address oneself solely to their cognitive deficits. It is our impression that the intervention programs most likely to achieve success are those which address themselves simultaneously to the children's cognitive development and to the emotional development with which it interacts. We are skeptical of programs which attempt to improve the learning patterns of children in this population solely by means of educational drill (Bereiter and Engelmann, 1966; Bereiter, 1967) or even via more sophisticated cognitive training (Deutsch, 1967; Kohlberg, 1970) which is not supported by attention to the children's emotional problems. We are not the first, of course, to arrive at this conclusion (Biber and Franklin, 1967; Malone, *et al.*, 1967). It is also obvious from our account that we do not believe that it is enough to work with emotional problems only.

Secondly, we believe that the consultation we provided to the director and his staff would not have been so effective had we not provided the additional services we have described. Not only did those services reinforce the points we were trying to get across to the staff by directly demonstrating their practical applicability, but they met a need which it would have been unrealistic to expect the teachers to be able to fill on their own. It also would have been unrealistic to expect that more than a few of the children who required specialized assistance beyond what the teachers could offer could have obtained it elsewhere. What we did in a sense was to bring the clinic to the center for those children who could not have gone to an outside clinic to obtain that assistance. Only time will tell how well the children we have worked with and come to know at the center will do, educationally and personally, but we are pleased to have been able to contribute to efforts to give them a good start.

<h2 style="text-align:center">REFERENCES</h2>

Bereiter, C.: Instructional planning in early compensatory education. In Hellmuth, Jerome (Ed.): *Disadvantaged Child.* New York, Brunner-Mazel, 1967, vol. 1, pp. 339-347.

Bereiter, C. and Engelmann, S.: *Teaching Disadvantaged Children in the Preschool.* Englewood Cliffs, P-H, 1966.

Biber, B. and Franklin, M. R.: The relevance of developmental and psychodynamic concepts to the education of the preschool child. In Hellmuth, Jerome (Ed.): *Disadvantaged Child.* New York, Brunner-Mazel, 1967, vol. 1, pp. 305-323.

Deutsch, M., et al.: *The Disadvantanged Child.* New York, Basic, 1967.

Erikson, E. H.: Growth and crises of the healthy personality. In *Identity and the Life Cycle (Psychol Issues,* Monograph 1). New York, Intl Univs Pr, 1959.

Freud, A.: *The Ego and the Mechanisms of Defense.* New York, Intl Univs Pr, 1946.

Gordon, S.: Are we seeing the right patients? Child guidance intake: the sacred cow. *Am J Orthopsychiatry,* 35:131-137, 1965.

Harrison, S. I., McDermott, J. F., Jr., Wilson, P. T. and Schrager, J.: Social class and mental illness in children: Choice of treatment. *Arch Gen Psychiatry,* 13:411-417, 1965.

Hersch, C.: Mental-health services and the poor. *Psychiatry,* 29:236-245, 1966.

Herzog, E. and Lewis, H.: Children in poor families: Myths and realities. *Am J Orthopsychiatry,* 40:375-387, 1970.

Hollingshead, A. and Redlich, F. C.: *Social Class and Mental Illiness: A Community Study.* New York, Wiley, 1958.

Inhelder, B. and Piaget, J.: *The Early Growth of Logic in the Child: Classification and Seriation.* New York, Norton, 1969.

Joint Commission on Mental Health of Children: *Crisis in Child Mental Health: Challenge for the 1970's.* New York, Har-Row, 1969.

Kohlberg, L.: Early education: A cognitive-developmental view. *Child Dev, 38*:1013-1075, 1968. Reprinted in Ornstein, Allan C. (Ed.): *Educating the Disadvantaged*. New York: AMS Pr, 1970, vol. 1, pt. 1.

Malone, C. A., Pavenstedt, E., Mattick, I., Bandler, L. S., Stein, M. R. and Mintz, N. L.: *The Drifters: Children of Disorganized Lower-Class Families*, Pavenstedt, E. (Ed.). Boston, Little, 1967.

Marmor, J.: Social action and the mental health professional. *Am J Orthopsychiatry, 40*:373-374, 1970.

Mayer, H. and Schamess, G.: The importance of maintaining long-term treatment services for the economically deprived family. Presented at the 45th Annual Meeting of the American Orthopsychiatric Association, Chicago, 1968.

McDermott, J. F., Jr., Harrison, S. I., Schrager, J., Lindy, J. and Killins, E.: Social class and mental illness in children: The question of childhood psychosis. *Am J Orthopsychiatry, 37*:548-557, 1967.

Piaget, J.: *Science of Education and the Psychology of the Child*. New York, Orion Pr. Grossman, 1970.

Schneiderman, L.: Social class, diagnosis and treatment. *Am J Orthopsychiatry, 35*:99-105, 1965.

Silverman, M. and Wolfson, E.: Early intervention and social class: diagnosis and treatment of preschool children in a day-care center. *J Am Acad Child Psychiatry, 10*:603-618, 1971.

Silverman, M. and Wolfson, E.: The use of small educational-therapeutic groups in a program for disadvantaged preschoolers. *Psychosocial Process, 1*:47-59, 1970.

Spurlock, J. and Cohen, R. S.: Should the poor get none? *J Am Acad Child Psychiatry, 8*:16-35, 1969.

Wilhelms, F. T.: The influence of environment and education. *National Association of Secondary School Principals*, April 1969, pp. 1-36. Reprinted in Ornstein, Allan C. (Ed.): *Educating the Disadvantaged*. New York, AMS Pr 1970, vol. 1, pt. 1, pp. 21-56.

INDEX

243